Federal Style Patterns
1780-1820
Interior Architectural Trim and Fences

Interior Doors, Doorways, and Arches
Window and Door Casings
Window Sills and Aprons
Cornices in Five Types
Room Designs
Baseboards
Chair Rails
Mantels
Fences

WILEY

Illustrations and Text by
Lawrence D. Smith and MaryBeth Mudrick

i

Published by John Wiley & Sons, Inc., Hoboken, New Jersey
Published simultaneously in Canada

For general information on our other products and services or for technical support, please contact our Customer Care Department within the United States at 800-762-2974, outside the United States at (317) 572-3993 or fax (317) 572-4002.

Wiley also publishes its books in a variety of electronic formats. Some content that appears in print may not be available in electronic books.

Library of Congress Cataloging-in-Publication Data:

Smith, Lawrence D., 1938-
  Federal style patterns 1780-1820 : interior architectural trim & fences /
illustrations and text by Lawrence D. Smith and MaryBeth Mudrick.
     p. cm.
  Includes bibliographical references and index.
  ISBN 0-471-69419-3 (cloth : alk. paper)
  1. Interior architecture--United States--New England--History--18th century. 2. Interior
architecture--United States--New England--History--19th century. 3. Decoration and ornament--United
States--New England--Federal style. I. Mudrick, MaryBeth. II. Title.
  NA2850.S63 2005
  729'.0974'09034--dc22

                                                    2004023269

Printed in the United States of America

10 9 8 7 6 5 4 3 2 1

Table of Contents

Acknowledgments

The authors wish to express their appreciation and gratitude to the following people whose assistance was vital to the creation of this book: Libby Nemota, Supervisor of Interlibrary Loans for the Palm Beach County Library System, went to extraordinary efforts on our behalf, making it possible for us to receive every book we requested through interlibrary loan. Without her assistance, there would have been no book. Brian Huculak of Huculak & Associates <www.caddpower.com> provided his insightful and precise knowledge of computers, software, and related hardware, and clear and workable instructions that helped us over many hurdles. Kathryn Hart and Iñaki Zubizarreta of Zubi Graphics <www.zubi.com> offered invaluable technical directions that enabled us to compile this book into digital form.

Preface

A tour of the historic house museums in Savannah, Georgia, prompted our interest in the American Federal Style, 1780-1820, but even in Federal Style house museums, we could find very little readily available information about its specific characteristics. Relying on a computer, library card, and a willing interlibrary loan department, we started a long journey through old books, microfilms, photographs, and measured drawings. We began with the drawings and text by ancient classic Roman architect Vitruvius, Italian Renaissance architects Vignola and Palladio, 18th Century English architects Sir William Chambers and Robert Adam, and New England architects Samuel McIntire, Asher Benjamin, and Charles Bulfinch. We studied; visited Federal Style museum homes in the New England area; took photographs; constructed samples of Federal Style architectural orders, cornices, chair rails, window and door casings, baseboards, mantles, and fences; and amassed a library of information from many scattered sources. We came to realize that a modern pattern book illustrating the form, character, scale and proportion, and ornament of the style was not available in a single volume. From a careful examination of accurately measured drawings and photographs of historic homes and period pattern books, we created some 300 drawings rendered in the American Federal Style and present them here.

TERMS

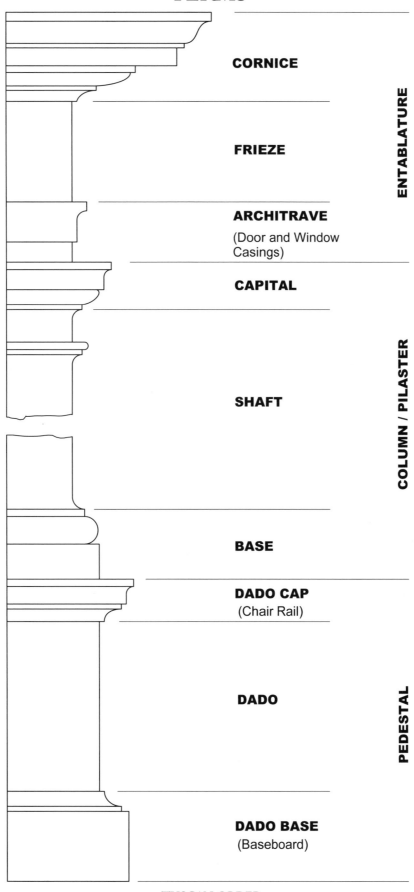

CORNICE

FRIEZE

ARCHITRAVE

(Door and Window
Casings)

CAPITAL

SHAFT

BASE

DADO CAP

(Chair Rail)

DADO

DADO BASE

(Baseboard)

ENTABLATURE

COLUMN / PILASTER

PEDESTAL

TUSCAN ORDER
as conceived by Federal Style Architect/Builder
ASHER BENJAMIN

About Federal Style Architecture

The neoclassic American Federal Style achieves its appeal by faithful adherence to classic Roman proportioning (Golden Section), reducing the monumental scale of Roman public architecture and introducing great variety and uniqueness in decoration and molding arrangements not found in ancient Rome's monumental architecture. It is the delicate and decorative interior treatment perfectly matched to the 8' room heights of our era.

At the end of the 18th century, the new merchant leadership of New England was captivated by the delicacy and grace of the newly imported neoclassic Adam Style. New England architects, carpenters, and carvers modified that sometimes flamboyant style into a simple, elegant, personal, and original form and rejected any subsequent imports of new English styles. In their hands, proportions became more eye-pleasing at closer distances, column and pilaster shafts became more slender, cornices increased and decreased in projection and height, friezes lengthened, architraves shortened, surfaces were flattened, muted colors were favored, and endless contrasts were provided by the use of flower motifs, circles, ellipses, squares, rectangles, and diamonds. Federal Style ornament was carved, cut, or gouged in wood or formed by filling molds with composition material, plaster, or papier-mâché. No brief description of this style is complete without giving note to its special ornament. "Federal style ornament marks the ultimate refinement of classical taste in American architecture. Supremely rhythmic, wire-fine, and delicately scaled, its attenuated ranks of geometric and natural motifs are drawn in elegant but circumscribed patterns, like the resilient threads of a spiderweb, across the taut surfaces of the spatial volumes. It is chaste, serene, and controlled." William H. Pierson, Jr. (*AMERICAN BUILDINGS AND THEIR ARCHITECTS, VOL. I, The Colonial and Neoclassical Styles*, New York, Oxford University Press, 1986, p. 221).

The Federal Style came to America through the English pattern books of Robert Adam's style and by American architects who toured England and Europe. Samuel McIntire, carver/architect/builder; Charles Bulfinch, architect; and Asher Benjamin, architect/builder/ theorist, are figures most associated with the creation of the Federal Style. Asher Benjamin is noteworthy because he created uniquely American pattern books based on the English Adam Style pattern books. Benjamin's books were widely sold and effected the proliferation of the style in the New England area. Charles Bulfinch toured England and brought back the Adam Style as evidenced by the three Harrison Gray Otis houses in Boston, Massachusetts. Samuel McIntire was influenced by the English Adam Style pattern books and his professional association with Charles Bulfinch. McIntire's preeminence as an architect is seen in the Gardner-White-Pingree House in Salem, Massachusetts, and his skill as a carver of Federal Style ornament is unequaled.

The Federal Style changed in character because prominent architects brought new insights to bear upon neoclassicism, regional tastes adopted variations of Adam's work, and new styles imported from England were influencing the earlier Federal Style. The focus of our book is on what William H. Pierson, Jr. calls "The Traditional Phase" of American Neoclassicism. "The Traditional Phase" flourished in the New England region, resisting stylistic modifications from England as well as other American regional stylistic changes from the beginning to the ending of the Federal Style period. Pierson stated, "The Traditional Phase of American Neoclassicism was both the earliest and the least aggressive. In its staunch conservatism it was, in fact, little more than a provincial transformation of the first phase of English Neoclassicism. At the same time, in its basic characteristics it did not represent a radical break from the architecture of the late colonial era. Fundamental building types were modified only slightly, if at all, and those changes which did occur were primarily refinements in proportion and scale. The greatest innovations appeared in the interior decoration, where new motifs, many of them derived indirectly from ancient classical sources, were used with restrained elegance. It is this delicate and refined mode of design which we will identify as the Federal Style,....)." Our work focuses entirely on the interior architectural trim of this phase as practiced in the New England region. We have included some drawings from other American regions that seem to have had their inspiration from the New England region.

MOLDINGS

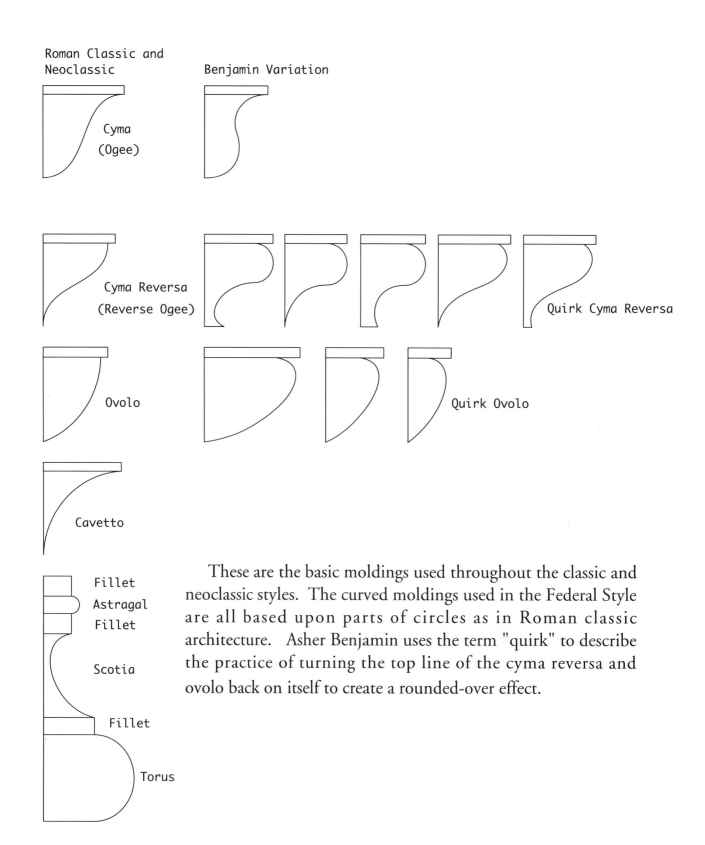

Roman Classic and Neoclassic

Benjamin Variation

Cyma (Ogee)

Cyma Reversa (Reverse Ogee)

Quirk Cyma Reversa

Ovolo

Quirk Ovolo

Cavetto

Fillet
Astragal
Fillet

Scotia

Fillet

Torus

These are the basic moldings used throughout the classic and neoclassic styles. The curved moldings used in the Federal Style are all based upon parts of circles as in Roman classic architecture. Asher Benjamin uses the term "quirk" to describe the practice of turning the top line of the cyma reversa and ovolo back on itself to create a rounded-over effect.

About the Drawings

Almost 200 years have passed since the Federal Style dominated American architecture. Our purpose is to reintroduce the beauty of neoclassic proportions and decoration used in the Federal Style to architects, designers, craftsmen, and the general public. In these pages, it is our wish that you join us for a fresh look at this American Style and find design inspiration, new ideas, and, most of all, a springboard for your own creative imagination.

All of our drawings were created using the dimensions found in accurately measured historic drawings or were based on historic pattern book guides and the Golden Rectangle. We retain the same height-to-projection dimensions, molding arrangements, molding types, and proportions found in the original designs. However, we held the minimum measurement to 1/32", altered some of the large curves of ovolo moldings to emulate neoclassic rather than classic practices, altered the "quirked" parts of ovolo moldings that could not be fabricated by rotating cutters, eliminated some ornament that would be difficult to reproduce, changed the tangent lines of ogee and reverse ogee moldings to fit more closely with neoclassic practices as required, and made new drawings of all applied and carved moldings based on the dimensions and character of the original drawings. All of these alterations are minor in themselves but produce a satisfying, neoclassic, architectural element.

It was not our intention to draw all of the interior architectural elements at original room height scale. The drawings in the cornice, door and window casings, chair rail, and baseboard sections have been proportionately scaled for an 8' room height and presented at half size with full size dimensions. For these sections of the book, we chose an 8' room height rather than the original room height for a variety of reasons. Our desire was to show the neoclassic scale, proportions, and delicate character of the style at a familiar room height. We encourage people to copy our drawings, tape those copies to the walls of their rooms to see which is most pleasing, and take the copies to their architect or cabinet maker for fabrication and/or installation.

We also found severe problems with reducing the drawings to fit the book size when the drawings were completed at the original room height (i.e., much of the detail was lost). Original drawings at an 8' room height totally eliminated the problem. The primary purpose of any historic pattern book is to provide drawings to be replicated and fabricated. Because they all give methods of reproducing the architectural elements at any room height, no historic pattern books use specific room heights. These books provide a scaling system for any room height that we discuss at the beginning of each section. But how the Federal Style evolved is not the subject for a pattern book but another book.

You may easily change our drawings of the cornice, chair rail, door and window casings, and baseboard architectural elements to conform in proportion and scale to any room height by determining the scaling percentage with a foot/inch calculator and using a computer scaling tool and printer, ordinary copier, or local copying service. If you want to scale and proportion one of our cornice drawings for a 9' room height, the procedure is simple. First, because these book sections are presented at half size to reduce the number of book pages required, increase the size of the drawing by enlarging the book sample by 100% to full size. Divide 9' by 8' to find 1.125 or 12.5%. Proportionately rescale upward the full cornice size copy by 12.5% to find the correct neoclassic scale and proportions for a 9' room. By using the captions for each drawing or going to the Index to the Figures (p. 238), you can go to the original source material of historic house drawings, determine the original room size, and rescale our drawings to original dimensions using the method outlined above.

We include many drawings of the work of English/Scottish architect Robert Adam in this book. Our drawings were based on the dimensions provided in historic records. Adam's work was a major inspirational source for the Federal Style as practiced in the New England region, and the character of his drawings dovetails with this New England style.

Golden Section Rectangle ratios dominated 18th century neoclassic design. The width and height relationship of every architectural element and part of that element can be understood by applying a specific Golden Rectangle ratio. The Golden Section of a line length is represented by the Greek letter phi (ø) and written as 1.618. A line length of 2" x 1.618 equals 3 1/4" line length or divided by 1.618 equals 1 1/4" line length. The new line lengths are in Golden Section proportion to the original line length. The math to produce the Golden Section ratio is 1: (1 + √5) ÷ 2 = 1.618. There are other ratios that are related to, common to, derived from, and visually proportionate with 1.618 (and, consequently, each other) that determine all Federal Style designs: 2.618, 3.618, 2.427 (1.5 x ø), 2.236 (√5), .539 (ø ÷ 3), 1:2, 1.414 (√2), 1.272 (√ø), .809 (ø ÷ 2), and 1.118 (√5 ÷ 2). The Golden Rectangle is identical to the Golden Section ratios but used to produce rectangles that are in Golden Section width and height proportions. Any design that fills the inside of the rectangle or at least touches the opposite corners of the long side of the rectangle is in Golden Section proportion. To demonstrate Golden Rectangle use in Federal Style architecture, we provide the following elements from the Cornice Plus design, at Fig. 107.

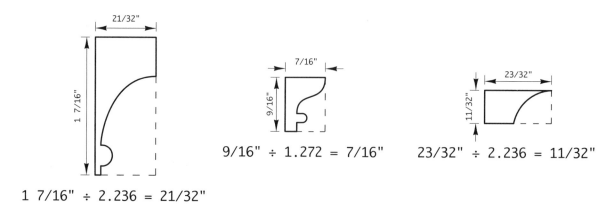

1 7/16" ÷ 2.236 = 21/32"

9/16" ÷ 1.272 = 7/16"

23/32" ÷ 2.236 = 11/32"

Assume that the dimension of the longest side of the rectangle represents a square of that dimension. Multiply or divide the dimension by any of the ratio numbers to find the desired rectangle in which you will draw a design. At the end of this section, we provide a graph of the division and multiplication of a 3/4" square for each of the ratios. Any of the rectangles may be mixed with the others, making the total design in Golden Section relationship.

The "contemporary" drawings found throughout the book are our designs based on these Golden Rectangle ratios, and we provide this information for each applicable design. For the contemporary drawings in the Type B cornice section, for example, we reduced the projection length of several Asher Benjamin designs to fit with Type B cornices by dividing the projection by one of the ratios listed above.

"The proportion of chimney pieces we are obliged to leave to the judgment of the workman; for, in our opinion, no exact rule can be laid down that will answer for every room. A room, however small, must have a fireplace large enough to be useful, and should the same proportion be used in a room of twenty feet high, and in large proportion, it would be so large as not to look well, and be too high in the opening for the smoke to ascend without spreading into the room." (Asher Benjamin and Daniel Raynerd, *The American Builder's Companion*, Dover Publications, 1969, Reprint of Sixth edition, 1827, p. 77.) In the Mantel section, we present the drawings at the height and width of the original historic drawing and present them at full book page size to allow the details to be shown. In the introduction to the Mantel section, we provide a rescaling procedure to a standard scale for each drawing. Period mantels were commonly constructed of the easily carved, stable, and widely available white pine and were, as with all interior architectural elements, meant to be painted. Applied ornament was made of wood, plaster, composition material, or papier-mâché. Both molded and wooden ornaments are appropriate choices for the patterns illustrated here and, as evidenced by period examples, may be freely combined to produce the desired effect.

Historically, two proportioning systems have been used to achieve overall design harmony among the architectural elements. If pilasters or columns are in use, the widest width of the column/pilaster shaft is the determining dimension for all other parts. This method is far too large to be covered in this volume and will have to be the subject of another book. It is important for the serious designer and student of Federal Style architecture to understand how the changes in column/pilaster design created this style and to use capitals and pilasters in modern neoclassic design.

The second proportioning system uses room height and door and window width divided into a specified number of parts. One or more of those parts are then assigned to each element: cornice, casing, etc. This latter method is used in this work. The original designer determined the dividing number for measured historic houses. If you wish to determine the dividing number for historic measured drawings or our drawings, find the height of the cornice drawing and divide the cornice height dimension into the room height. For our purpose of designing for 8' room heights, we rely on Asher Benjamin's height and width divider numbers. His method is described in the introduction to each appropriate book section. Benjamin's system also allows for more than one height and width for the applicable sections of our book. Previously, we provided an operation for rescaling our drawings to any room height and, now, an operation to rescale the book drawings to other sizes provided by the pattern book. When using Benjamin's guides, for example, Type A cornices allow for an 8' room height at these heights: 4 13/16", 4 3/8", 4", and 3 11/16". If our drawing is at 3 11/16" height and you wish to see it at 4 13/16", we provide this operation: divide the book drawing height into the new height, find the appropriate percentage, and rescale the book drawing (4 13/16" ÷ 3 11/16" = 30.5% - 3 11/16" + 30.5% = 4 13/16").

All of the drawings in this book were created using Engineered Software's PowerCadd drawing program <www.engsw.com> and Apple computers. The Companion CD contains the drawings in the following formats: PowerCadd version 6, DXF version R13, Adobe PDF, and PostScript. The PDF drawings can be opened and manipulated using Adobe Illustrator.

Golden Rectangle	3/4" Square	Golden Rectangle
21/32" = 1.118 ÷		× 1.118 = 27/32"
5/8" = .809 ÷		× .809 = 15/16"
19/32" = 1.272 ÷		× 1.272 = 31/32"
17/32" = 1.414 ÷		× 1.414 = 1 1/16"
15/32" = 1.618 ÷		× 1.618 = 1 7/32"
13/32" = .539 ÷		× .539 = 1 13/32"
3/8" = 2 ÷		× 2 = 1 1/2"
11/32" = 2.236 ÷		× 2.236 = 1 11/16"
5/16" = 2.427 ÷		× 2.427 = 1 13/16"
9/32" = 2.618 ÷		× 2.618 = 1 31/32"
7/32" = 3.618 ÷		× 3.618 = 2 23/32"

9

Ornaments Omitted

Federal Style ornament is rich in detail and used abundantly by many of the original designers. But a taste for the plain and less ornamented is also evidenced. The more richly decorated cornice, chair rail, and mantle designs are probably based on the influence of the highly colorful and ornate Adam Style. The plainer, less ornamented, and unornamented designs are certainly based on uniquely American sensibilities and taste. The next pages present highly ornamented drawings of a mantel, cornice, and cornice plus accompanied by drawings using less ornament than the original. Any drawing in this book can be altered to fit your taste and remain within the unique proportions and scale of the American Federal Style.

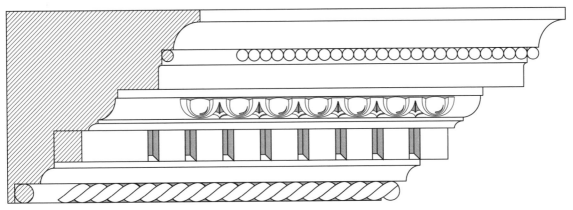

Original Cornice Type A Design
Fig. 17

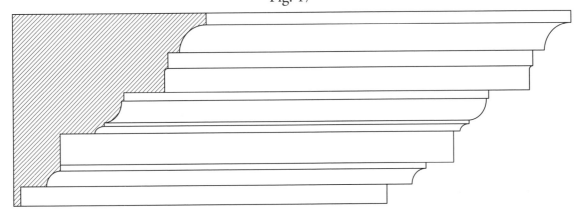

Variation #1

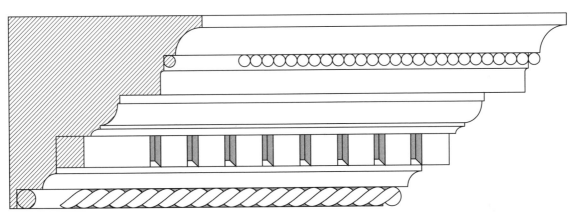

Variation #2

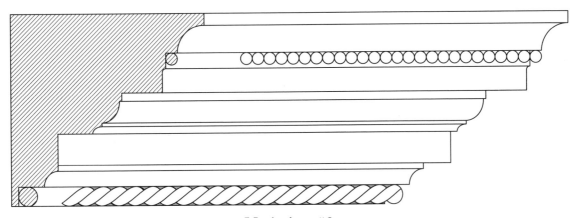

Variation #3

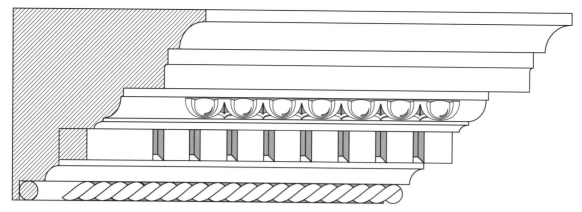

Variation #4

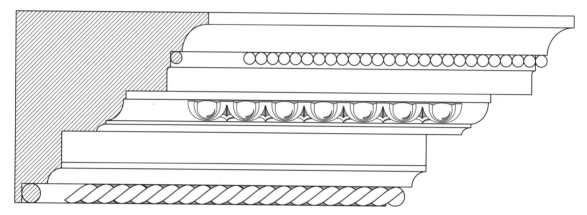

Variation #5

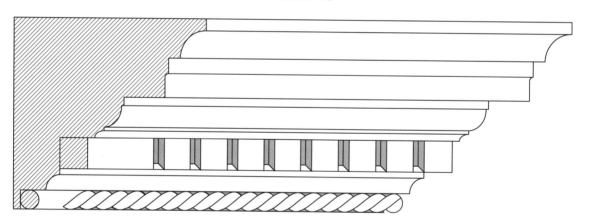

Variation #6

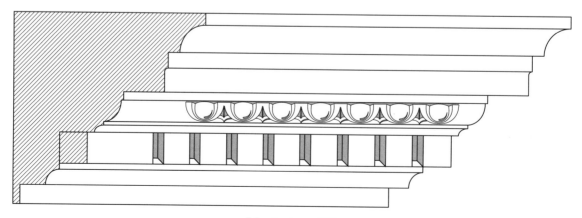

Variation #7

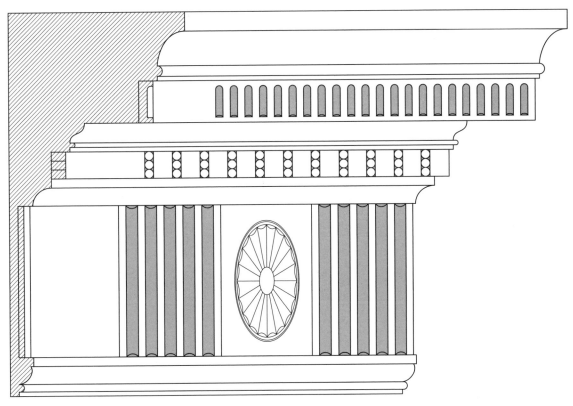

Original Cornice Plus Design
Fig. 107

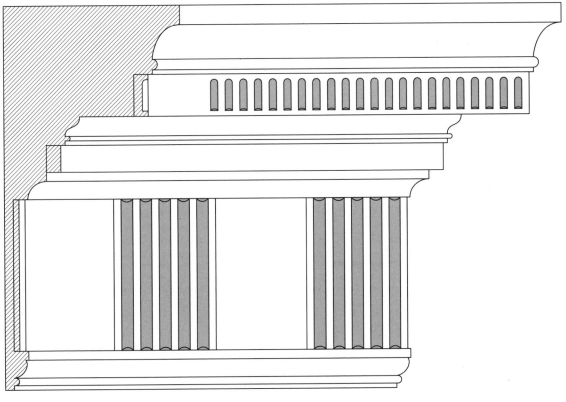

Variation #1

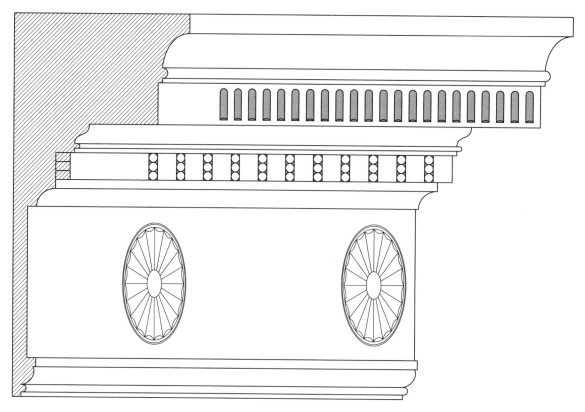

Variation #2

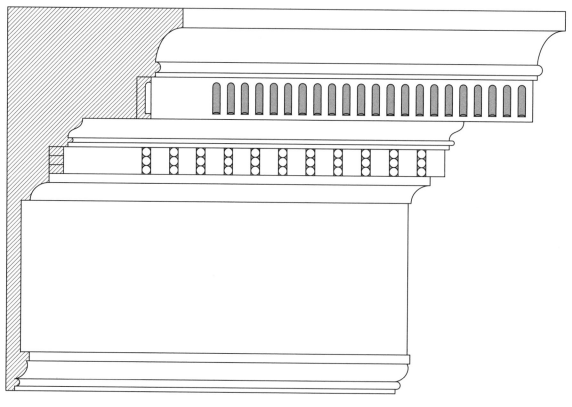

Variation #3

14

Original Mantel Design, Fig. 274

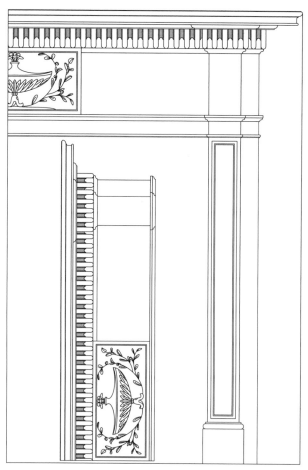

Variation #1

Variation #2

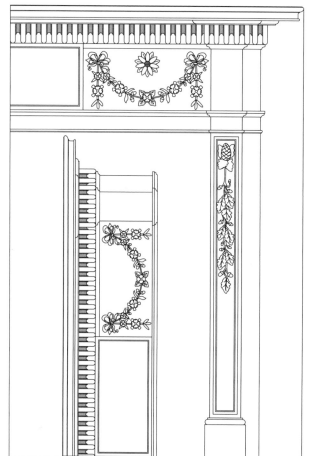

Variation #3

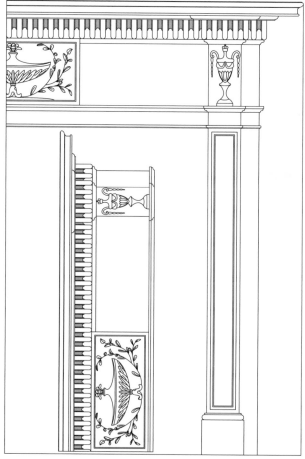

Variation #4

CORNICE TYPES

A

4 3/8"

4 3/8"

B

2 3/8"

4 3/8"

C

5"

2 11/16"

Cornice Plus

3 1/2"

6 1/2"

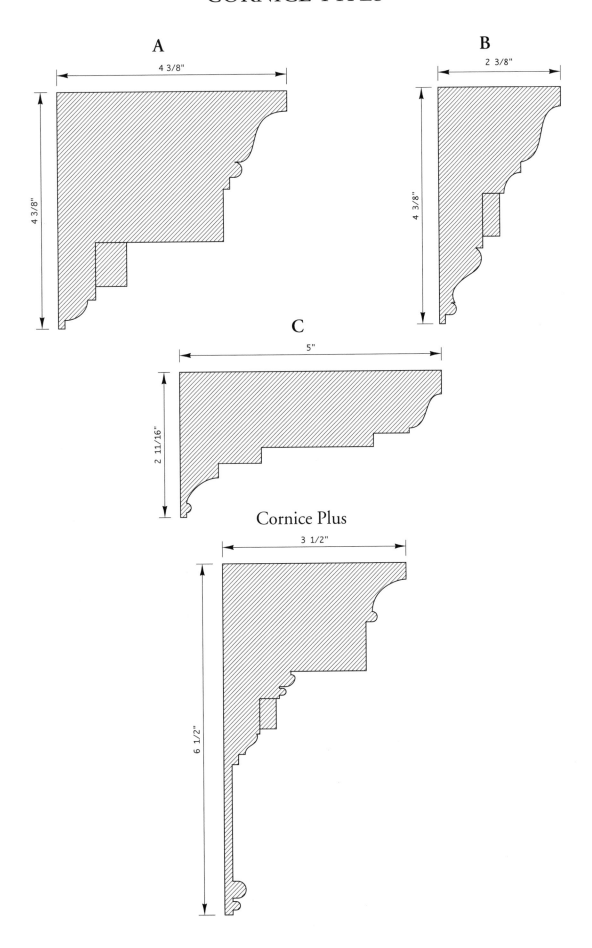

17

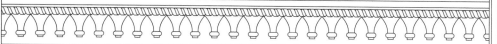

Cornices

Period pattern books and measured drawings of historic homes establish that these cornice moldings can be grouped into three Types based on height and projection. Type A cornices are of nearly equal length in height and projection (Figs. 2, 20, and 25 are exceptions that are due to the large ornament), Type B cornices have a shorter projection length in comparison to their height, and Type C cornices have a longer projection length in comparison to their height. These Types produce strikingly different visual effects, provide a great variety of design choices, and are firmly rooted in neoclassic design. Cornice Plus is a group of cornice designs with added frieze and architrave elements. The Cornice Plus is considered by many to be the most elegant and decorative of all the cornice treatments in the American Federal Style and emulates the highest form of the Adam Style. The drawings in the Palace of Diocletian section call attention to an ancient Italian source of the Federal Style. The ruins of this palace were a major inspiration for Robert Adam in the formation of the neoclassic style bearing his name. The Adam Style, in turn, was the inspiration for the Federal Style.

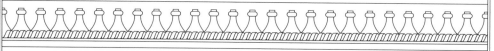

Type A Cornices

Type A cornices have been proportionally rescaled from the original drawings for an 8' room height and presented at half size with full size dimensions. According to Benjamin's pattern books, the height of Type A cornices may be determined by dividing the room height into **22, 24, 26**, or, occasionally, **20** parts, with one part taken for the cornice height. An 8' room height yields the following: 20 = 4 13/16", 22 = 4 3/8", 24 = 4", and 26 = 3 11/16". The projection is of approximately equal length and calculated from wall line, frieze line, or front face of the bottom molding. When the original measured drawing was unclear or did not furnish a room height dimension, we chose the pattern books' guides. Height dimensions differing from Benjamin's guides were taken from measured drawings clearly indicating room height. To rescale to any room height, refer to the instructions contained in the About the Drawings section (p. 5).

Fairly equal height and projection dimensions produce a cornice face angle of approximately 45°. This condition is basic to the classic orders of architecture, except in instances in which ornaments project outside this 45° angle (see Figs. 2, 20, and 25). The Type B and Type C cornices that follow are neoclassic variations of the classic orders based on a reexamination of the ruins of ancient Italy. These variations dramatically alter the height-to-width relationship of classic architecture.

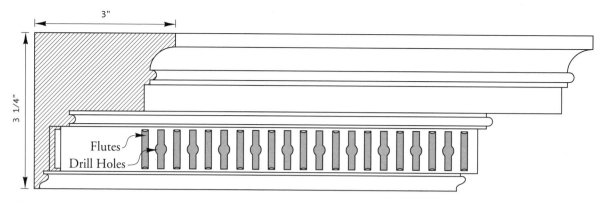

Fig. 1 Cook-Oliver House, Salem, MA, 1804, Mullins, *Architectural Treasures,* vol. I, p. 168.

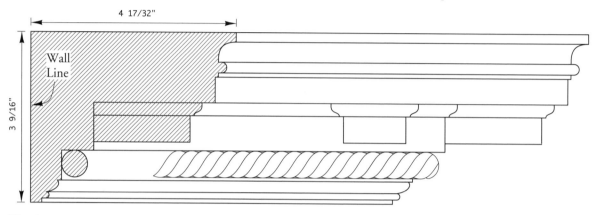

Fig. 2 Woodbridge-Short House, Salem, MA, 1810, Mullins, *Architectural Treasures*, vol. X, p. 157.
3 9/16" x ratio 1.272 = 4 17/32" from Wall Line.

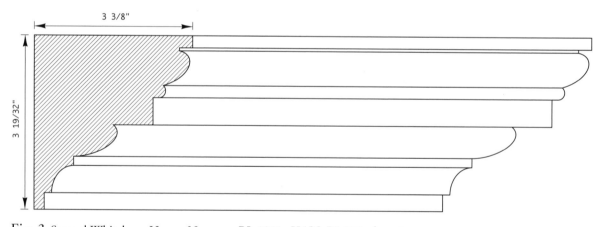

Fig. 3 Samuel Whitehorn House, Newport, RI, 1811, *HABS*, RI-323, sheet 9.

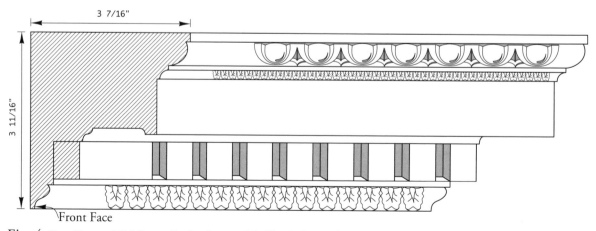

Fig. 4 Sion House, Middlesex, England, remodeled by Robert Adam 1762-1769, Adam, *Works,* 1975 reprint, p. 83,
vol. II, no. IV, pl. V. 3 11/16" ÷ ratio 1.118 = 3 5/16" from Front Face.

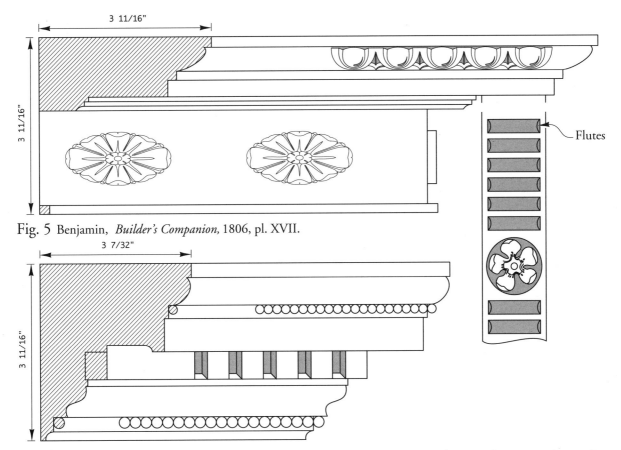

Fig. 5 Benjamin, *Builder's Companion,* 1806, pl. XVII.

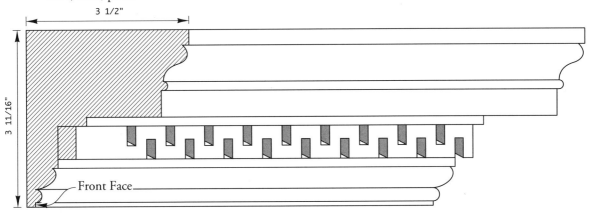

Fig. 6 Sion House, Middlesex, England, remodeled by Robert Adam 1762-1769, Adam, *Works,* 1975 reprint, p. 69, vol. I, no. I, pl. II.

Fig. 7 Oak Hill Rooms, Peabody, MA, 1800-1801, now in the Boston Museum of Fine Arts, Hipkiss, *Three McIntire Rooms,* p. 87. 3 11/16" ÷ ratio 1.118 = 3 5/16" from Front Face.

Fig. 8 Portsmouth, NH, date of original house unknown, Howe and Fuller, *Details,* pl. XVII.
3 11/16" ÷ ratio 1.118 = 3 9/32" from Wall Line.

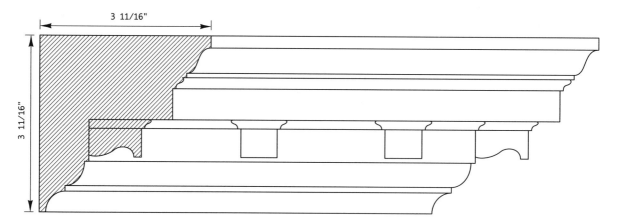

Fig. 9 Benjamin, *Country Builder's Assistant*, 1797, pl. V.

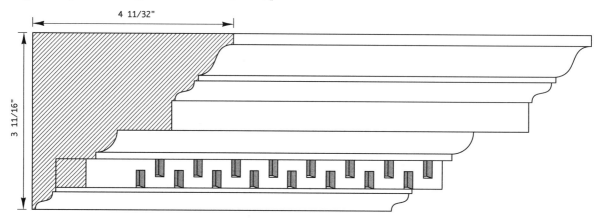

Fig. 10 Benjamin, *Builder's Companion*, 1827, pl. XXI.

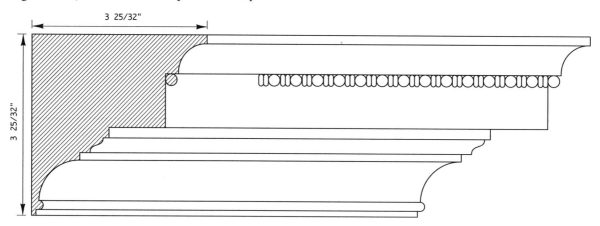

Fig. 11 Captain Leonard House, Agawam, MA, 1807, *HABS*, MA-2-50, sheet 9.

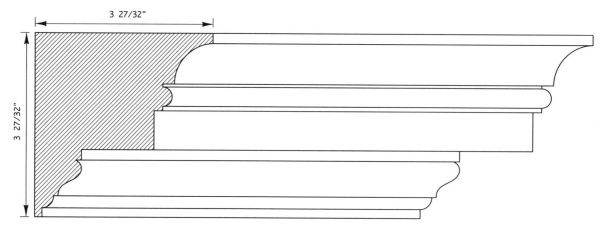

Fig. 12 Jonathan Woodbridge House, Worthington, MA, 1806, *HABS*, MA-124, sheet 20.

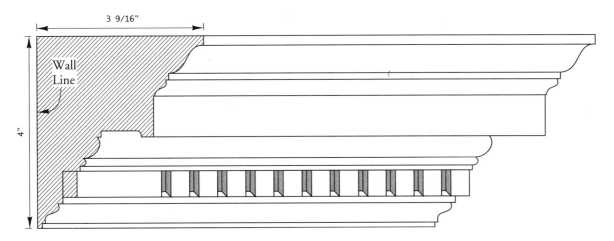

Fig. 13 Shelburne House, London, England, built by Robert Adam 1762-1768, Adam, *Works*, 1975 reprint, p. 126, vol. II, no. III, pl. III. 4" ÷ ratio 1.118 = 3 9/16" from Wall Line.

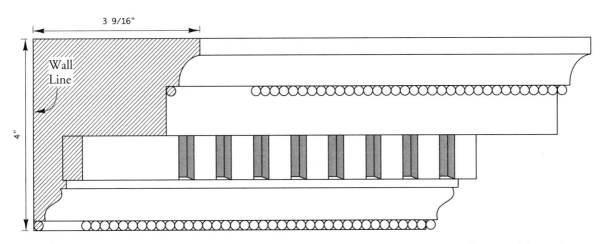

Fig. 14 Kenwood House, Middlesex, England, remodeled by Robert Adam 1767-1769, Adam, *Works,* 1975 reprint, p. 93, vol. I, no. II, pl. IV. 4" ÷ ratio 1.118 = 3 9/16" from Wall Line.

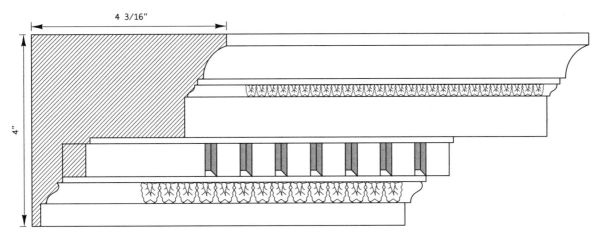

Fig. 15 Sion House, Middlesex, England, remodeled by Robert Adam 1762-1769, Adam, *Works*, 1975 reprint, p. 78, vol. II, no. IV, pl. II.

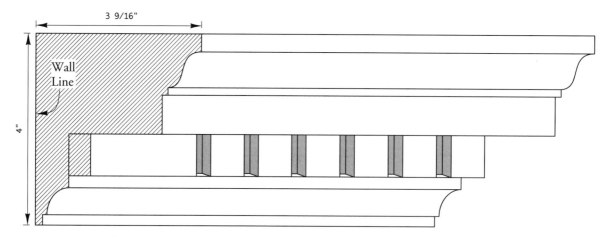

Fig. 16 Sion House, Middlesex, England, remodeled by Robert Adam 1762-1769, Adam, *Works*, 1975 reprint, p. 138, vol. I, no. III, pl. VI. 4" ÷ ratio 1.118 = 3 9/16" from Wall Line.

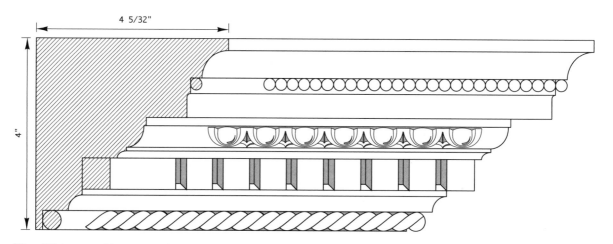

Fig. 17 Date and location unknown, Wallis, *American Architecture,* pl. X.

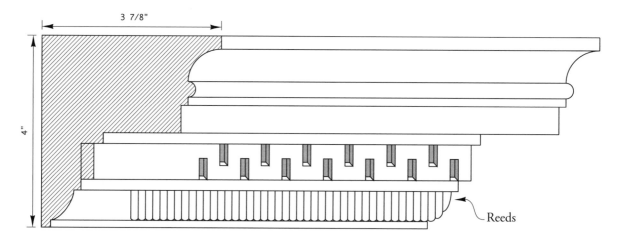

Fig. 18 Pierce-Nichols House, Salem, MA, 1801, Mullins, *Architectural Treasures,* vol. XVI, p. 90.

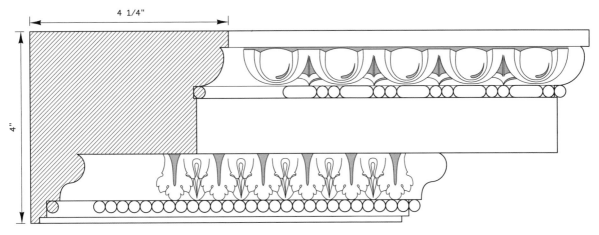

Fig. 19 Sion House, Middlesex, England, remodeled by Robert Adam 1762-1769, Adam, *Works,* 1975 reprint, p. 77, vol. I, no. I, pl. VII.

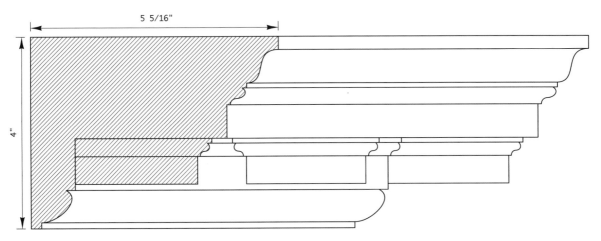

Fig. 20 Benjamin, *Country Builder's Assistant,* 1797, pl. IV.

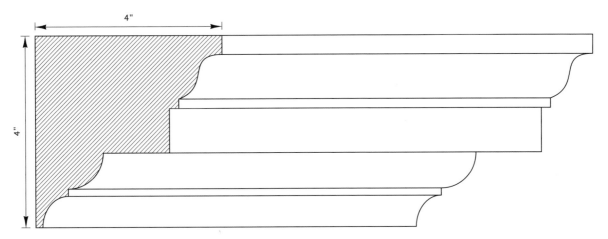

Fig. 21 Benjamin, *Country Builder's Assistant,* 1797, pl. III.

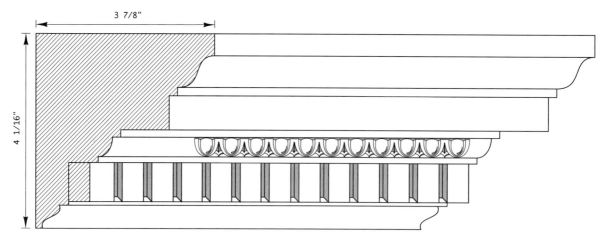

Fig. 22 Harrison Gray Otis House (first), Boston, MA, 1796, Mullins, *Architectural Treasures,* vol. I, p. 169.

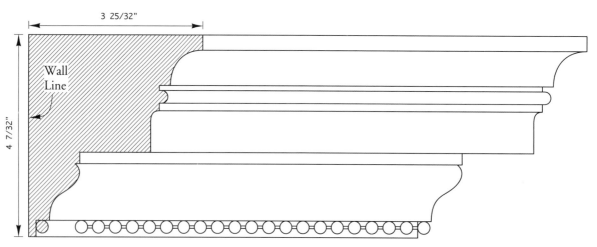

Fig. 23 Jonathan Woodbridge House, Worthington, MA, 1806, *HABS*, MA-124, sheet 21.
4 7/32" ÷ ratio 1.118 = 3 25/32" from Wall Line.

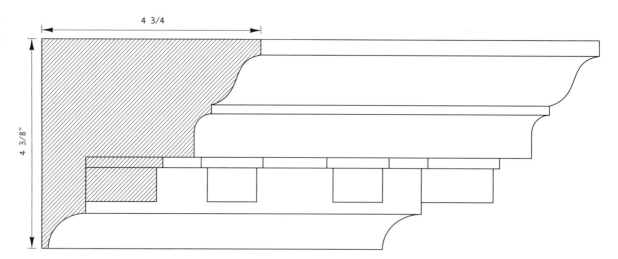

Fig. 24 Benjamin, *Builder's Companion,* 1827, pl. XXI.

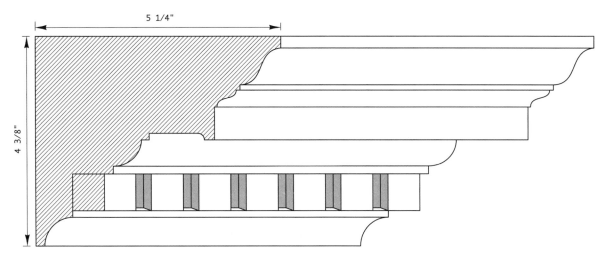

Fig. 25 Benjamin, *Builder's Companion,* 1827, pl. XXI.

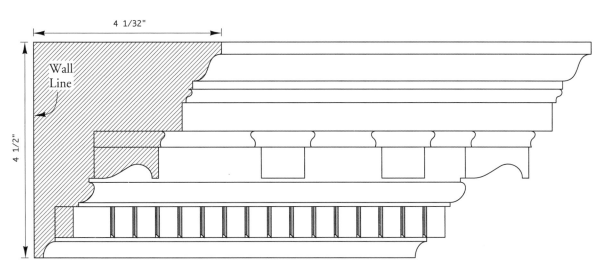

Fig. 26 Coleman-Hollister House, Greenfield, MA, 1796, *HABS,* MA-2-19, sheet 17.
4 1/2" ÷ ratio 1.118 = 4 1/32" from Wall Line.

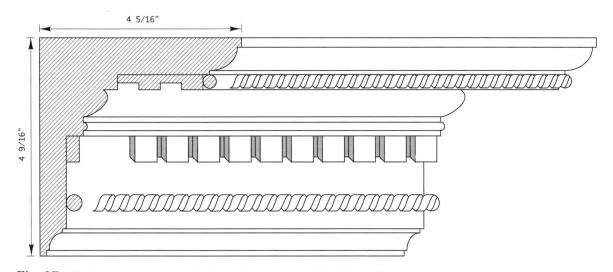

Fig. 27 Wheeler-Beecher House, Bethany, CT, 1801, *HABS,* CT-68, sheet 22.

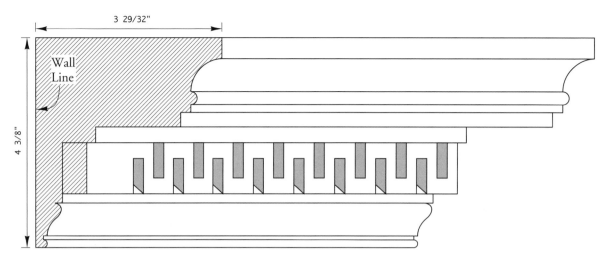

Fig. 28 Oak Hill Rooms, Peabody, MA, 1800-1801, now in the Boston Museum of Fine Arts, Hipkiss, *Three McIntire Rooms,* p. 87. 4 3/8" ÷ 1/118 = 3 29/32" from Wall Line.

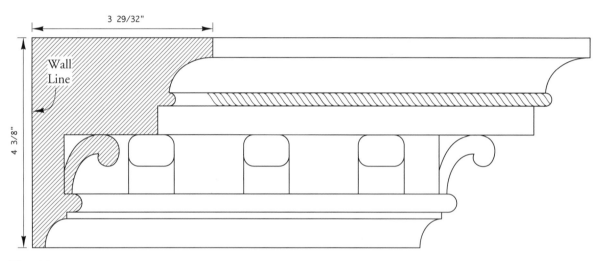

Fig. 29 Cambridge, MA, date of original house unknown, Howe and Fuller, *Details,* pl. XVII.
4 3/8" ÷ 1/118 = 3 29/32" from Wall Line.

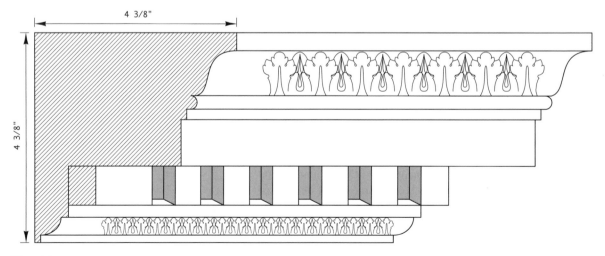

Fig. 30 Wynn House, London, England, remodeled by Robert Adam 1772-1774, Adam, *Works,* 1975 reprint,
p. 115, vol. II, no. II, pl. V.

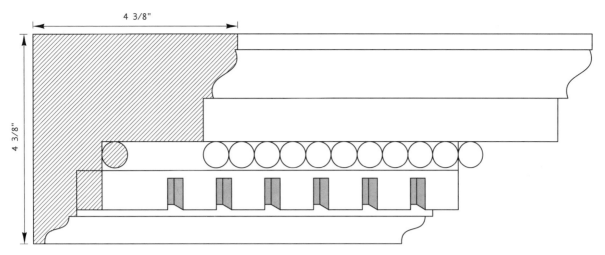

Fig. 31 Coleman-Hollister House, Greenfield, MA, 1796, *HABS*, MA-2-19, sheet 15.

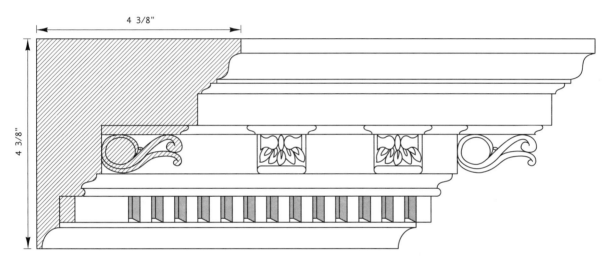

Fig. 32 Benjamin, *Country Builder's Assistant*, 1797, pl. 7.

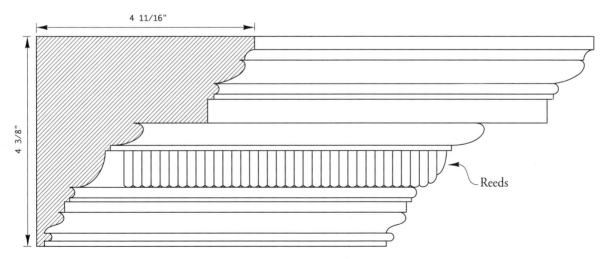

Reeds

Fig. 33 Gideon Tucker House, Salem, MA, 1806, Mullins, *Architectural Treasures,* vol. I, p. 168.

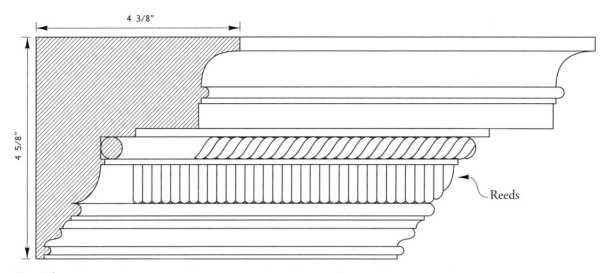

Fig. 34 Gideon Tucker House, Salem, MA, 1806, Mullins, *Architectural Treasures,* vol. I, p. 168.

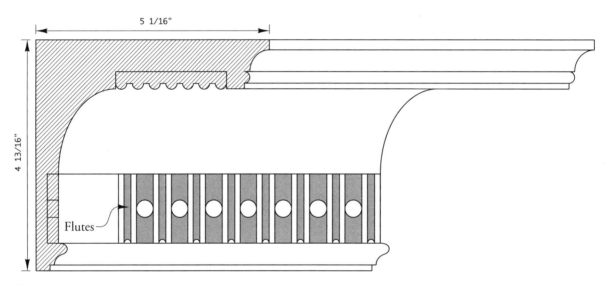

Fig. 35 Nathan Dean House, East Taunton, MA, 1810 addition, *HABS,* MA-143, sheet 12.

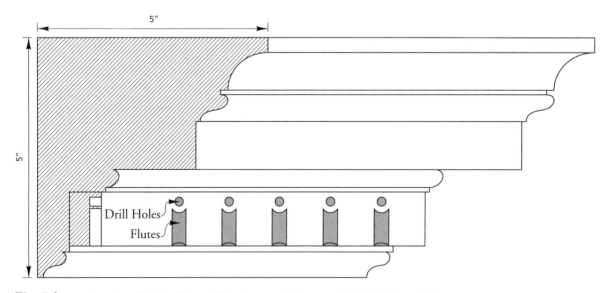

Fig. 36 Jonathan Woodbridge House, Worthington, MA, 1806, *HABS*, MA-124, sheet 12.

Type B Cornices

The height of Type B cornices is also determined in the manner used in Type A cornices, but the shortened projection compared to height was determined by the original designer and can be understood by applying Golden Section ratios. The length of the projection can be calculated by **dividing** the height of the cornice by one of the following ratios: **.539, 1.272, 1.618, 1.414, 2.236,** or **.809.** The projection dimensions are calculated from wall line, frieze line, or front face of the bottom molding. When the original measured drawing was unclear or did not furnish a room height dimension, we chose the pattern books' guides. Height dimensions differing from Benjamin's guides were taken from measured drawings clearly indicating room height. To rescale to any room height, refer to the instructions contained in the About the Drawings section (p.5). Reducing the projection of several Benjamin Type A designs to Type B designs created "contemporary" cornices. We provide the ratio for the "contemporary" cornices and also indicate the Golden Section ratio to understand the projection reduction for each of the other Type B designs. Type B cornices have been proportionally rescaled for an 8' room height and presented at half size with full size dimensions.

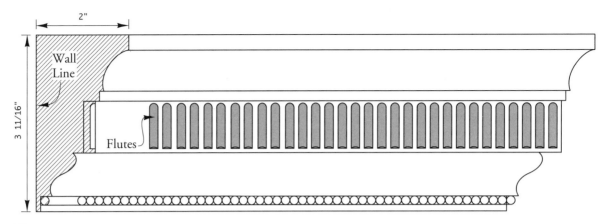

Fig. 37 Shelburne House, London, England, built by Robert Adam 1762-1768, Adam, *Works,* 1975 reprint, p. 83, vol. II, no. 4, pl. V. 3 11/16" ÷ ratio .539 = 2" from Wall Line.

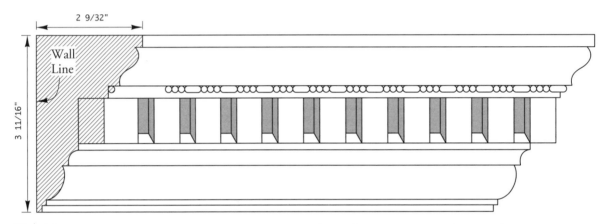

Fig. 38 Sion House, Middlesex, England, remodeled by Robert Adam 1762-1769, Adam, *Works,* 1975 reprint, p. 83, vol. II, no. 4, pl. V. 3 11/16" ÷ ratio 1.618 = 2 9/32" from Wall Line.

Fig. 39 Contemporary design by The Federal Style Orders, 2003, based on a design for a cornice by Benjamin, *Country Builder's Assistant,* 1797, pl. XVI. 3 11/16" ÷ ratio 1.618 = 2 9/32" from Front Face.

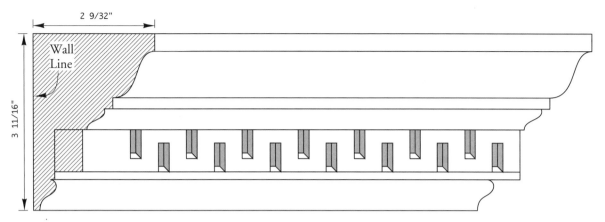

Fig. 40 Charlestown, MA, date of original house source unknown, Howe and Fuller, *Details*, pl. 42.
3 11/16" ÷ ratio 1.618 = 2 9/32" from Wall Line.

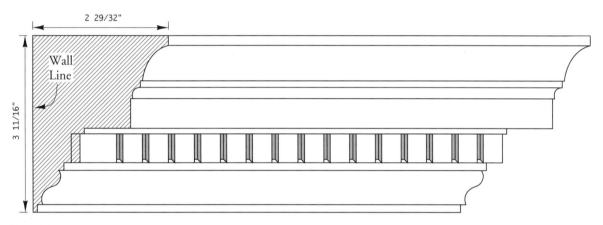

Fig. 41 Luton Park, Beds, England, built by Robert Adam, 1767-1775, Adam, *Works*, 1975 reprint, p. 137.
3 11/16" ÷ ratio 1.272 = 2 29/32" from Wall Line.

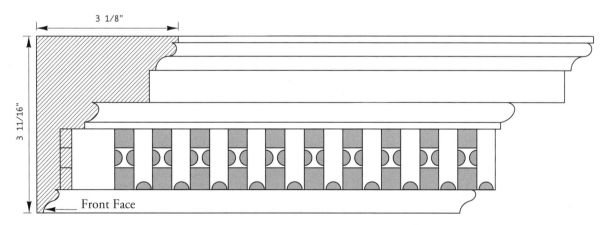

Fig. 42 Contemporary design by The Federal Style Orders, 2003, based on a design for a cornice by Benjamin,
Country Builder's Assistant, 1797, pl. XVI. 3 11/16" ÷ ratio 1.272 = 2 29/32" from Front Face.

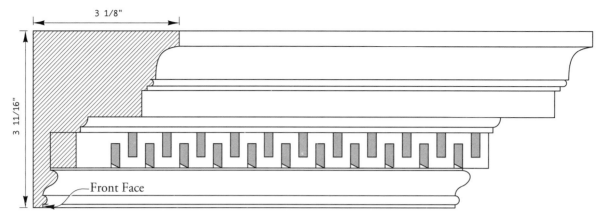

Fig. 43 Oak Hill Rooms, Peabody, MA, 1800-1801, now in the Boston Museum of Fine Arts, Hipkiss,
Three McIntire Rooms, p. 93. 3 11/16" ÷ ratio 1.272 = 2 29/32" from Front Face.

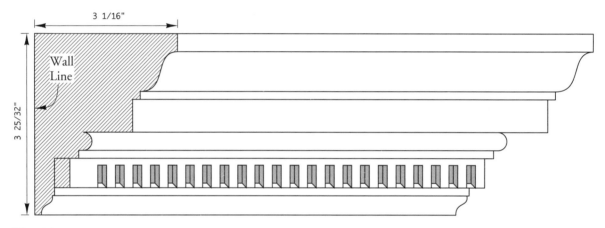

Fig. 44 Harrison Gray Otis House (first), Boston, MA, 1796, Mullins, *Architectural Treasures*, vol. I, p. 169.
3 25/32" ÷ ratio .809 = 3 1/16" from Wall Line.

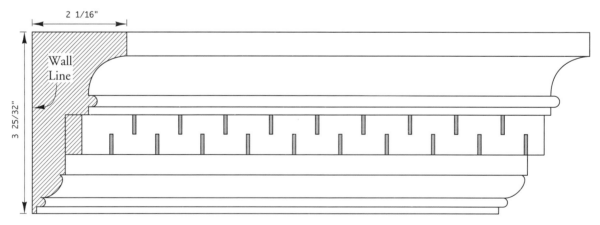

Fig. 45 Sayward-Holmes House, Alfred, ME, 1802, *HABS*, ME-32, sheet 11.
3 25/32" ÷ ratio .539 = 2 1/16" from Wall Line.

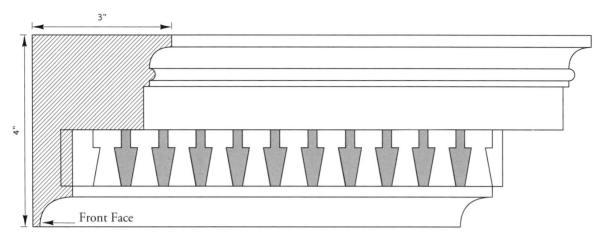

Fig. 46 Contemporary design by The Federal Style Orders, 2003, based on a design for a cornice by Benjamin, *Country Builder's Assistant*, 1797, pl. 16. 4" ÷ ratio 1.414 = 2 27/32" from Front Face.

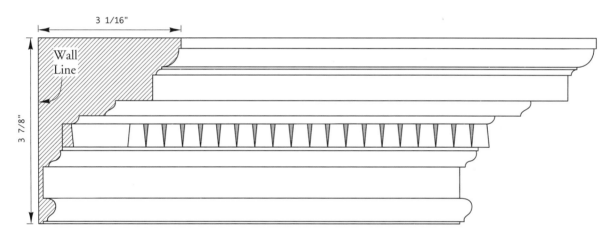

Fig. 47 Coleman-Hollister House, Greenfield, MA, 1796, *HABS*, MA-2-19, sheet 15.
3 7/8" ÷ ratio 1.272 = 3 1/16" from Wall Line.

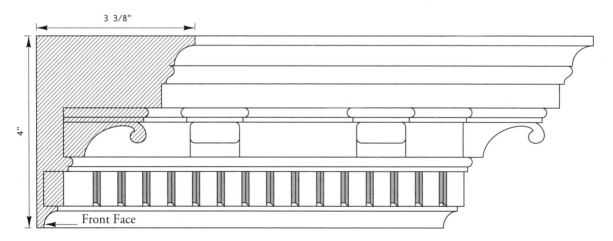

Fig. 48 Charlestown, MA, date of original house unknown, Howe and Fuller, *Details*, pl. XVII.
4" ÷ ratio .809 = 3 1/4" from Front Face.

35

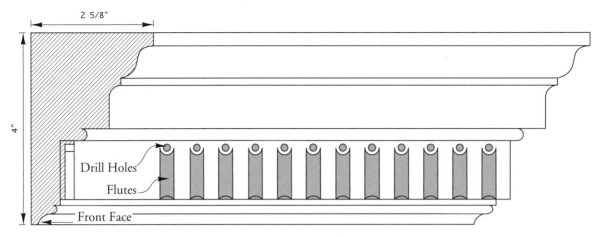

Fig. 49 Contemporary design by The Federal Style Orders, 2003, based on a design for a cornice by Benjamin, *Country Builder's Assistant*, 1797, pl. 16. 4" ÷ ratio 1.618 = 2 15/32" from Front Face.

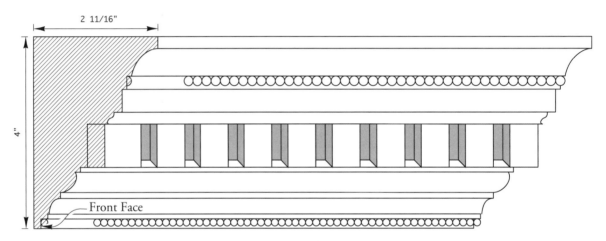

Fig. 50 Sion House, Middlesex, England, remodeled by Robert Adam 1762-1769 and 1773, Adam, *Works,* 1975 reprint, p. 69, vol. II, no. I, pl. II. 4" ÷ ratio 1.618 = 2 15/32" from Front Face.

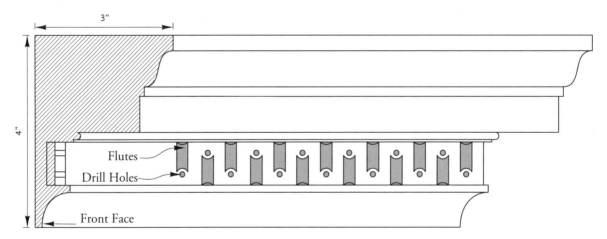

Fig. 51 Charlestown, MA, date of original house source unknown, Howe and Fuller, *Details,* pl. 42. 4" ÷ ratio 1.414 = 2 13/16" from Front Face.

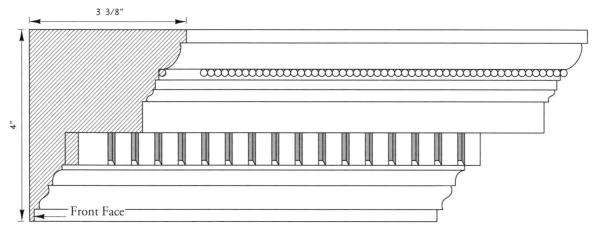

Fig. 52 Kenwood, Middlesex, England, remodeled by Robert Adam 1767-1769, Adam, *Works,* 1975 reprint, p. 93, vol. I, no. II, pl. IV. 4" ÷ ratio .809 = 3 1/4" from Front Face.

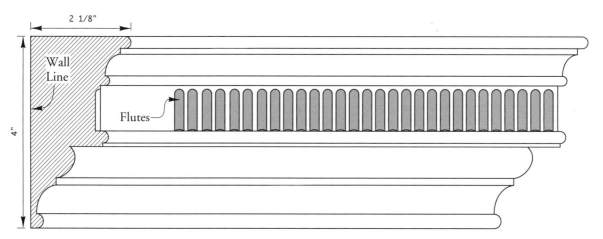

Fig. 53 Contemporary design by The Federal Style Orders, 2003, based on a design for a cornice by Benjamin, *Country Builder's Assistant,* 1797, pl. XVI. 4" ÷ ratio .539 = 2 1/8" from Wall Line.

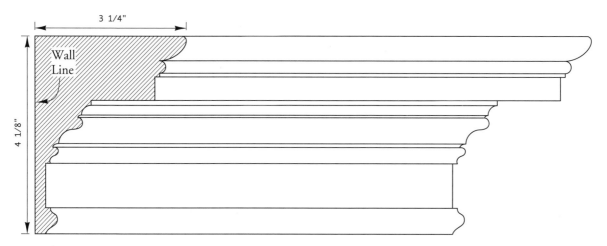

Fig. 54 Coleman-Hollister House, Greenfield, MA, 1795, *HABS,* MA-2-19, sheet 20. 4 1/8" ÷ ratio 1.272 = 3 1/4" from Wall Line.

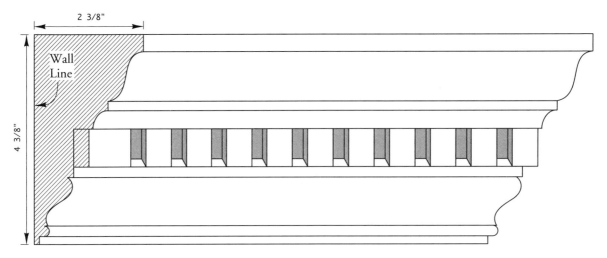

Fig. 55 Luton Park, Beds, England, built by Robert Adam 1767-1775, Adam, *Works,* 1975 reprint, p. 138, vol. I, no. III, pl. IV. 4 3/8" ÷ ratio .539 = 2 3/8" from Wall Line.

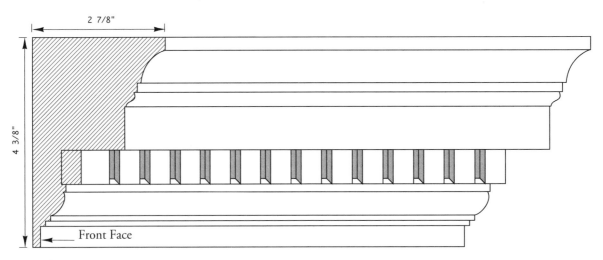

Fig. 56 Shelburne House, London, England, built by Robert Adam 1762-1768, Adam, *Works,* 1975 reprint, p. 130, vol. III, no. III, pl. V. 4 3/8" ÷ ratio 1.618 = 2 11/16" from Front Face.

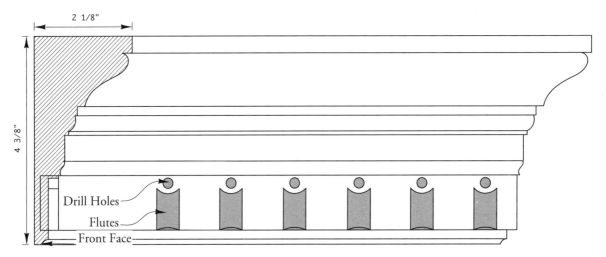

Fig. 57 South Yarmouth, MA, date of original house source unknown, Howe and Fuller, *Details,* pl. XVII. 4 3/8" ÷ ratio 2.236 = 1 15/16" from Front Face.

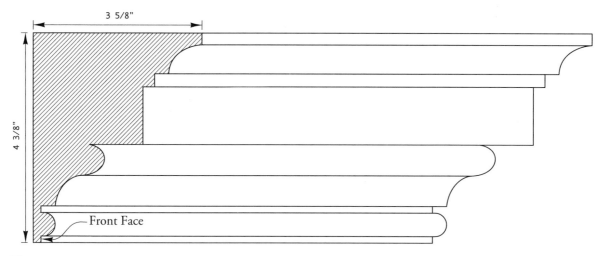

3 5/8"

4 3/8"

Front Face

Fig. 58 Contemporary design by The Federal Style Orders, 2003, based on a design for a cornice by Benjamin, *Country Builder's Assistant*, 1797, pl. XVI. 4 3/8" ÷ ratio 1.272 = 3 7/16" from Front Face.

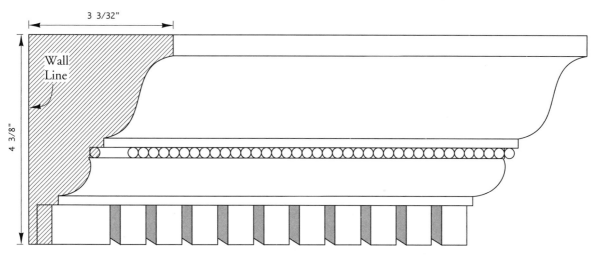

3 3/32"

4 3/8"

Wall Line

Fig. 59 Sion House, Middlesex, England, remodeled by Robert Adam 1762-1769 and 1773, Adam, *Works*, 1975 reprint, p. 77, vol. I, no. I, pl. VII. 4 3/8" ÷ ratio 1.414 = 3 3/32" from Wall Line.

2 3/8"

4 3/8"

Wall Line

Fig. 60 Contemporary design by The Federal Style Orders, 2003, based on a design for a cornice by Benjamin, *Country Builder's Assistant*, 1797, pl. XVI. 4 3/8" ÷ ratio .539 = 2 3/8" from Wall Line.

Fig. 61 Contemporary design by The Federal Style Orders, 2003, based on a design for a cornice by Benjamin, *Country Builder's Assistant*, 1797, pl. XVI. 4 3/8" ÷ ratio .539 = 2 3/8" from Front Face.

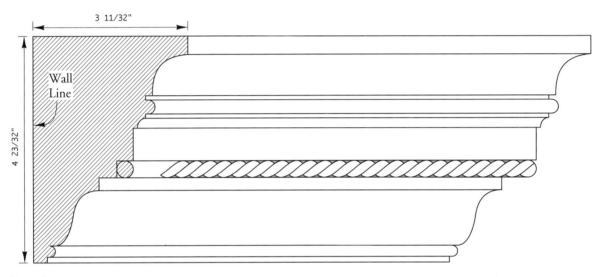

Fig. 62 General Salem Towne House, Charlton, MA, 1796, Mullins, *Architectural Treasures*, vol. X, p. 156.
4 23/32" ÷ ratio 1.414 = 3 11/32" from Wall Line.

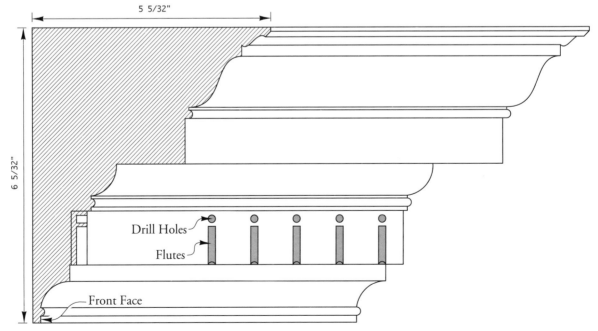

Fig. 63 Sayward-Holmes House, Alfred, ME, 1802, *HABS*, ME-32, sheet 13.
6 5/32" ÷ ratio .809 = 5" from Front Face.

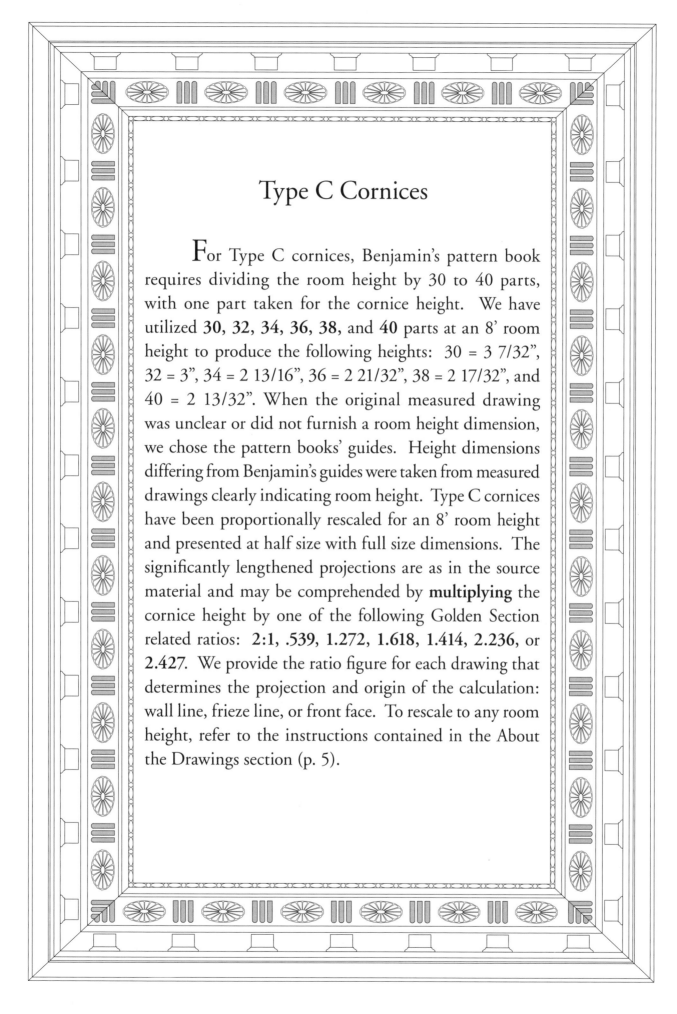

Type C Cornices

For Type C cornices, Benjamin's pattern book requires dividing the room height by 30 to 40 parts, with one part taken for the cornice height. We have utilized **30, 32, 34, 36, 38,** and **40** parts at an 8' room height to produce the following heights: 30 = 3 7/32", 32 = 3", 34 = 2 13/16", 36 = 2 21/32", 38 = 2 17/32", and 40 = 2 13/32". When the original measured drawing was unclear or did not furnish a room height dimension, we chose the pattern books' guides. Height dimensions differing from Benjamin's guides were taken from measured drawings clearly indicating room height. Type C cornices have been proportionally rescaled for an 8' room height and presented at half size with full size dimensions. The significantly lengthened projections are as in the source material and may be comprehended by **multiplying** the cornice height by one of the following Golden Section related ratios: **2:1, .539, 1.272, 1.618, 1.414, 2.236,** or **2.427.** We provide the ratio figure for each drawing that determines the projection and origin of the calculation: wall line, frieze line, or front face. To rescale to any room height, refer to the instructions contained in the About the Drawings section (p. 5).

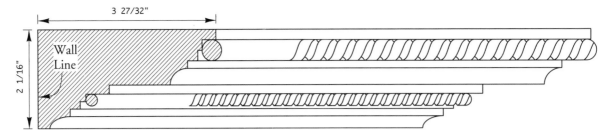

Fig. 64 Captain Barnes House, Portsmouth, NH, 1807, *HABS*, NH-26, sheet 45.
2 1/16" x ratio .539 = 3 27/32" from Wall Line.

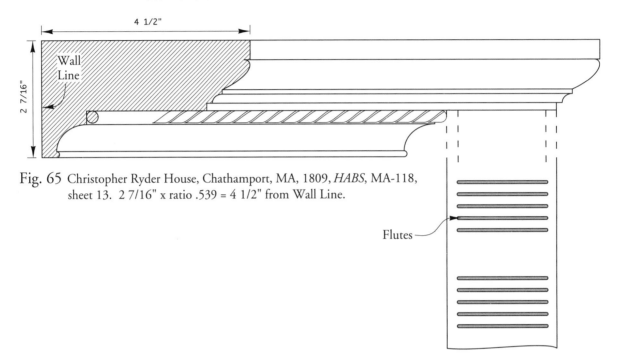

Fig. 65 Christopher Ryder House, Chathamport, MA, 1809, *HABS*, MA-118,
sheet 13. 2 7/16" x ratio .539 = 4 1/2" from Wall Line.

Flutes

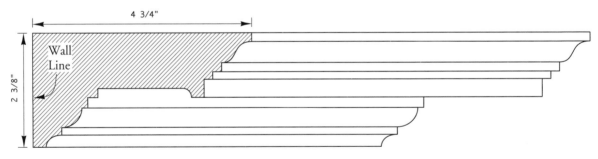

Fig. 66 Edward Carrington House, Providence, RI, 1812, *HABS*, RI-19, sheet 51.
2 3/8" x ratio 2:1 = 4 3/4" from Wall Line.

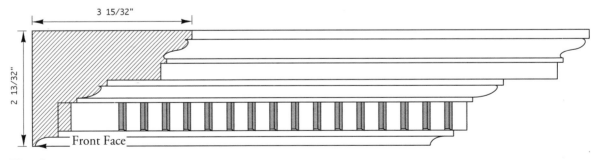

Fig. 67 Benjamin, *Builder's Companion*, 1806, pl. XII. 2 13/32" x ratio 1.414 =
3 13/32" from Front Face.

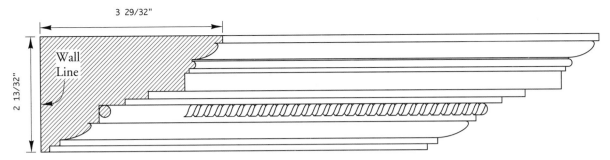

Fig. 68 Benjamin, *Builder's Companion,* 1806, pl. XII. 2 13/32" x ratio 1.618 = 3 29/32" from Wall Line.

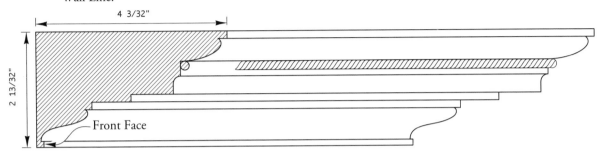

Fig. 69 Benjamin, *Builder's Companion,* 1806, pl. XII. 2 13/32" x ratio 1.618 = 3 29/32" from Front Face.

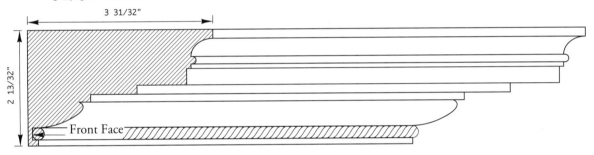

Fig. 70 Benjamin, *Builder's Companion,* 1806, pl. XIII. 2 13/32" x ratio 1.618 = 3 29/32" from Front Face.

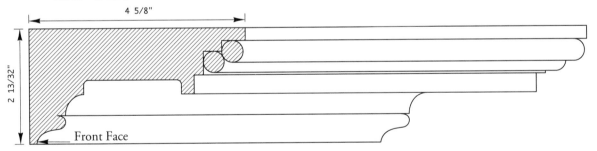

Fig. 71 Edward Carrington House, 1812, Providence, RI, *HABS*, RI-19, sheet 53. 2 13/32" x .539 = 4 15/32" from Front Face.

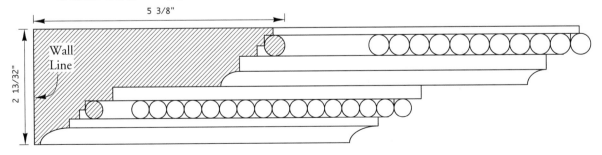

Fig. 72 Benjamin, *Builder's Companion,* 1806, pl. XIII. 2 13/32" x ratio 2.236 = 5 3/8" from Wall Line.

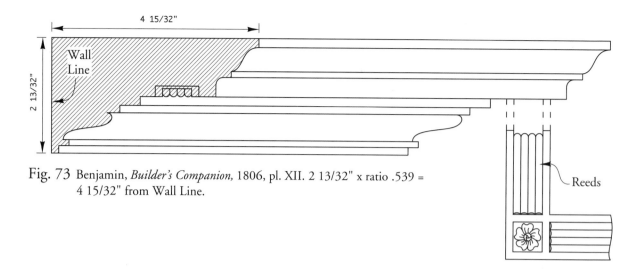

Fig. 73 Benjamin, *Builder's Companion,* 1806, pl. XII. 2 13/32" x ratio .539 =
4 15/32" from Wall Line.

Reeds

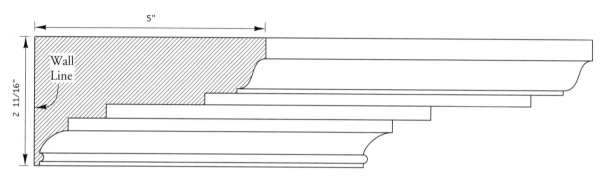

Fig. 74 Governor Woodbury Mansion, Portsmouth, NH, 1809, *HABS,* NH-20, sheet 33.
2 11/16" x ratio .539 = 5" from Wall Line.

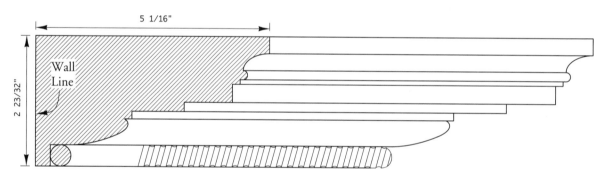

Fig. 75 Captain Barnes House, Portsmouth, NH, 1807, *HABS,* NH-26, sheet 46.
2 23/32" x ratio .539 = 5 1/16" from Wall Line.

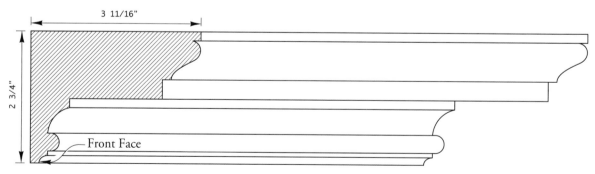

Fig. 76 Edward Carrington House, Providence, RI, 1812, *HABS,* RI-19, sheet 53.
2 3/4" x ratio 1.272 = 3 1/2" from Front Face.

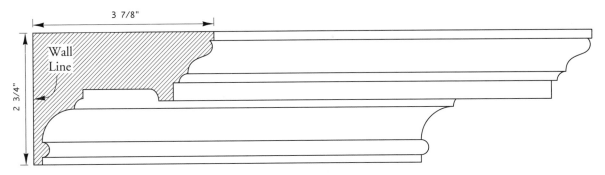

Fig. 77 Edward Carrington House, Providence, RI, 1812, *HABS,* RI-19, sheet 52.
2 3/4" x ratio 1.414 = 3 7/8" from Wall Line.

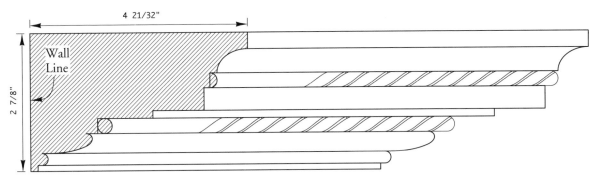

Fig. 78 Hyde-Lincoln House, Charlestown, MA, 1801, *HABS,* MA-299, sheet 8.
2 7/8" x ratio 1.618 = 4 21/32" from Wall Line.

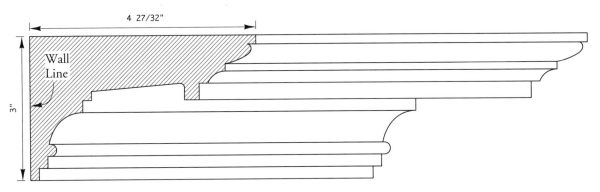

Fig. 79 Edward Carrington House, Providence, RI, 1812, *HABS*, RI-19, sheet 53.
3" x ratio 1.618 = 4 27/32" from Wall Line.

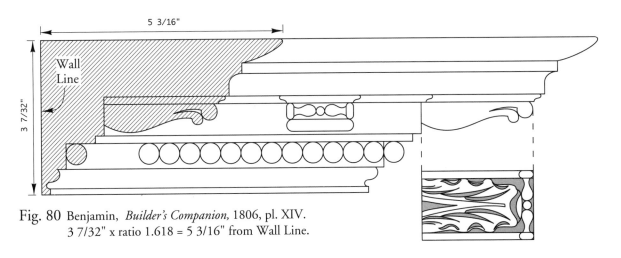

Fig. 80 Benjamin, *Builder's Companion,* 1806, pl. XIV.
3 7/32" x ratio 1.618 = 5 3/16" from Wall Line.

45

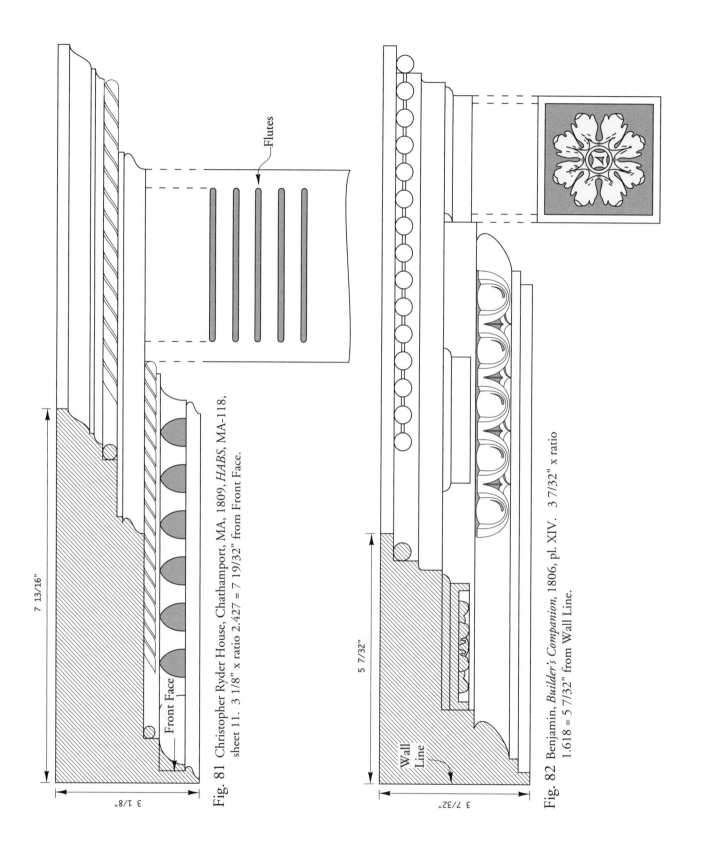

Flutes

Front Face

Fig. 81 Christopher Ryder House, Chathamport, MA, 1809, *HABS*, MA-118, sheet 11. 3 1/8" x ratio 2.427 = 7 19/32" from Front Face.

7 13/16"

3 1/8"

Wall Line

Fig. 82 Benjamin, *Builder's Companion*, 1806, pl. XIV. 3 7/32" x ratio 1.618 = 5 7/32" from Wall Line.

5 7/32"

3 7/32"

46

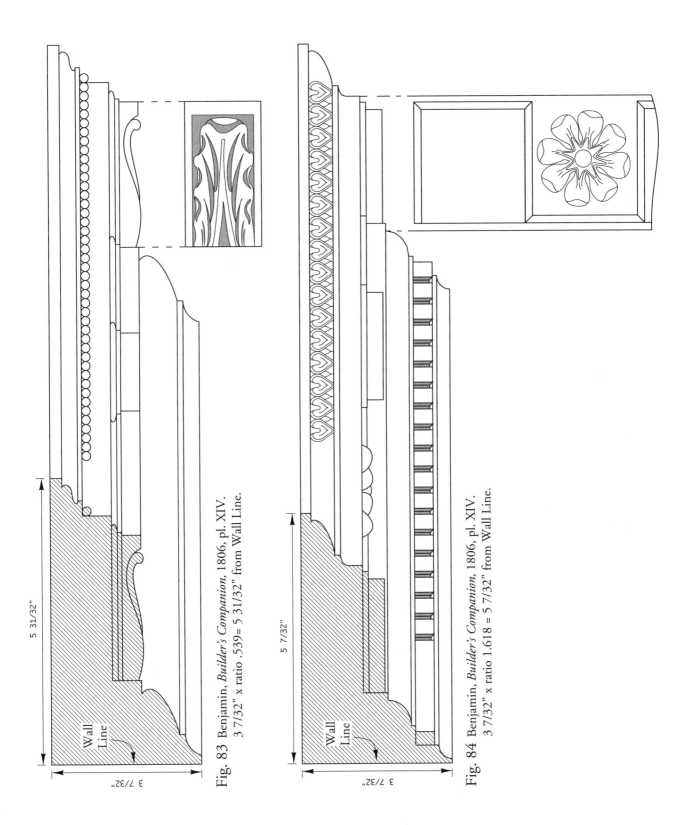

Fig. 83 Benjamin, *Builder's Companion*, 1806, pl. XIV.
3 7/32" x ratio .539 = 5 31/32" from Wall Line.

Fig. 84 Benjamin, *Builder's Companion*, 1806, pl. XIV.
3 7/32" x ratio 1.618 = 5 7/32" from Wall Line.

5 31/32"

3 7/32"

Wall Line

5 7/32"

3 7/32"

Wall Line

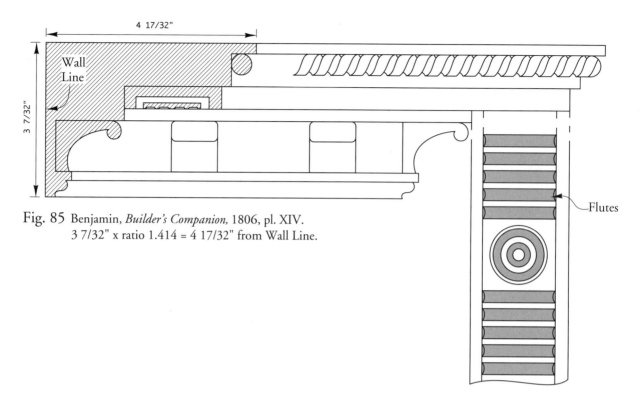

Fig. 85 Benjamin, *Builder's Companion,* 1806, pl. XIV.
3 7/32" x ratio 1.414 = 4 17/32" from Wall Line.

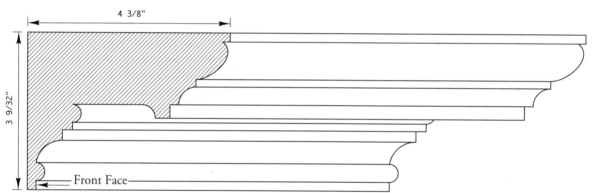

Fig. 86 Edward Carrington House, Providence, RI, 1812, *HABS,* RI-19, sheet 53.
3 9/32" x ratio 1.272 = 4 3/16" from Front Face.

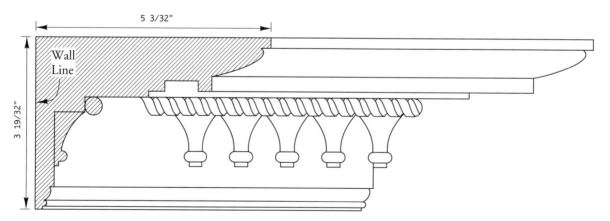

Fig. 87 Captain Barnes House, Portsmouth, NH, 1807, *HABS,* NH-26, sheet 40.
3 19/32" x ratio 1.414 = 5 3/32" from Wall Line.

Cornice Plus Cornices

The Cornice Plus type combines a cornice with a shortened frieze and architrave to provide a full entablature. The Cornice Plus is considered by many to be the most elegant and decorative of all the cornice treatments in the American Federal Style and emulates the highest form of the Adam Style. Since period pattern books provide no guidelines for Cornice Plus designs, the dimensions were determined entirely from measured drawings of historic buildings. If the original designs did not provide dimensions, we chose a height of 5 3/4". The designs are appropriate for an 8' room height and presented at half size with full size dimensions. The length of the projection can be calculated by **dividing** the height of the Cornice Plus by one of the following Golden Section ratios: **.539, 1.618, 2.236, 2.618, 3.618, 2:1,** or **2.427.** The projection dimensions are calculated from wall line, frieze line, or front face of the bottom molding. We provide this information with each design.

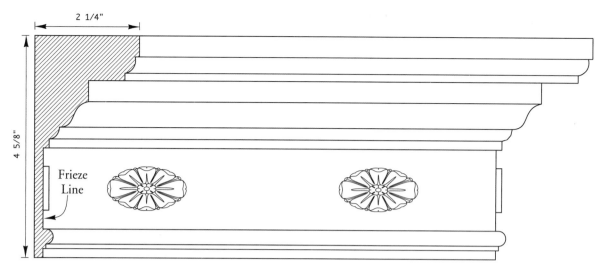

Fig. 88 Samuel Whitehorne House, Newport, RI, 1811, *HABS*, RI-323, sheet 12.
   4 5/8" ÷ ratio 2.236 = 2 1/16" from Frieze Line.

Fig. 89 Samuel Whitehorn House, Newport, RI, 1811, *HABS*, RI-323, sheet 12.
   4 15/16" ÷ ratio 3.618 = 1 3/8" from Front Face.

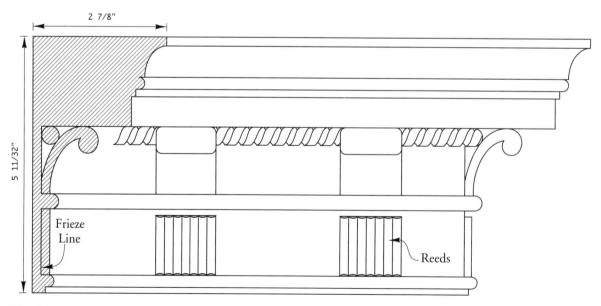

Fig. 90 Gardner-White-Pingree House, Salem, MA, 1804, Mullins, *Architectural Treasures*, vol. XVI, p. 104.
   5 11/32" ÷ ratio 2:1 = 2 11/16" from Frieze Line.

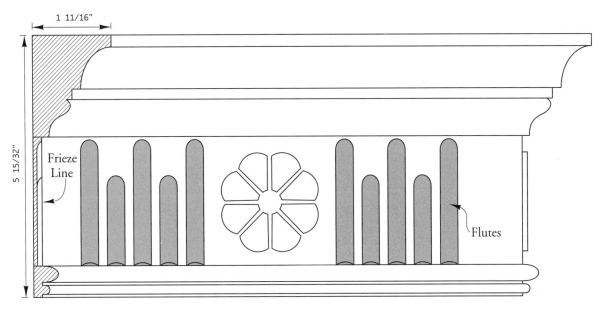

Fig. 91 Lt. Governor Martin House, Seekonk, MA, 1810, *HABS*, MA-2-90, sheet 19.
5 15/32" ÷ ratio 3.618" = 1 1/2" from Frieze Line.

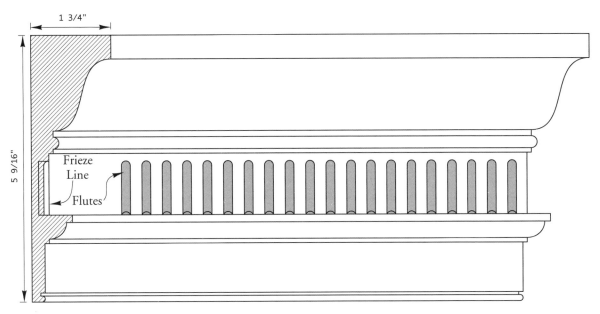

Fig. 92 General Salem Towne House, Charlton, MA, 1796, *HABS*, MA-2-38, sheet 16.
5 9/16" ÷ ratio 3.618" = 1 17/32" from Frieze Line.

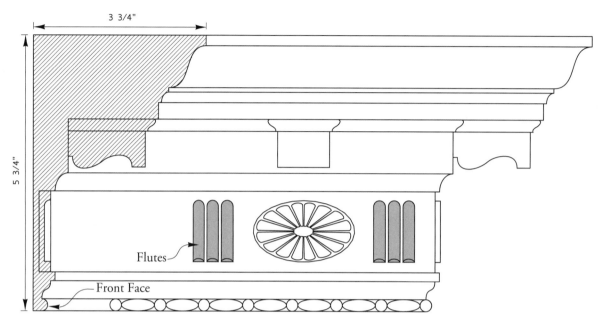

Fig. 93 Date and location of original house unknown, Wallis, *American Architecture,* pl. 10.
5 3/4" ÷ 1.618 = 3 9/16" from Front Face.

Fig. 94 Salem, MA, date of original house unknown, Mullins, *Architectural Treasures,* vol. XVI, p. 92.
5 3/4" ÷ ratio 2.618 = 2 1/4" from Wall Line.

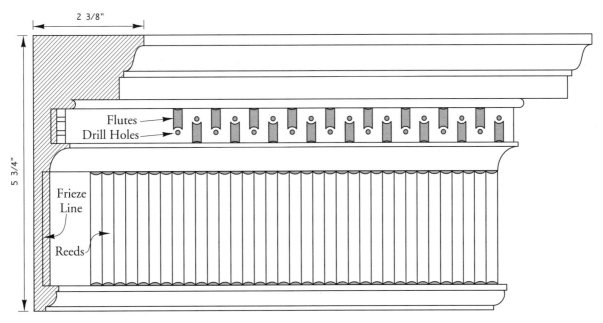

Fig. 95 Charlestown, MA, date of original house unknown, Howe and Fuller, *Details,* pl. 42.
    5 3/4" ÷ ratio 2.618 = 2 3/16" from Frieze Line.

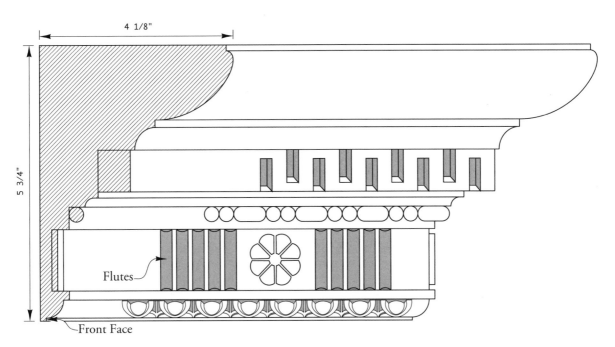

Fig. 96 Date and location of original house unknown, Wallis, *American Architecture,* pl. X.
    5 3/4" ÷ ratio 1.414 = 4 1/16" from Front Face.

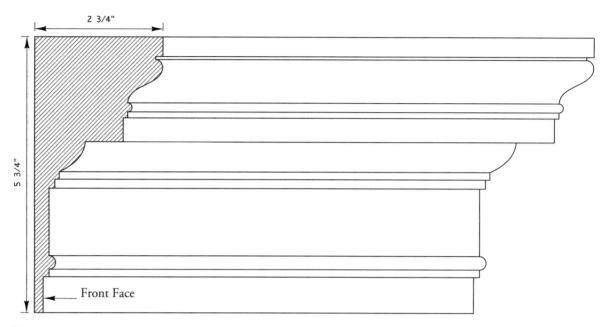

Fig. 97 Thibault House, Newburyport, MA, 1815, *HABS*, MA-123, sheet 3.
5 3/4" ÷ ratio 2.236 = 2 9/16" from Front Face.

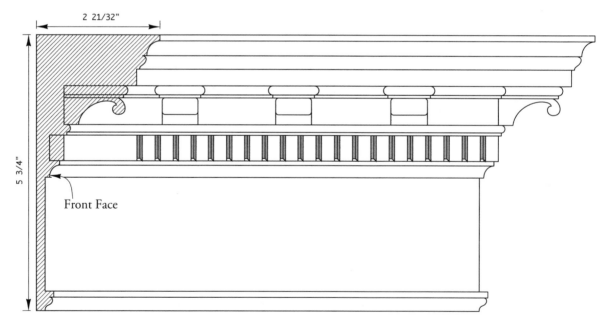

Fig. 98 Charlestown, MA, date of original house unknown, Howe and Fuller, *Details*, pl. X.
5 3/4" ÷ ratio 2.427 = 2 3/8" from Front Face.

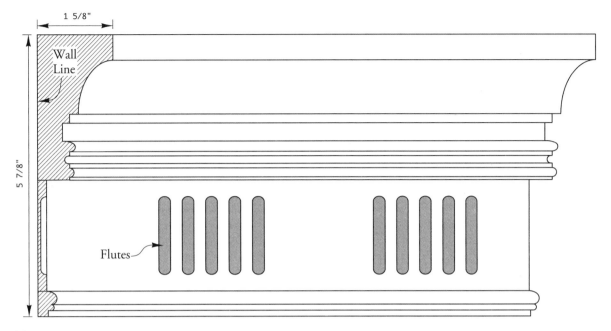

Fig. 99 Lt. Governor Martin House, Seekonk, MA, 1810, *HABS,* MA-2-90, sheet 18.
5 7/8" ÷ ratio 3.618 = 1 5/8" from Wall Line.

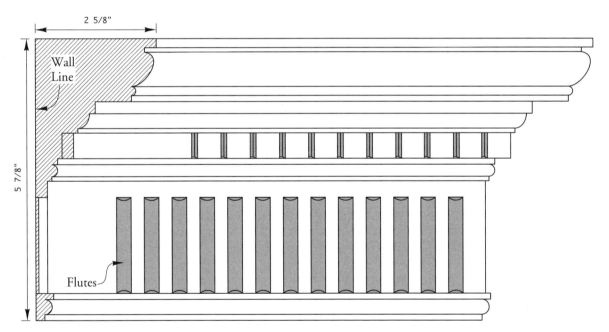

Fig. 100 Samuel Whitehorne House, Newport, RI, 1811, *HABS,* MA-323, sheet 8.
5 7/8" ÷ ratio 2.236 = 2 5/8" from Wall Line.

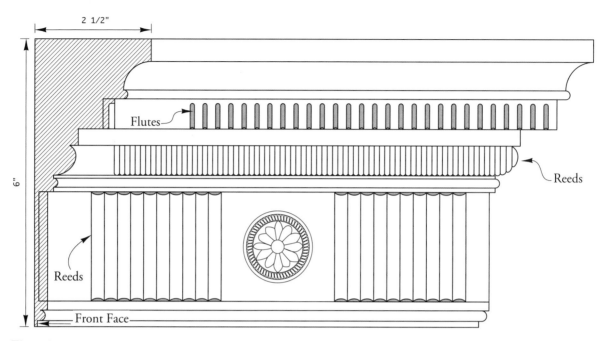

Fig. 101 Samuel Whitehorne House, Newport, RI, 1811, *HABS,* MA-323, sheet 8.
6" ÷ ratio 2.427 = 2 15/32" from Front Face.

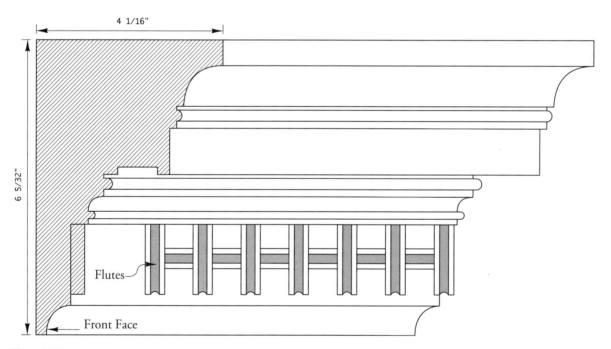

Fig. 102 Bezaleel Mann House, North Attleboro, MA, 1790, Mullins, *Architectural Treasures,* vol. X, p. 156.
6 5/32" ÷ ratio 1.618 = 3 13/16" from Front Face.

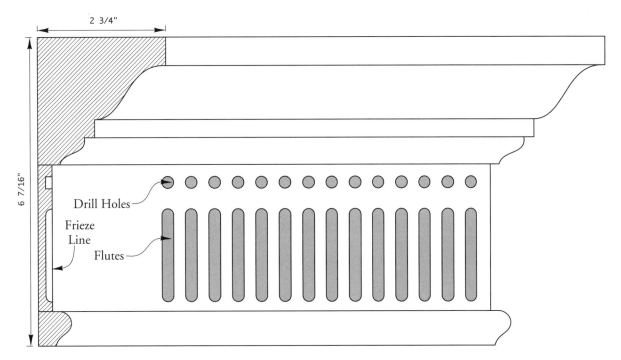

Fig. 103 Holmes-Sayward House, Alfred, ME, 1802, *HABS*, ME-32, sheet 12.
6 7/16" ÷ ratio 2.618 = 2 7/16" from Frieze Line.

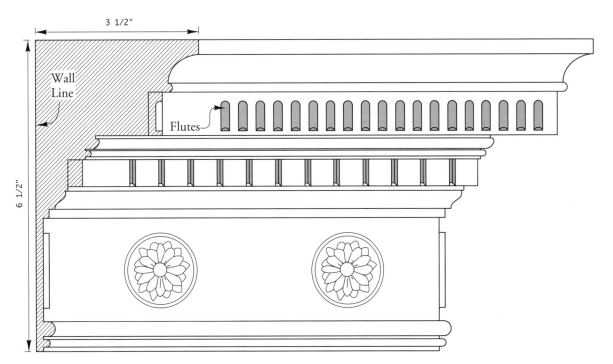

Fig. 104 Lt. Governor Martin House, Seekonk, MA, 1810, *HABS,* MA-2-90, sheet 12.
6 1/2" ÷ ratio .539 = 3 1/2" from Wall Line.

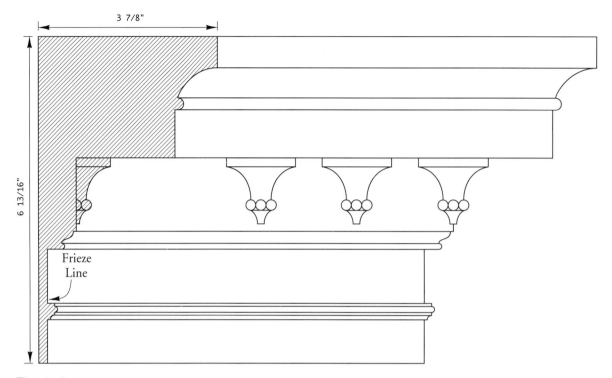

Fig. 105 Henry Pettis House, Somerset, MA, 1810, *HABS,* MA-2-52, sheet 8.
6 13/16" ÷ ratio .539 = 3 11/16" from Frieze Line.

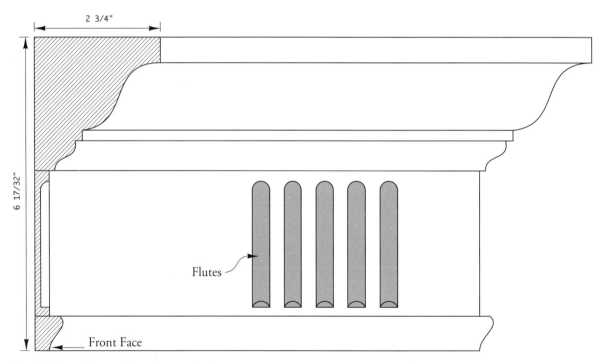

Fig. 106 Hyde-Worthen House, Charlestown, MA, 1800, *HABS,* MA-19-2, sheet 5.
6 17/32" ÷ ratio 2.618 = 2 1/2" from Front Face.

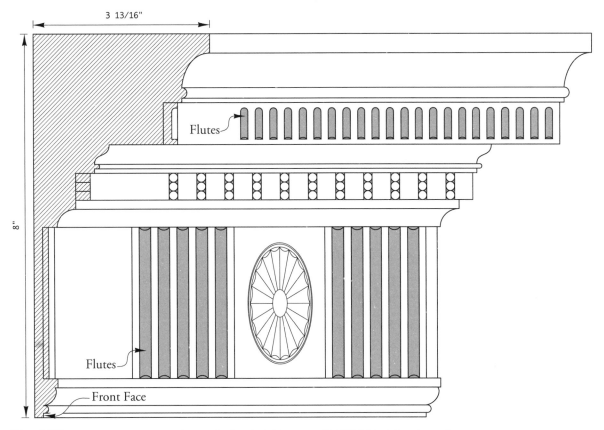

Fig. 107 Lt. Governor Martin House, Seekonk, MA, 1810, *HABS,* MA-2-90, sheet15.
      8 " ÷ ratio 2.236 = 3 19/32" from Front Face.

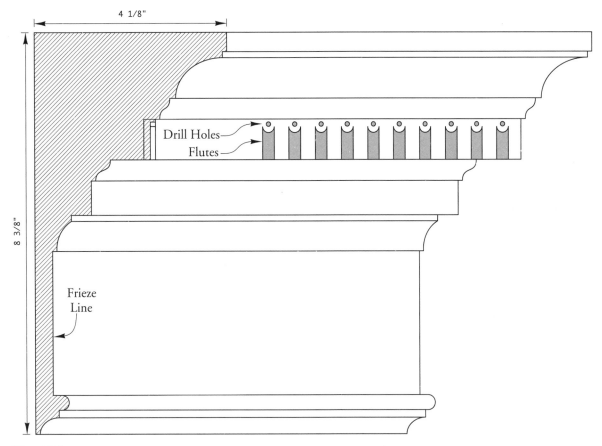

Fig. 108 Henry Pettis House, Somerset, MA, 1800, *HABS,* MA-2-52, sheet 9.
      8 3/8" ÷ ratio 2.236 = 3 3/4" from Frieze Line.

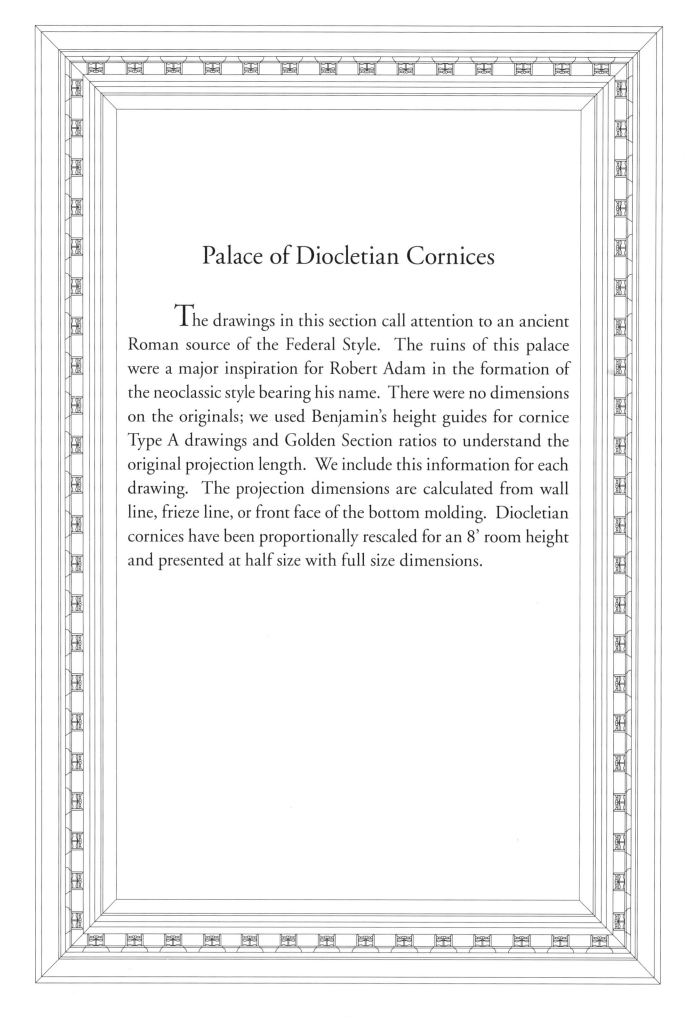

Palace of Diocletian Cornices

The drawings in this section call attention to an ancient Roman source of the Federal Style. The ruins of this palace were a major inspiration for Robert Adam in the formation of the neoclassic style bearing his name. There were no dimensions on the originals; we used Benjamin's height guides for cornice Type A drawings and Golden Section ratios to understand the original projection length. We include this information for each drawing. The projection dimensions are calculated from wall line, frieze line, or front face of the bottom molding. Diocletian cornices have been proportionally rescaled for an 8' room height and presented at half size with full size dimensions.

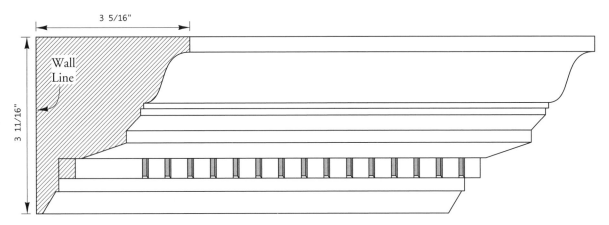

Fig. 109 Palace of Diocletian, Spalato, Croatia, Adam, *Ruins of the Palace,* pl. XXX.
3 11/16" ÷ ratio 1.118 = 3 5/16" from Wall Line.

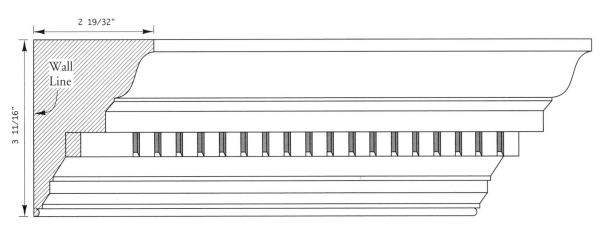

Fig. 110 Palace of Diocletian, Spalato, Croatia, Adam, *Ruins of the Palace,* pl. LXXXVI.
3 11/16" ÷ ratio 1.414 = 2 19/32" from Wall Line.

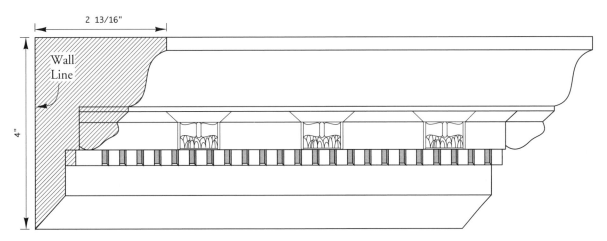

Fig. 111 Palace of Diocletian, Spalato, Croatia, Adam, *Ruins of the Palace,* pl. XXXV.
4" ÷ ratio 1.414 = 2 13/16" from Wall Line.

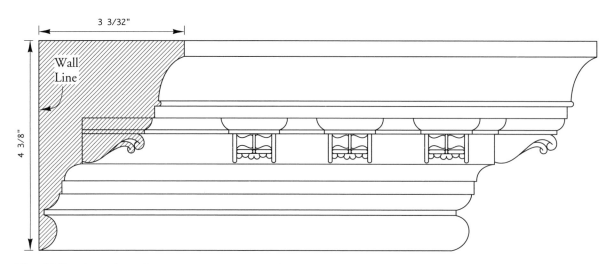

Fig. 112 Palace of Diocletian, Spalato, Croatia, Adam, *Ruins of the Palace,* pl. XLVIII.
4 3/8" ÷ ratio 1.414 = 3 3/32" from Wall Line.

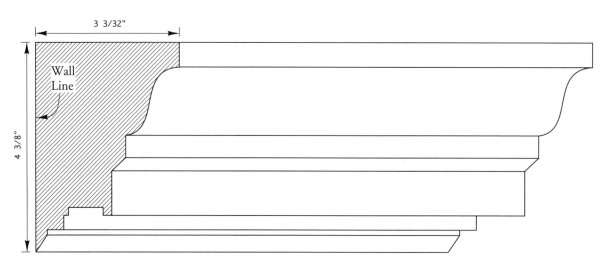

Fig. 113 Palace of Diocletian, Spalato, Croatia, Adam, *Ruins of the Palace,* pl. XXVII.
4 3/8" ÷ ratio 1.414 = 3 3/32" from Wall Line.

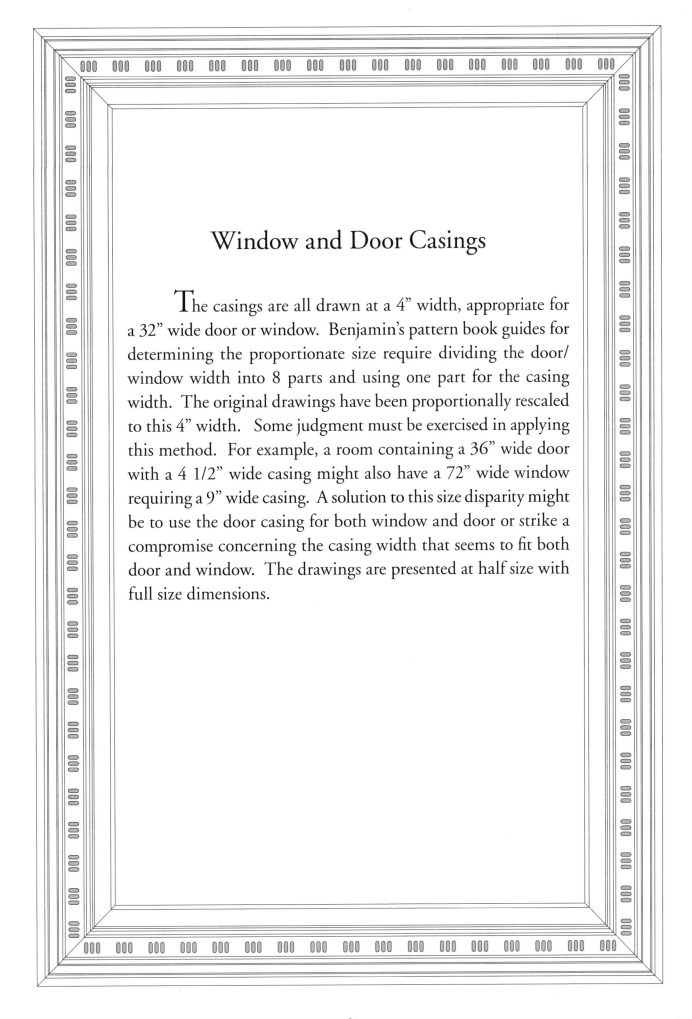

Window and Door Casings

The casings are all drawn at a 4" width, appropriate for a 32" wide door or window. Benjamin's pattern book guides for determining the proportionate size require dividing the door/ window width into 8 parts and using one part for the casing width. The original drawings have been proportionally rescaled to this 4" width. Some judgment must be exercised in applying this method. For example, a room containing a 36" wide door with a 4 1/2" wide casing might also have a 72" wide window requiring a 9" wide casing. A solution to this size disparity might be to use the door casing for both window and door or strike a compromise concerning the casing width that seems to fit both door and window. The drawings are presented at half size with full size dimensions.

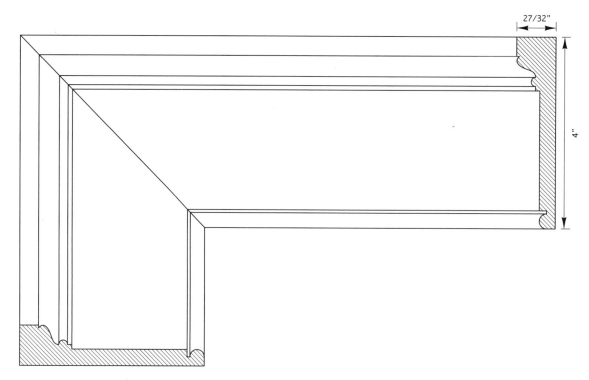

Fig. 114 Amory-Ticknor House, Boston, MA, 1804, *HABS,* MA-175, sheet 12.

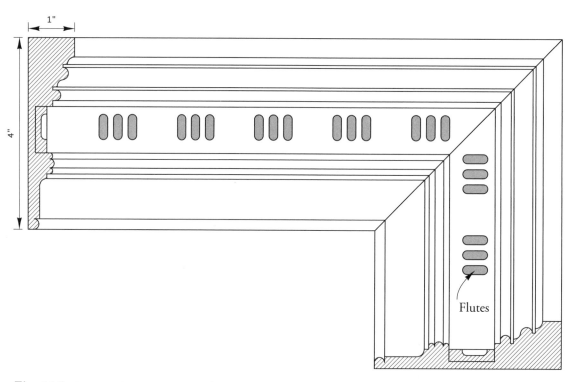

Fig. 115 Harrison Gray Otis House (first), Boston, MA, 1796, Mullins, *Architectural Treasures,* vol. I, p. 169.

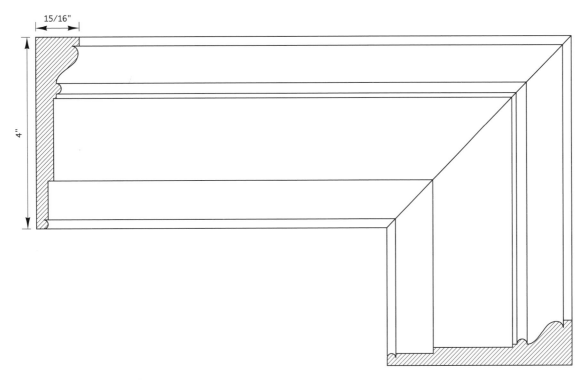

Fig. 116 Hyde-Lincoln House, Charlestown, MA, 1801, *HABS*, MA-299, sheet 8.

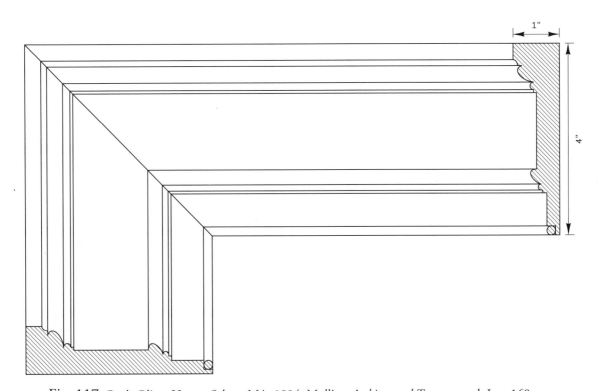

Fig. 117 Cook-Oliver House, Salem, MA, 1804, Mullins, *Architectural Treasures*, vol. I, p. 168.

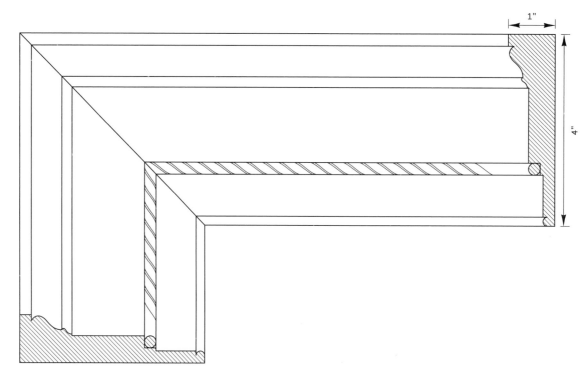

Fig. 118 Christopher Ryder House, Chathamport, MA, 1809, *HABS,* MA-118, sheet 13.

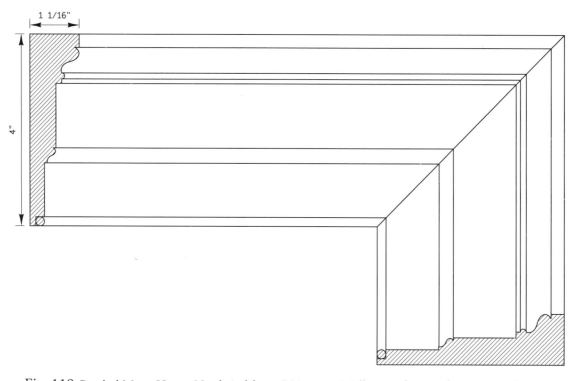

Fig. 119 Bezaleel Mann House, North Attleboro, MA, 1790, Mullins, *Architectural Treasures*, vol. X, p. 156.

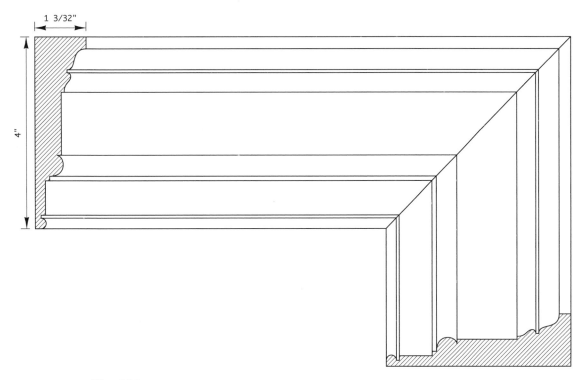

1 3/32"

4"

Fig. 120 Captain Leonard House, Agawam, MA, 1807, *HABS*, MA-2-50, sheet 9.

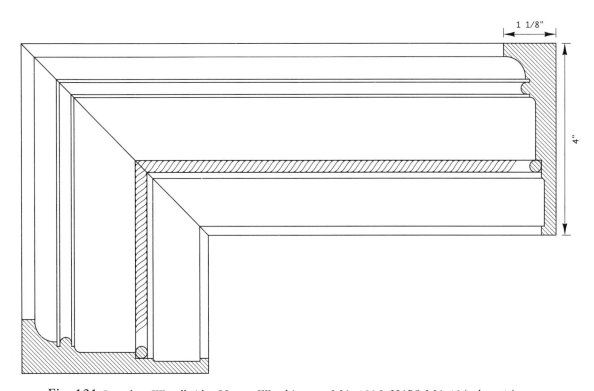

1 1/8"

4"

Fig. 121 Jonathan Woodbridge House, Worthington, MA, 1806, *HABS*, MA-124, sheet 14.

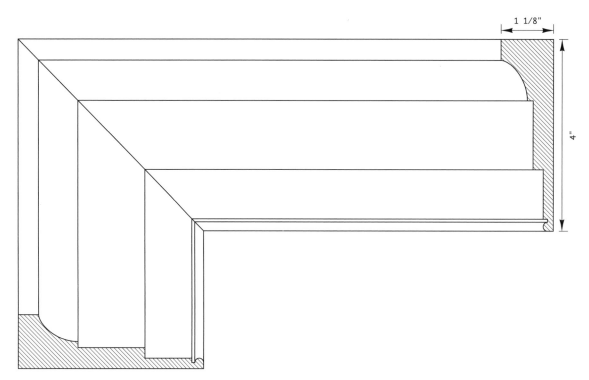

Fig. 122 Timothy Jackson House, Newton, MA, 1809, *HABS*, MA-139, sheet 8.

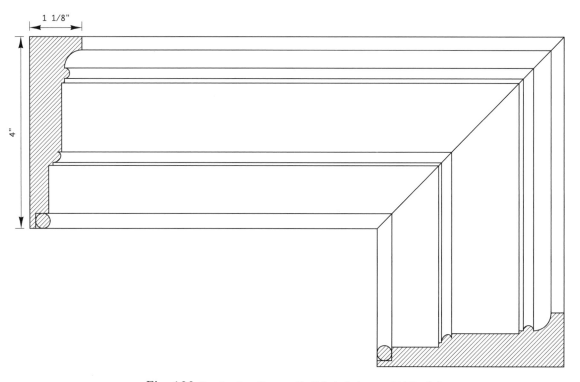

Fig. 123 Benjamin, *Country Builder's Assistant*, 1797, pl. I.

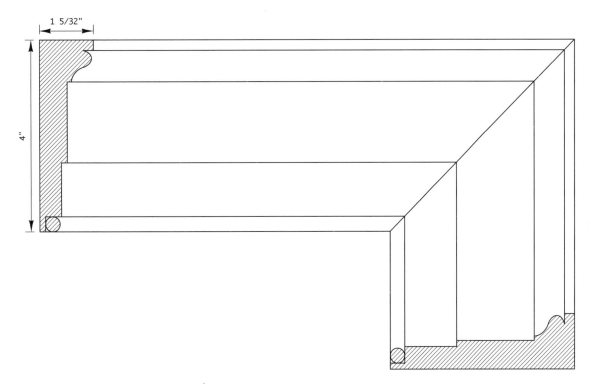

Fig. 124 Benjamin, *Country Builder's Assistant,* 1797, pl. I.

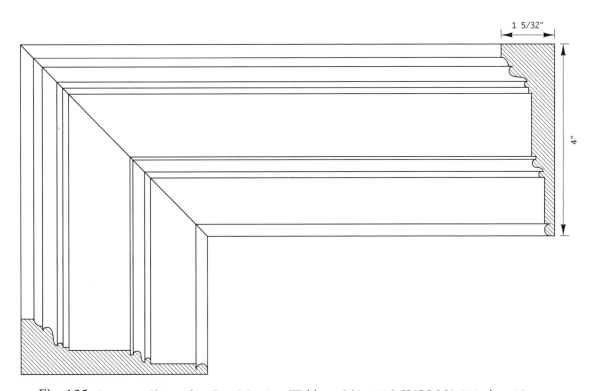

Fig. 125 Governor Christopher Gore Mansion, Waltham, MA, 1806, *HABS,* MA-210, sheet 13.

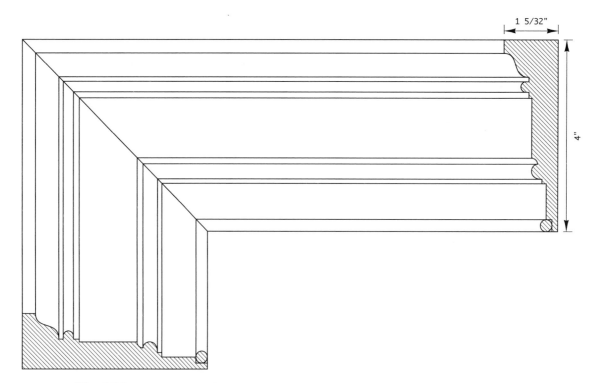

Fig. 126 Captain Leonard House, Agawam, MA, 1807, *HABS*, MA-2-50, sheet 9.

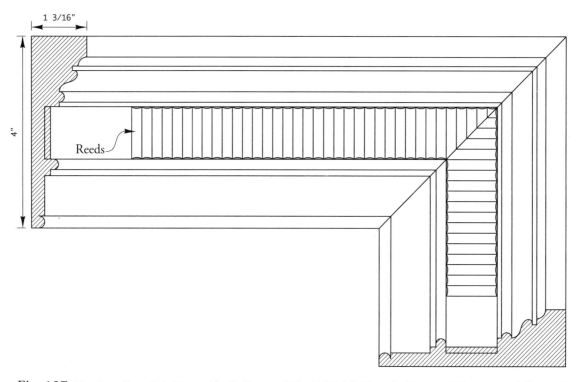

Fig. 127 Harrison Gray Otis House (first), Boston, MA, 1796, Mullins, *Architectural Treasures,* vol. I, p. 169.

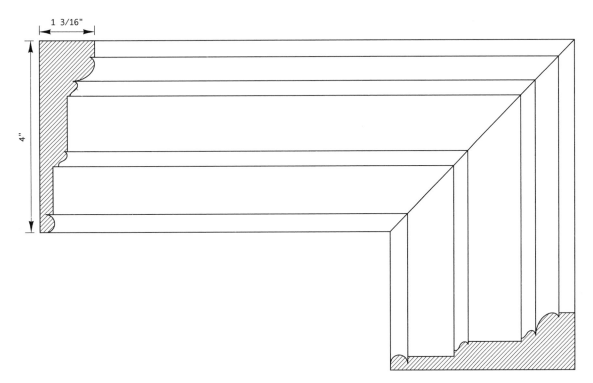

Fig. 128 Coleman-Hollister House, Greenfield, MA, 1796, *HABS*, MA-2-19, sheet 14.

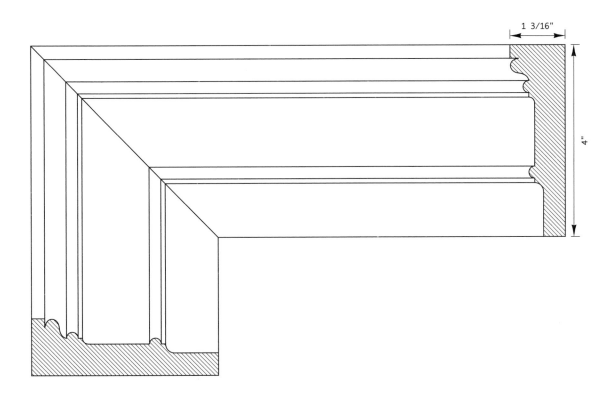

Fig. 129 Benjamin, *Country Builder's Assistant,* 1797, pl. I.

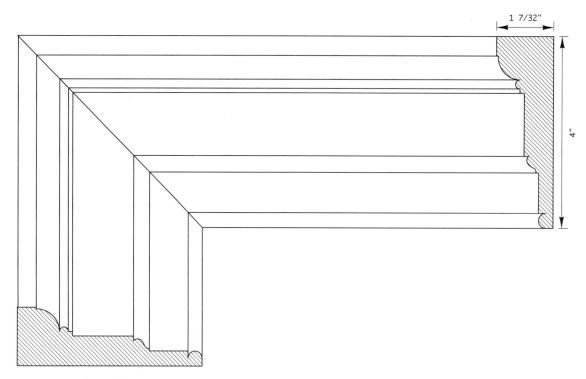

Fig. 130 Lt. Governor Martin House, Seekonk, MA, 1810, *HABS*, MA-2-90, sheet 18.

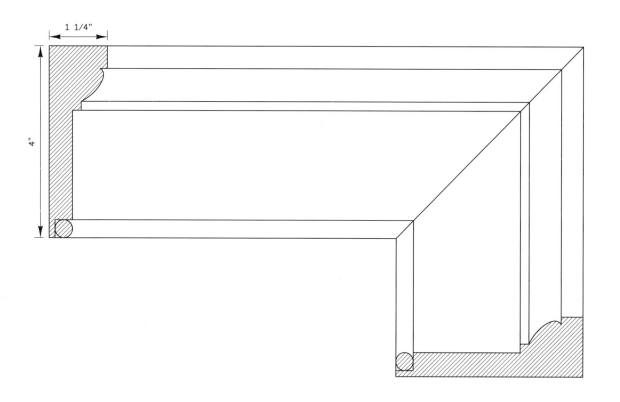

Fig. 131 Benjamin, *Builder's Companion,* 1806, pl. XI.

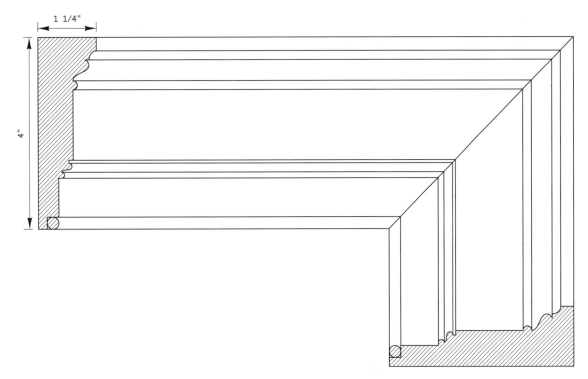

Fig. 132 Governor Christopher Gore Mansion, Waltham, MA, 1806, *HABS*, MA-210, sheet 19.

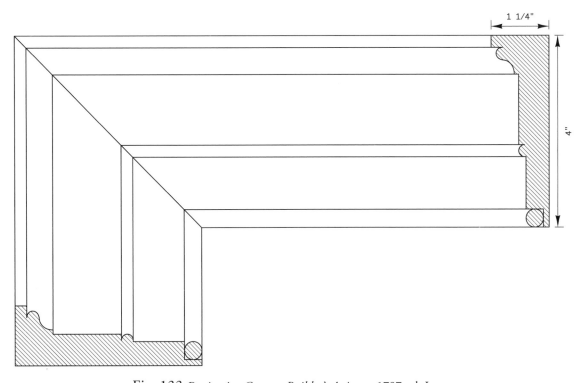

Fig. 133 Benjamin, *Country Builder's Assistant*, 1797, pl. I.

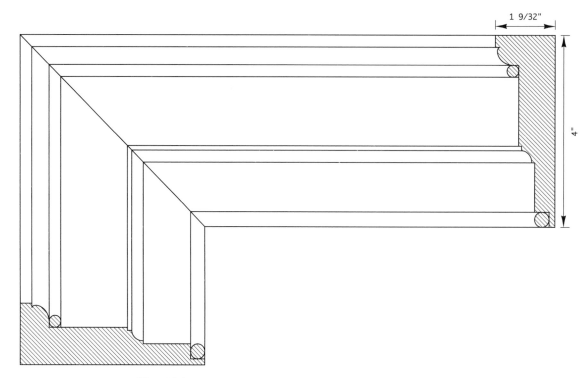

Fig. 134 Benjamin, *Country Builder's Assistant,* 1797, pl. I.

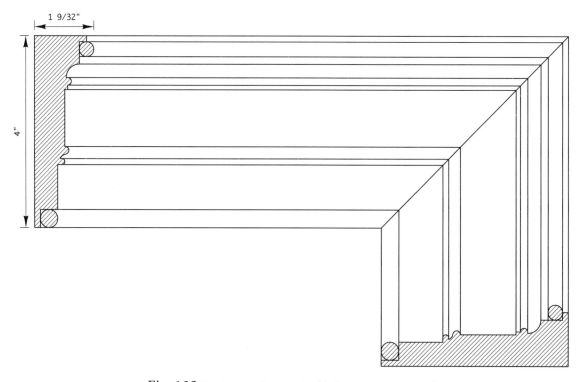

Fig. 135 Benjamin, *Country Builder's Assistant,* 1797, pl. I.

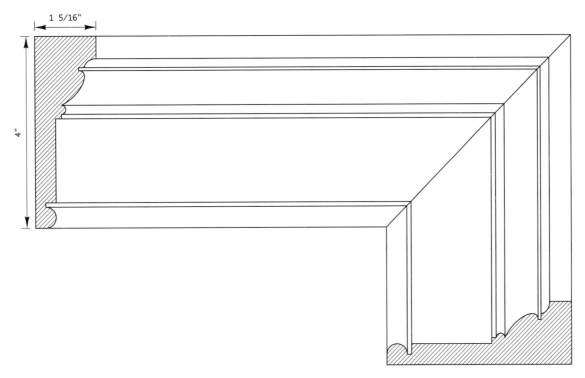

Fig. 136 Hyde-Worthen House, Charlestown, MA, 1800, *HABS,* MA-192, sheet 7.

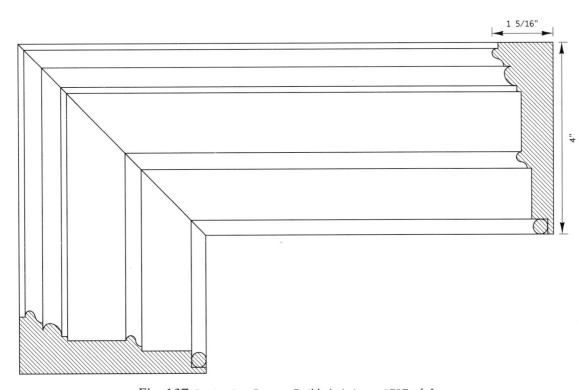

Fig. 137 Benjamin, *Country Builder's Assistant,* 1797, pl. I.

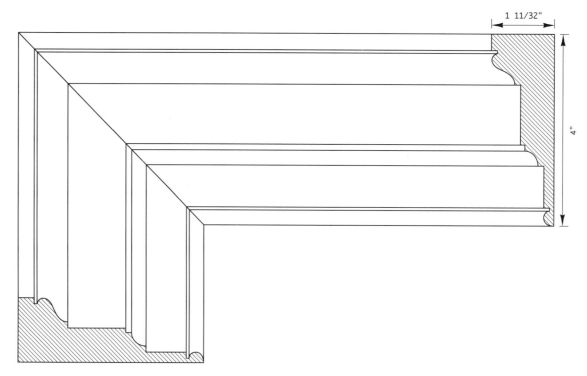

Fig. 138 Lt. Governor Martin House, Seekonk, MA, 1810, *HABS,* MA-2-90, sheet 19.

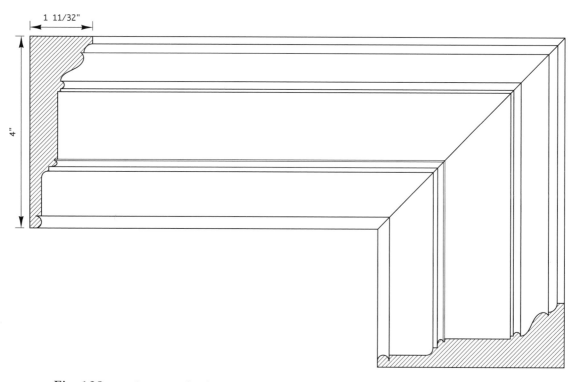

Fig. 139 Jonathan Woodbridge House, Worthington, MA, 1806, *HABS,* MA-124, sheet 15.

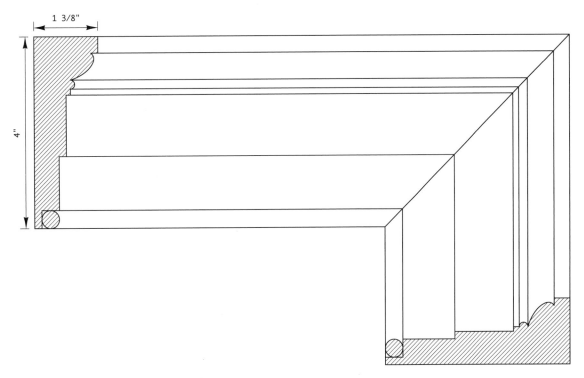

1 3/8"

4"

Fig. 140 Benjamin, *Builder's Companion*, 1806, pl. XI.

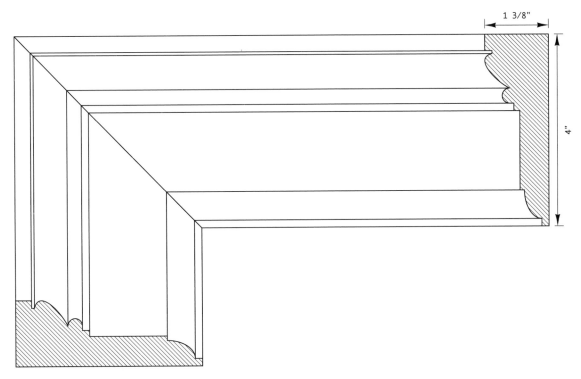

1 3/8"

4"

Fig. 141 Nathan Dean House, East Taunton, MA, 1810 addition, *HABS*, MA-143, sheet 11.

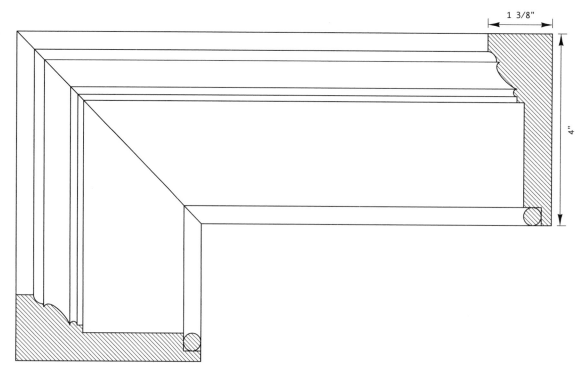

Fig. 142 Benjamin, *Builder's Companion,* 1806, pl. XI.

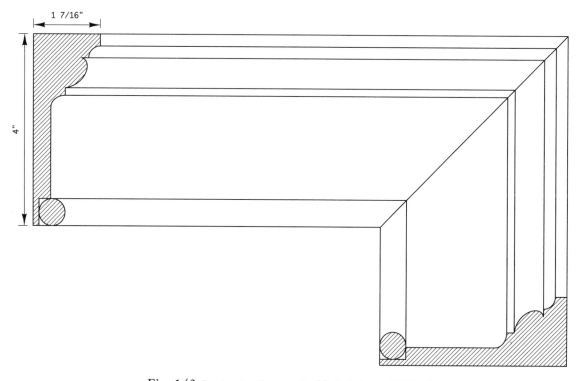

Fig. 143 Benjamin, *Country Builder's Assistant,* 1797, pl. I.

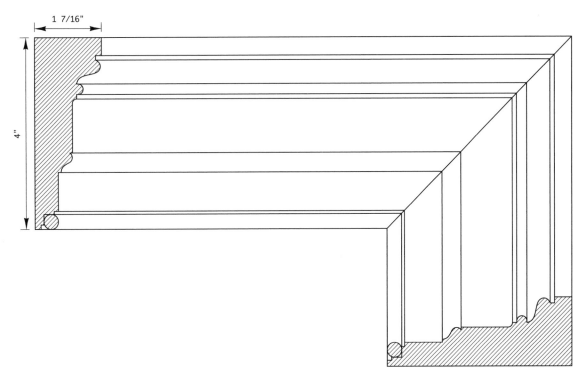

Fig. 144 Isaac Cooley House, Agawam, MA, 1807, *HABS,* MA-2-51, sheet 6.

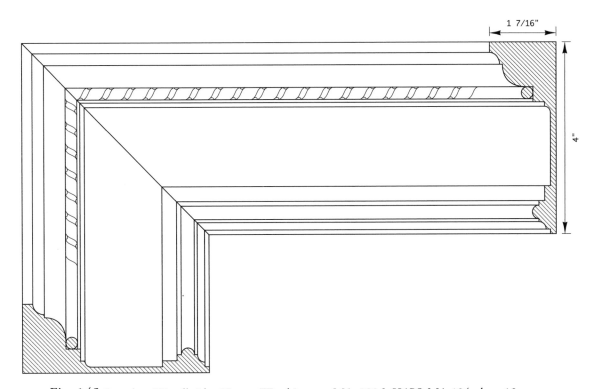

Fig. 145 Jonathan Woodbridge House, Worthington, MA, 1806, *HABS*, MA-124, sheet 13.

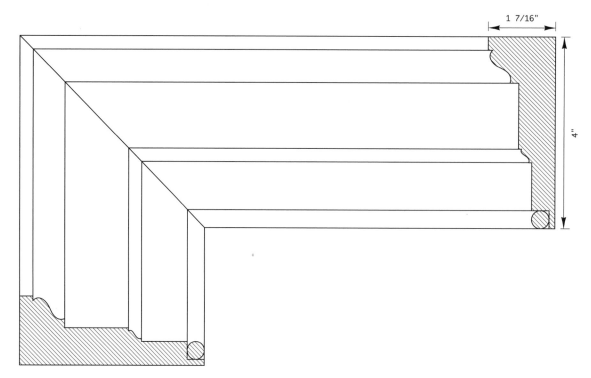

Fig. 146 Coleman-Hollister House, Greenfield, MA, 1795, *HABS*, MA-2-19, sheet 19.

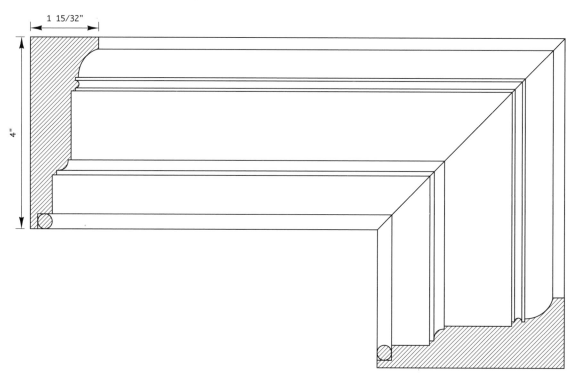

Fig. 147 Jonathan Woodbridge House, Worthington, MA, 1806, *HABS*, MA-124, sheet 20.

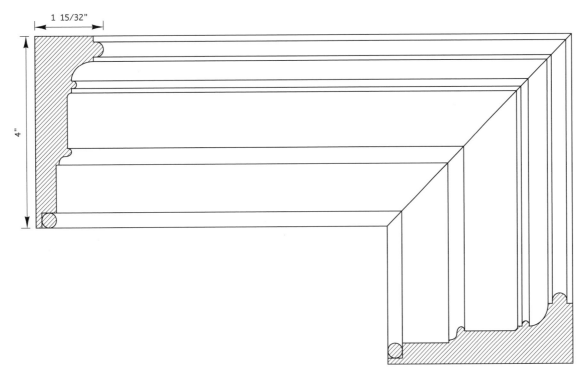

Fig. 148 Benjamin, *Country Builder's Assistant,* 1797, pl. 1.

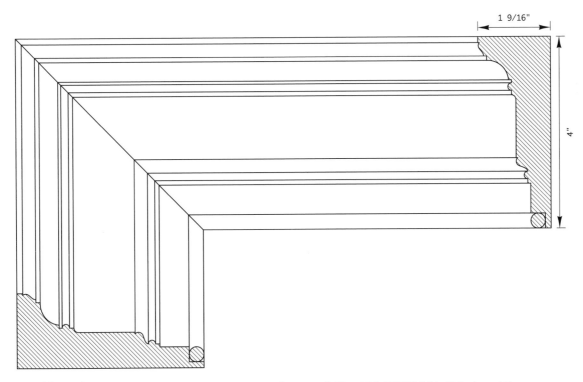

Fig. 149 Jonathan Woodbridge House, Worthington, MA, 1806, *HABS,* MA-124, sheet 17.

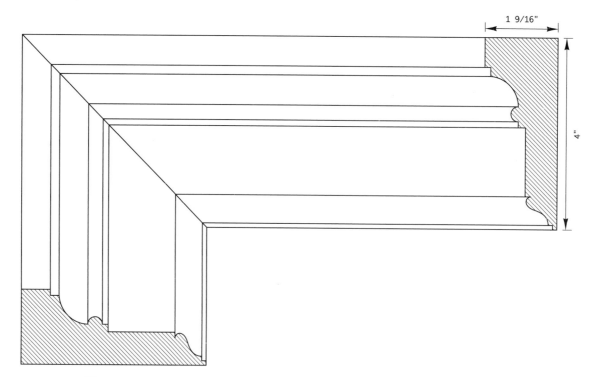

Fig. 150 Thibault House, Newburyport, MA, 1815, *HABS,* MA-123, sheet 3.

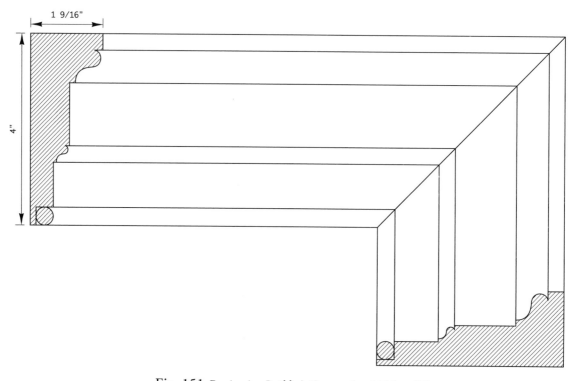

Fig. 151 Benjamin, *Builder's Companion,* 1806, p. XI.

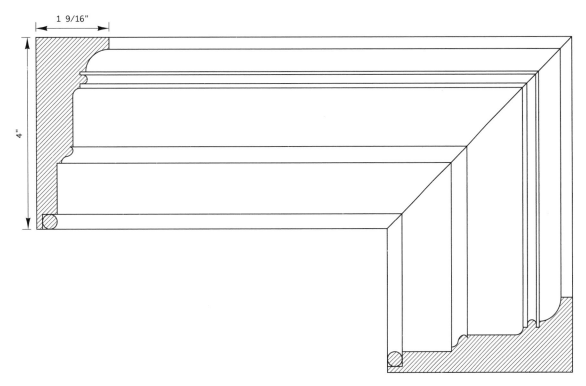

Fig. 152 Benjamin, *Country Builder's Assistant,* 1797, pl. I.

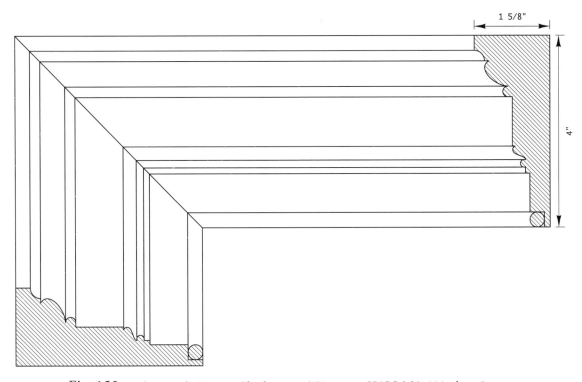

Fig. 153 Hyde-Lincoln House, Charlestown, MA, 1801, *HABS*, MA-299, sheet 8.

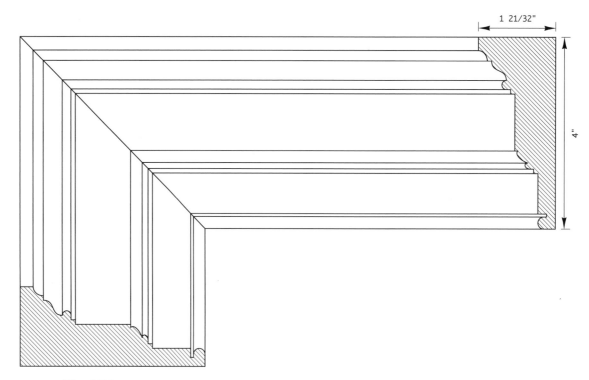

Fig. 154 Lt. Governor Martin House, Seekonk, MA, 1810, *HABS*, MA-2-90, sheet 15.

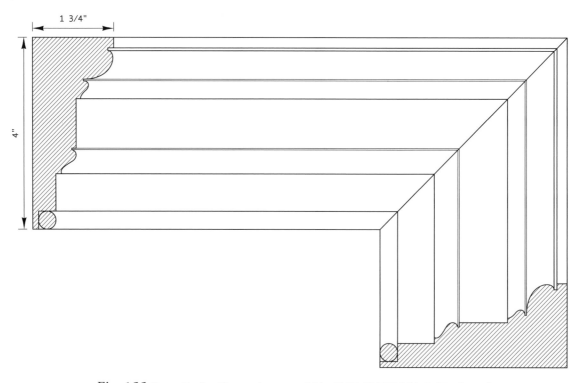

Fig. 155 Isaac Cooley House, Agawam, MA, 1807, *HABS,* MA-2-51, sheet 6.

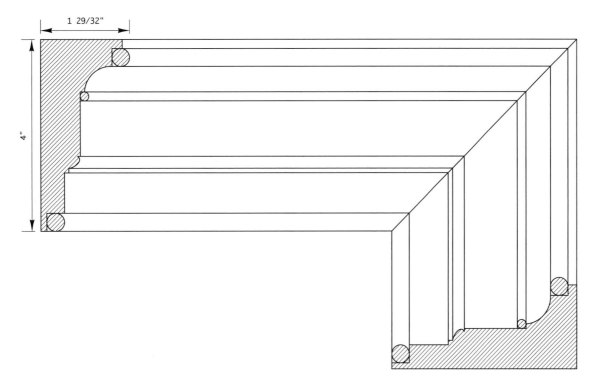

Fig. 156 Benjamin, *Builder's Companion,* 1806, pl. XI.

Window Sills and Aprons

Historic pattern books offer no guides for window sills or aprons. A careful examination of resource material reveals the window casings most often terminate at the top of the chair rail without any sill, floor, window seat, or floor plinth block. We have provided the historic sill and apron drawings that were found at the original dimensions and presented them at full size. We prepared some contemporary designs for sills and used chair rail designs found in the Chair Rail section for aprons (p. 98). The contemporary designs are appropriate for an 8' room height and are presented at full size.

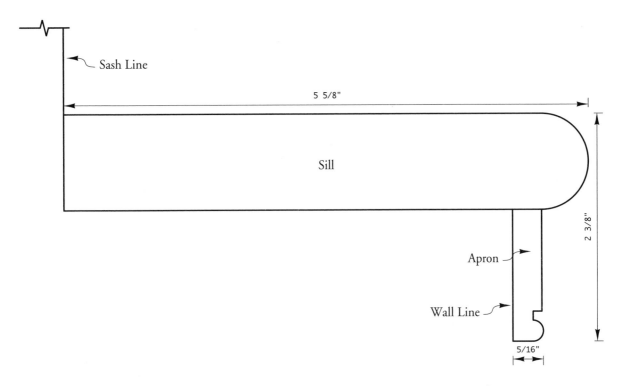

Fig. 157 Hyde-Lincoln House, Charlestown, MA, 1801, *HABS,* MA-299, sheet 7.

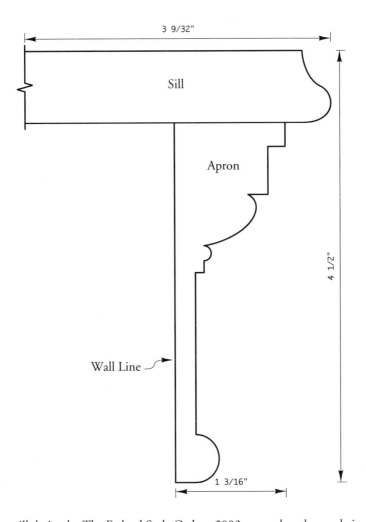

Fig. 158 Contemporary sill design by The Federal Style Orders, 2003, apron based on a chair rail design (see Fig. 210).

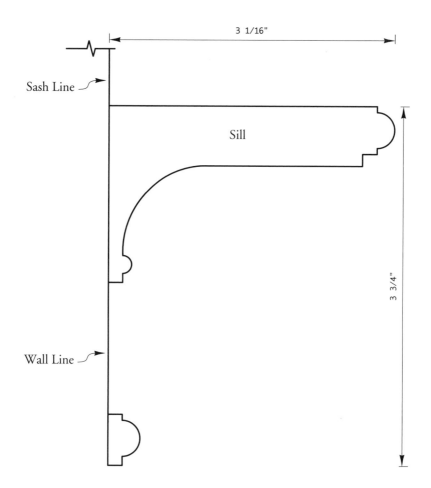

Fig. 159 Wheeler-Beecher House, Bethany, CT, 1801, *HABS*, CT-68, sheet 24.

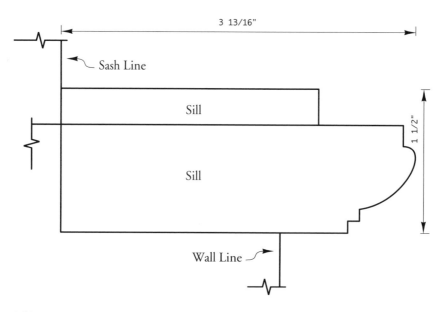

Fig. 160 Governor Woodbury Mansion, Portsmouth, NH, 1809, *HABS*, NH-20, sheet 48.

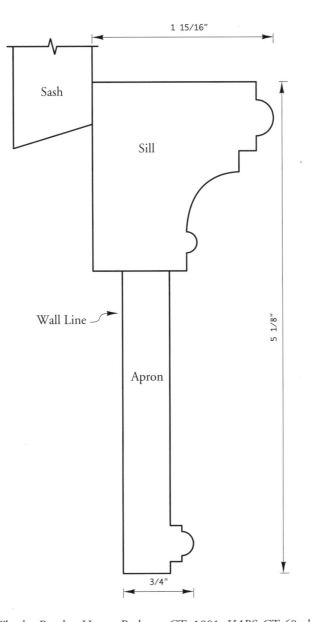

Fig. 161 Wheeler-Beecher House, Bethany, CT, 1801, *HABS,* CT-68, sheet 20.

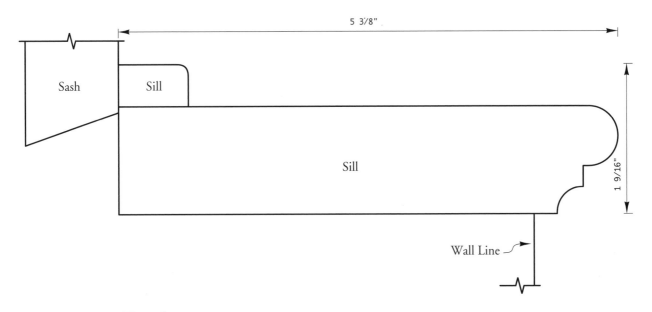

Fig. 162 Shaw-Souther House, Cohasset, MA, 1794, *HABS,* MA-231, sheet 5.

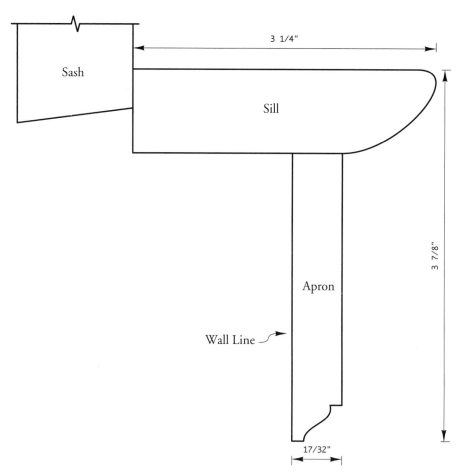

Fig. 163 Isaac Cooley House, Agawam, MA, 1807, *HABS,* MA-2-51, sheet 6.

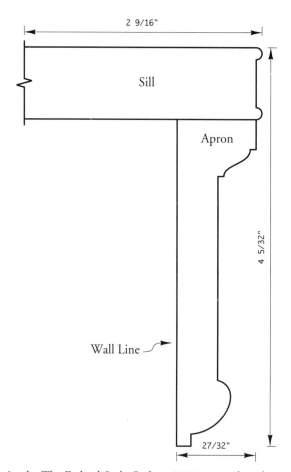

Fig. 164 Contemporary sill design by The Federal Style Orders, 2003, apron based on a chair rail design (see Fig. 197).

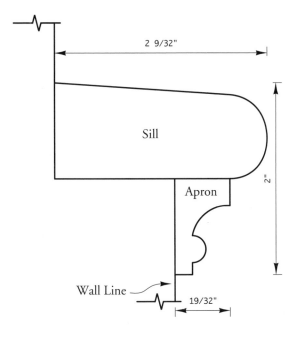

2 9/32"

Sill

Apron

2"

Wall Line

19/32"

Fig. 165 Hyde-Lincoln House, Charlestown, MA, 1801, *HABS,* MA-299, sheet 7.

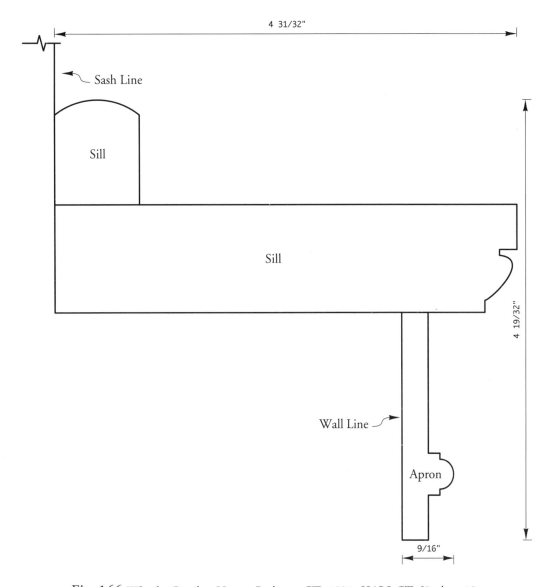

4 31/32"

Sash Line

Sill

Sill

4 19/32"

Wall Line

Apron

9/16"

Fig. 166 Wheeler-Beecher House, Bethany, CT, 1801, *HABS,* CT-68, sheet 19.

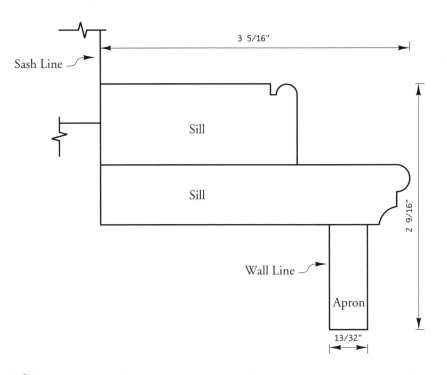

Sash Line

3 5/16"

Sill

Sill

2 9/16"

Wall Line

Apron

13/32"

Fig. 167 Governor Woodbury Mansion, Portsmouth, NH, 1809, *HABS*, NH-20, sheet 49.

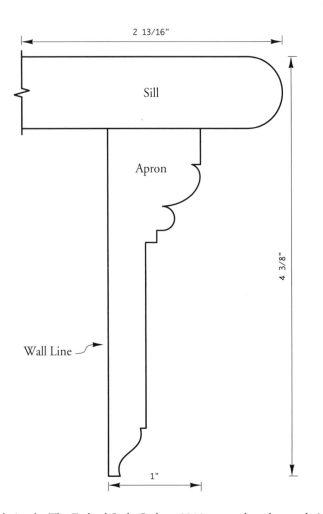

2 13/16"

Sill

Apron

4 3/8"

Wall Line

1"

Fig. 168 Contemporary sill design by The Federal Style Orders, 2003, apron based on a chair rail design (see Fig. 203).

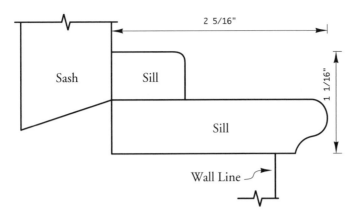

Fig. 169 Shaw-Souther House, Cohasset, MA, 1794, *HABS,* MA-231, sheet 6.

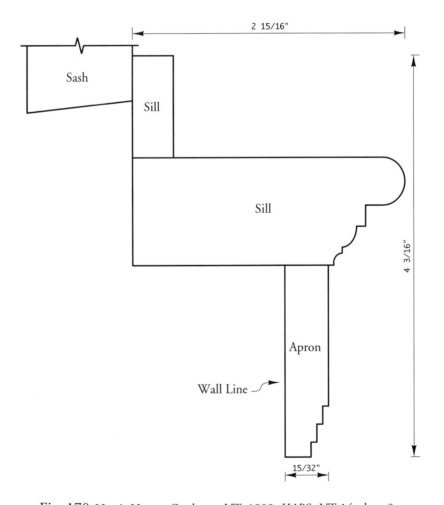

Fig. 170 Harris House, Castleton, VT, 1800, *HABS,* VT-14, sheet 9.

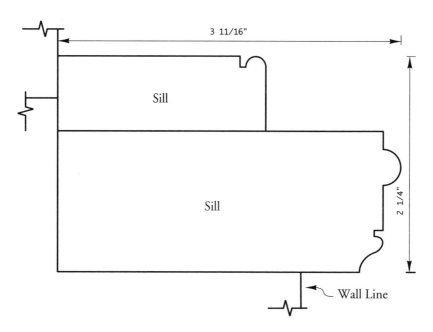

Fig. 171 Governor Woodbury Mansion, Portsmouth, NH, 1809, *HABS*, NH-20, sheet 49.

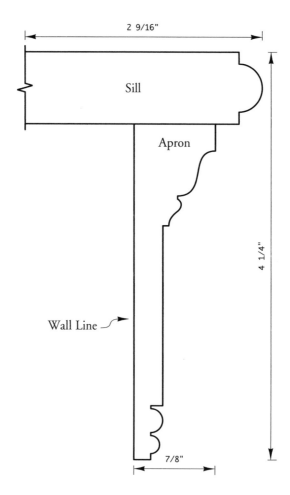

Fig. 172 Contemporary sill design by The Federal Style Orders, 2003, apron based on a chair rail design (see Fig. 200).

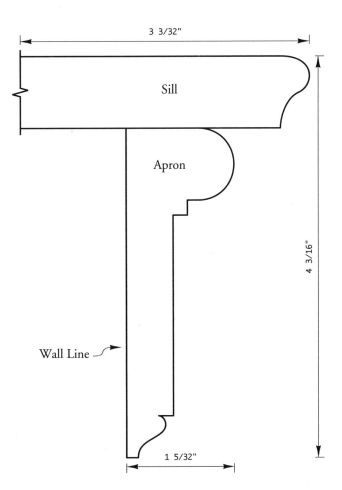

3 3/32"

Sill

Apron

Wall Line

4 3/16"

1 5/32"

Fig. 173 Contemporary sill design by The Federal Style Orders, 2003, apron based on a chair rail design (see Fig. 198).

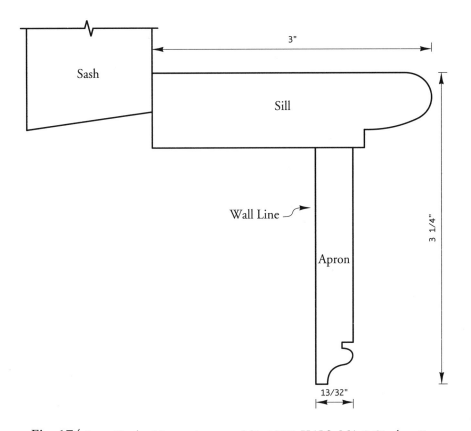

Sash

3"

Sill

Wall Line

Apron

3 1/4"

13/32"

Fig. 174 Isaac Cooley House, Agawam, MA, 1807, *HABS,* MA-2-51, sheet 7.

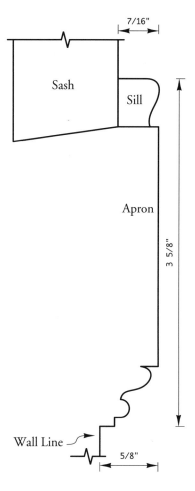

7/16"

Sash

Sill

Apron

3 5/8"

Wall Line

5/8"

Fig. 175 Isaac Cooley House, Agawam, MA, 1807, *HABS,* MA-2-51, sheet 6.

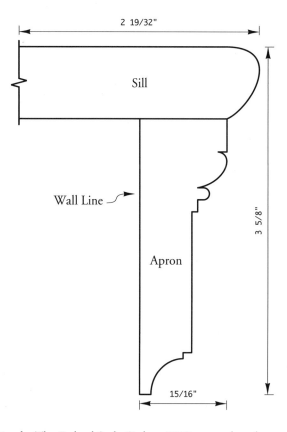

2 19/32"

Sill

Wall Line

3 5/8"

Apron

15/16"

Fig. 176 Contemporary sill design by The Federal Style Orders, 2003, apron based on a chair rail design (see Fig. 180).

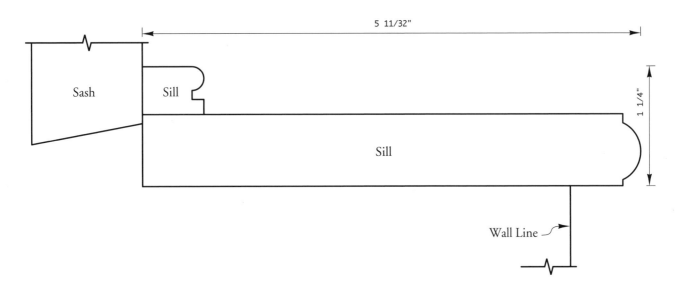

Fig. 177 Shaw-Souther House, Cohasset, MA, 1794, *HABS,* MA-231, sheet 5.

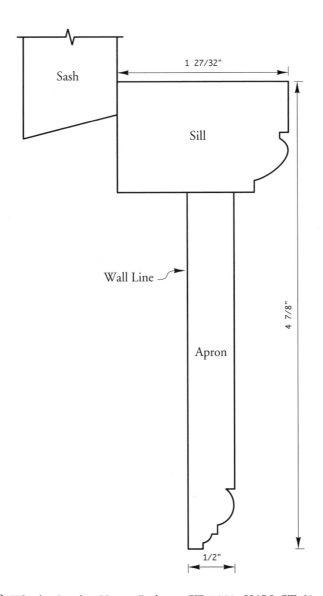

Fig. 178 Wheeler-Beecher House, Bethany, CT, 1801, *HABS,* CT-68, sheet 20.

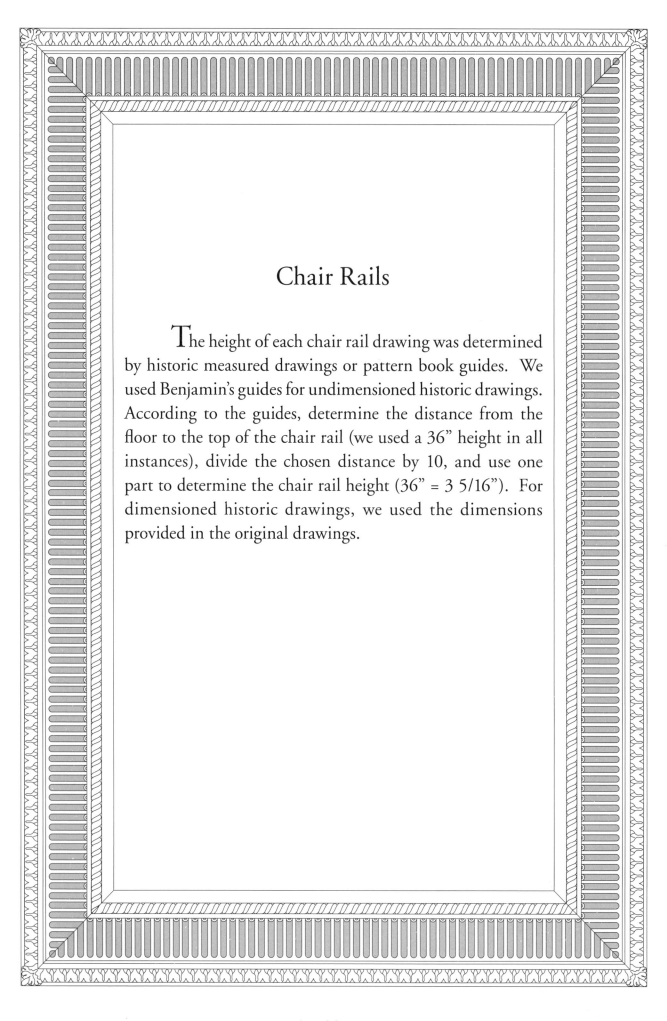

Chair Rails

The height of each chair rail drawing was determined by historic measured drawings or pattern book guides. We used Benjamin's guides for undimensioned historic drawings. According to the guides, determine the distance from the floor to the top of the chair rail (we used a 36" height in all instances), divide the chosen distance by 10, and use one part to determine the chair rail height (36" = 3 5/16"). For dimensioned historic drawings, we used the dimensions provided in the original drawings.

Fig. 179 Hyde-Lincoln House, Charlestown, MA, 1801, *HABS*, MA-299, sheet 8.

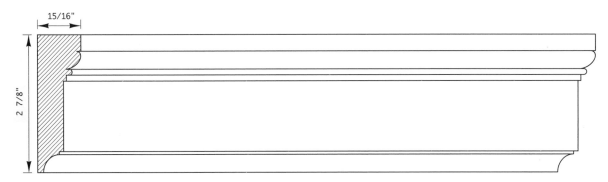

Fig. 180 Lt. Governor Martin House, Seekonk, MA, 1810, *HABS*, MA-2-90, sheet 17.

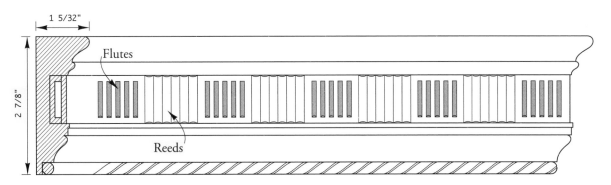

Fig. 181 Christopher Ryder House, Chathamport, MA, 1809, *HABS*, MA-118, sheet 13.

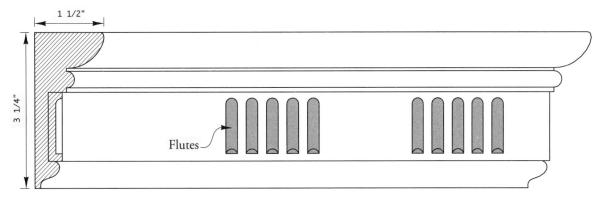

Fig. 182 Coleman-Hollister House, Greenfield, MA, 1796, *HABS,* MA-2-19, sheet 19.

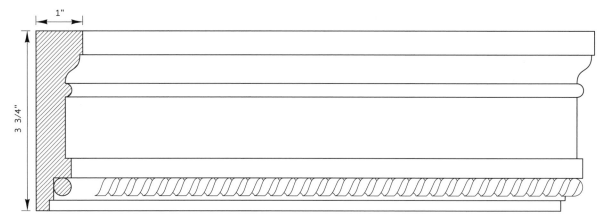

Fig. 183 General Salem Towne House, Charlton, MA, 1796, *HABS*, MA-2-38, sheet 16.

Fig. 184 Lt. Governor Martin House, Seekonk, MA, 1810, *HABS*, MA-2-90, sheet 12.

Fig. 185 Benjamin, *Country Builder's Assistant*, 1797, pl. XIX.

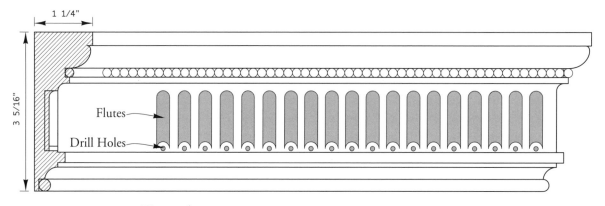

Fig. 186 Benjamin, *Country Builder's Assistant*, 1797, pl. XV.

Fig. 187 Henry Pettis House, Somerset, MA, 1800, *HABS*, MA-2-52, sheet 10.

Fig. 188 Benjamin, *Country Builder's Assistant*, 1797, pl. XV.

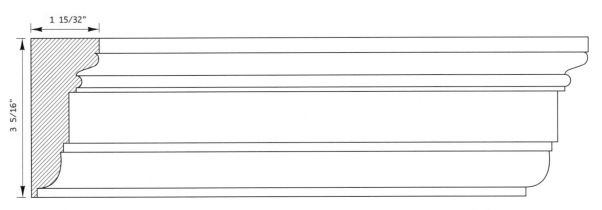

Fig. 189 Jonathan Woodbridge House, Worthington, MA, 1806, *HABS*, MA-124, sheet 20.

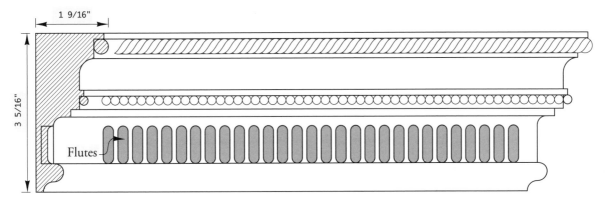

Flutes

Fig. 190 Benjamin, *Country Builder's Assistant,* 1797, pl. XV.

101

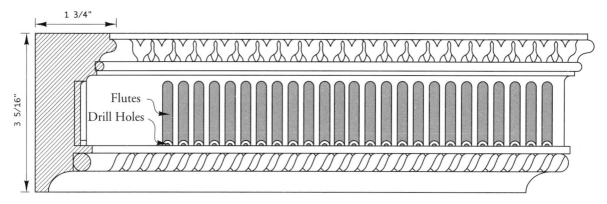

Fig. 191 Benjamin, *Country Builder's Assistant*, 1797, pl. XV.

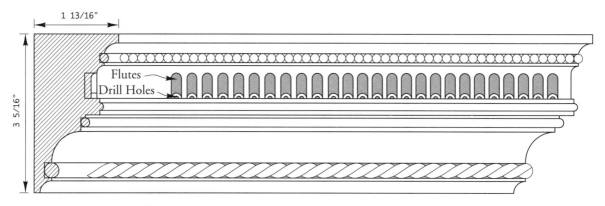

Fig. 192 Benjamin, *Country Builder's Assistant*, 1797, pl. XV.

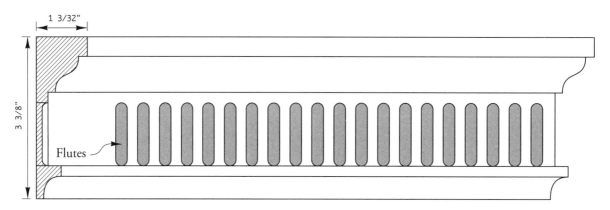

Fig. 193 General Salem Towne House, Charlton, MA, 1796, Mullins, *Architectural Treasures,* vol. X, p. 156.

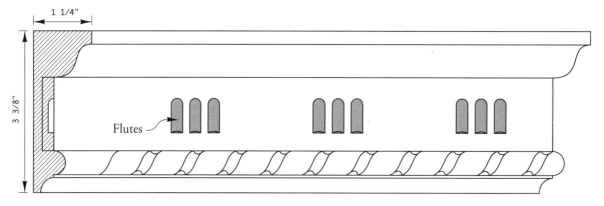

Fig. 194 Jonathan Woodbridge House, Worthington, MA, 1806, *HABS*, MA-124, sheet 14.

Fig. 195 Bezaleel Mann House, North Attleboro, MA, 1790, Mullins, *Architectural Treasures,* vol. X, p. 156.

Fig. 196 Woodbridge-Short House, Salem, MA, 1810, Mullins, *Architectural Treasures,* vol. X, p. 157.

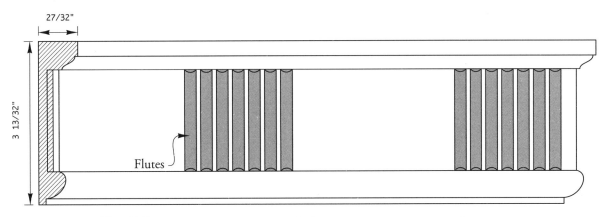

Fig. 197 Holmes-Sayward House, Alfred, ME, 1802, *HABS,* ME-32, sheet 13.

Fig. 198 Captain Leonard House, Agawam, MA, 1807, *HABS,* MA-2-50, sheet 11.

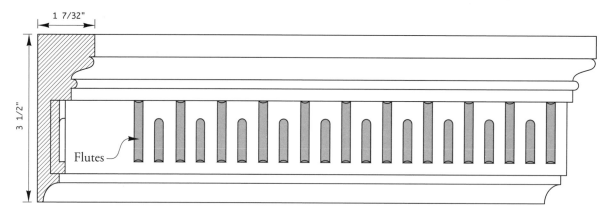

Fig. 199 Lt. Governor Martin House, Seekonk, MA, 1810, *HABS*, MA-2-90, sheet 12.

Fig. 200 Hyde-Lincoln House, Charlestown, MA, 1801, *HABS*, MA-299, sheet 8.

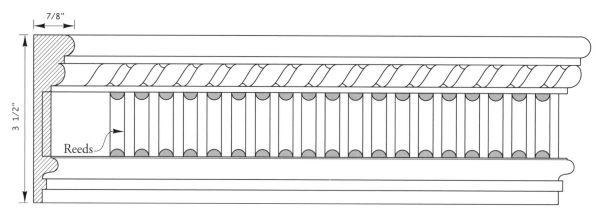

Fig. 201 Gardner-White-Pingree House, Salem, MA, 1804, Mullins, *Architectural Treasures,* vol. XVI, p. 104.

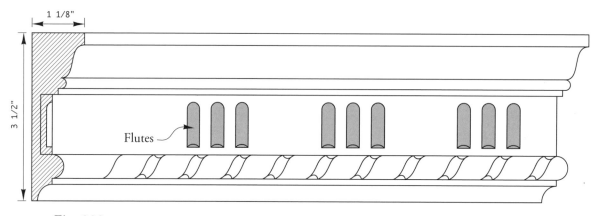

Fig. 202 Jonathan Woodbridge House, Worthington, MA, 1806, *HABS*, MA-124, sheet 12.

Fig. 203 Gideon Tucker House, Salem, MA, 1806, Mullins, *Architectural Treasures*, vol. I, p. 168.

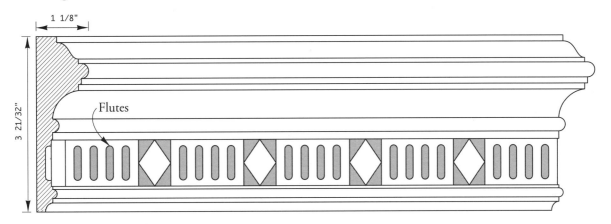

Flutes

Fig. 204 Henry Pettis House, Somerset, MA, 1800, *HABS*, MA-2-52, sheet 8.

Fig. 205 Governor Woodbury Mansion, Portsmouth, NH, 1809, *HABS*, NH-20, sheet 40.

Fig. 206 Captain Leonard House, Agawam, MA, 1807, *HABS*, MA-2-50, sheet 9.

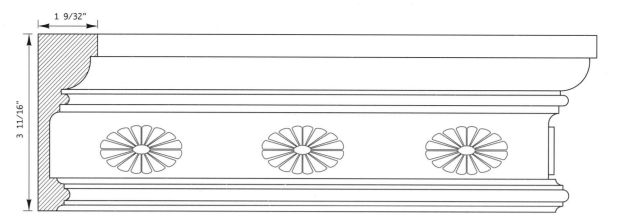

Fig. 207 Harrison Gray Otis House (first), Boston, MA, 1796, Mullins, *Architectural Treasures,* vol. I, p. 169.

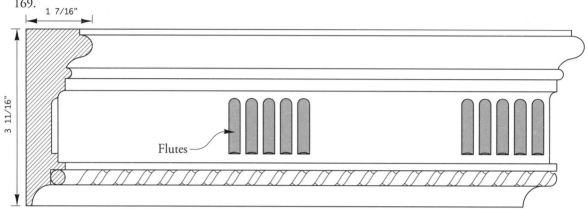

Flutes

Fig. 208 Captain Leonard House, Agawam, MA, 1807, *HABS*, MA-2-50, sheet 8.

Fig. 209 Edward Carrington House, Providence, RI, 1812, *HABS*, RI-19, sheet 50.

Fig. 210 Governor Woodbury Mansion, Portsmouth, NH, 1809, *HABS*, NH-20, sheet 40.

Fig. 211 Thibault House, Newburyport, MA, 1815, *HABS*, MA-123, sheet 3.

Fig. 212 Isaac Cooley House, Agawam, MA, 1807, *HABS*, MA-2-51, sheet 6.

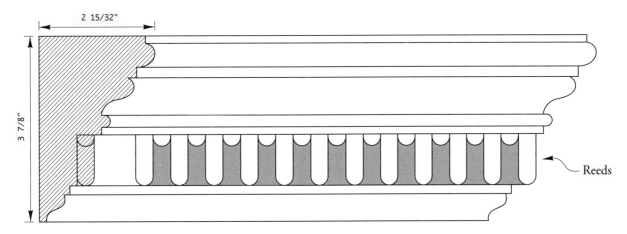

Reeds

Fig. 213 Major Israel Forster House, Manchester, MA, 1804, Mullins, *Architectural Treasures,* vol. I, p. 202.

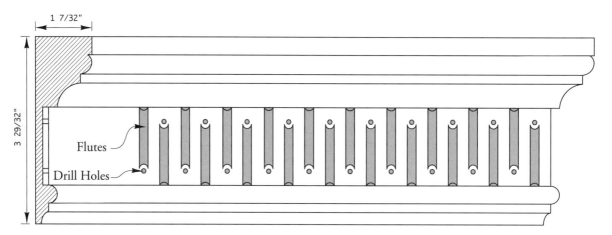

Fig. 214 Henry Pettis House, Somerset, MA, 1800, *HABS*, MA-2-52, sheet 9.

Fig. 215 Henry Pettis House, Somerset, MA, 1800, *HABS*, MA-2-52, sheet 7.

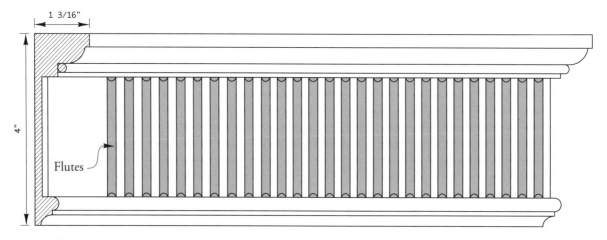

Fig. 216 Cook-Oliver House, Salem, MA, 1804, Mullins, *Architectural Treasures*, vol. I, p. 168.

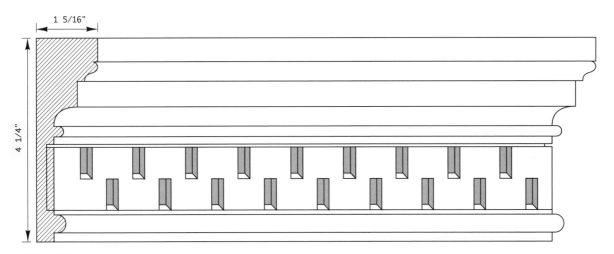

Fig. 217 Harrison Gray Otis House (first), Boston, MA, 1796, Mullins, *Architectural Treasures,* vol. I, p. 169.

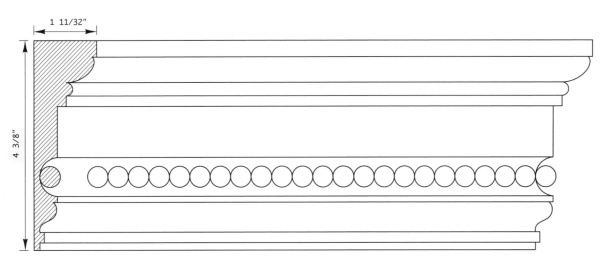

Fig. 218 Gardner-White-Pingree House, Salem, MA, 1804, Mullins, vol. XVI, p. 104.

Flutes

Fig. 219 Nathan Dean House, East Taunton, MA, 1810 addition, *HABS,* MA-143, sheet 11.

Baseboards

The baseboard drawings (moldings and plinth) have the same dimensions as found in historic measured drawings. If you are using a different chair rail height than the one in our samples, proportional rescaling should provide satisfying results. Benjamin's pattern books provide guides for sizing the baseboard as determined by the height of the chair rail. Assume a chair rail height of 36", divide by 10, and find 3 5/16". **Divide** 3 5/16" by 2 to find 1 21/32" for the height of the baseboard molding and **multiply** 3 5/16" by 1.33 to find 4 13/32" for the height of the plinth. Total baseboard height becomes 6 1/16".

31/32"

5"

Fig. 220 Henry Pettis House, Somerset, MA, 1800, *HABS*, MA-2-52, sheet 9.

7/8"

5 17/32"

Fig. 221 Hyde-Lincoln House, Charlestown, MA, 1801, *HABS*, MA-299, sheet 9.

Fig. 222 Hyde-Lincoln House, Charlestown, MA, 1801, *HABS*, MA-299, sheet 9.

Fig. 223 Hyde-Worthen House, Charlestown, MA, 1800, *HABS*, MA-192, sheet 7.

3/4"

6"

Fig. 224 Woodbridge-Short House, Salem, MA, 1810, Mullins, *Architectural Treasures,* vol. X, p. 157.

7/8"

6"

Fig. 225 Gideon Tucker House, Salem, MA, 1806, Mullins, *Architectural Treasures,* vol. I, p. 168.

Fig. 226 Captain Leonard House, Agawam, MA, 1807, *HABS*, MA-2-50, sheet 9.

Fig. 227 Hyde-Worthen House, Charlestown, MA, 1800, *HABS*, MA-192, sheet 5.

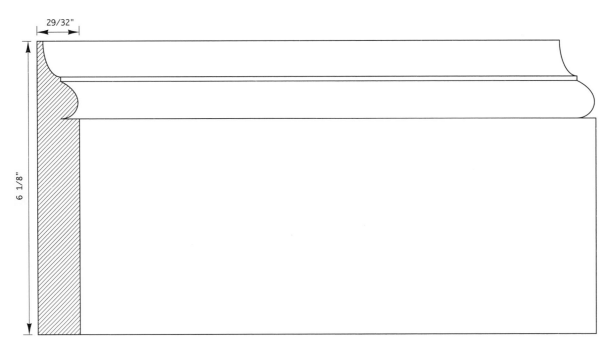

Fig. 228 Lt. Governor Martin House, Seekonk, MA, 1810, *HABS*, MA-2-90, sheet 17.

Fig. 229 Hyde-Lincoln House, Charlestown, MA, 1801, *HABS*, MA-299, sheet 8.

Fig. 230 Lt. Governor Martin House, Seekonk, MA, 1810, *HABS*, MA-2-90, sheet 16.

Fig. 231 Nathan Dean House, East Taunton, MA, 1810 addition, *HABS*, MA-143, sheet 12.

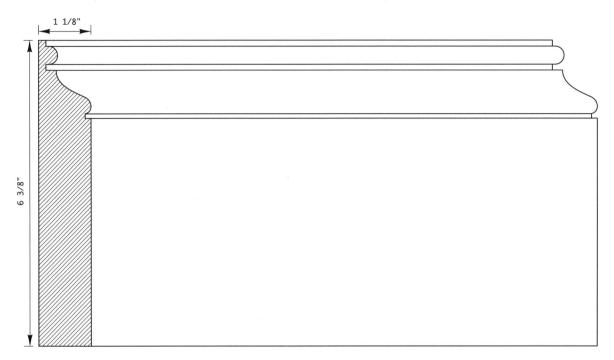

1 1/8"

6 3/8"

Fig. 232 Captain Leonard House, Agawam, MA, 1807, *HABS*, MA-2-50, sheet 11.

5/8"

6 1/2"

Fig. 233 Harrison Gray Otis House (first), Boston, MA, 1796, Mullins, *Architectural Treasures*, vol. X, p. 169.

27/32"

6 5/8"

Fig. 234 Harrison Gray Otis House (first), Boston, MA, 1796, Mullins, *Architectural Treasures*, vol. I, p. 168.

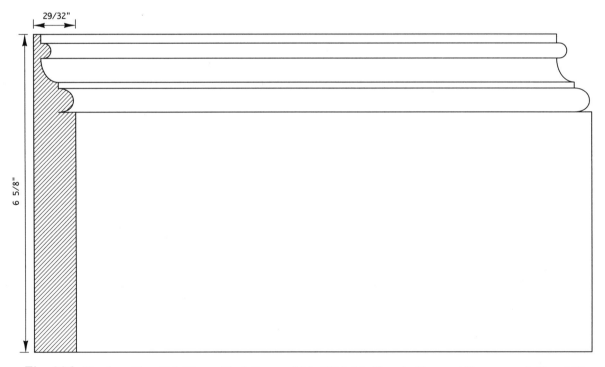

29/32"

6 5/8"

Fig. 235 Harrison Gray Otis House (first), Boston, MA, 1796, Mullins, *Architectural Treasures*, vol. X, p. 169.

3/4"

6 3/4"

Fig. 236 Christopher Ryder House, Chathamport, MA, 1809, *HABS*, MA-118, sheet 13.

7/8"

6 3/4"

Fig. 237 Holmes-Sayward House, Alfred, ME, 1802, *HABS*, ME-32, sheet 13.

Fig. 238 Captain Leonard House, Agawam, MA, 1807, *HABS*, MA-2-50, sheet 8.

Fig. 239 Woodbridge-Short House, Salem, MA, 1810, *HABS*, MA-124, sheet 17.

13/16"

6 7/8"

Fig. 240 Amory-Ticknor House, Boston, MA, 1804, *HABS*, MA-175, sheet 12.

Mantels

The mantel drawings are presented at full book size to show as much detail as possible, and the original height and width dimensions are included. The book page drawing is too small to provide small dimensions; we include the following information to enable our book drawings to be changed into measurable, standard scale documents: **6 in. = 1 ft. - 1:2, 3 in. = 1 ft. - 1:4, 1 1/2 in. = 1 ft. - 1:8, 3/4 in. = 1 ft. - 1:16, 1/2 in. = 1 ft. - 1:24, 1/4 in. = 1 ft. - 1:48,** and **3/16 in. = 1 ft. - 1:64.** We will use our Fig. 241 mantel drawing to create a standard scale drawing (1 1/2" = 1' - 1:8). Divide the mantel's given height dimension by 8 (58 1/2" ÷ 8 = 7 5/16") to find the height of the drawing at the chosen standard scale. Assume our book height of 10" and divide 7 5/16" by 10" to find 73.125%. Scale down the book drawing (using the accompanying CD) to 73.125% of the book page height to produce a scaled, 1 1/2" = 1', measurable document for computer use.

A strategy for producing scaled drawings from the book size drawings without the computer requires a different approach. Since the measurements will be taken from a scaled, printed version, the printout will have to be large enough to allow for easy measuring. A standard scale of 3" or 6" to 1' will probably have to be used. For this example, we divide the given height dimension [58 1/2" ÷ 4 (3" = 1' - 1:4)] to find the printed height of 14 5/8". Divide the printed height of 14 5/8" by the 10" book page height to find 46.25%. Because of the large paper size, you might need the services of a copy center or graphic reproduction outlet. Either business can proportionally rescale upward the book drawing by 46.25% and print a document that will be exact to the real dimensions at a scale of 3" to 1'. If the drawing is still too small to obtain accurate measurements, follow the above procedure but use the 6" to 1' scale.

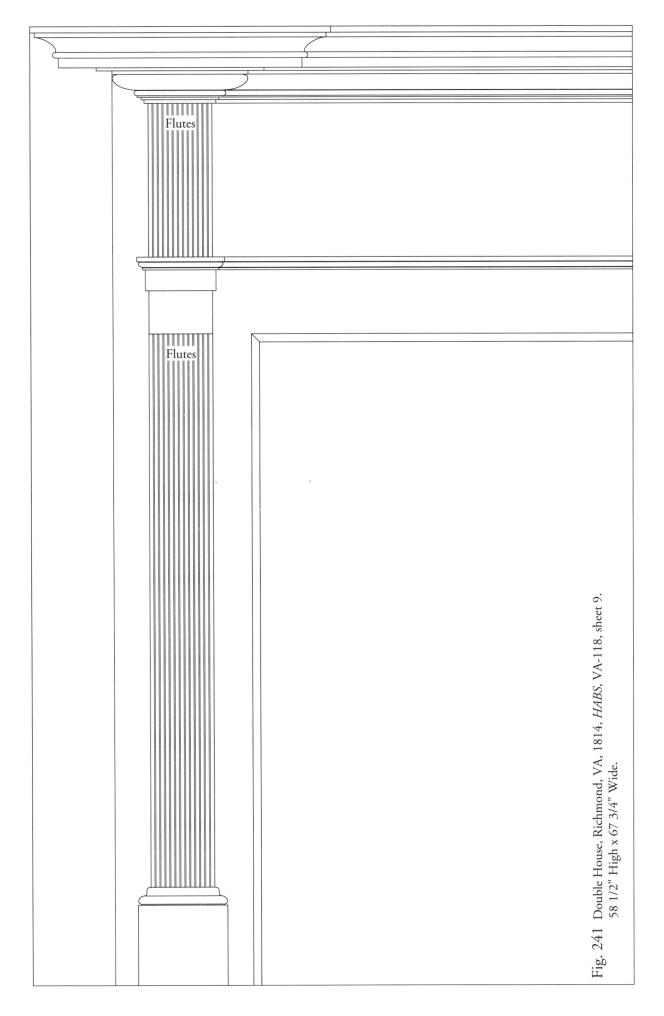

Flutes

Flutes

Fig. 241 Double House, Richmond, VA, 1814, *HABS*, VA-118, sheet 9.
58 1/2" High x 67 3/4" Wide.

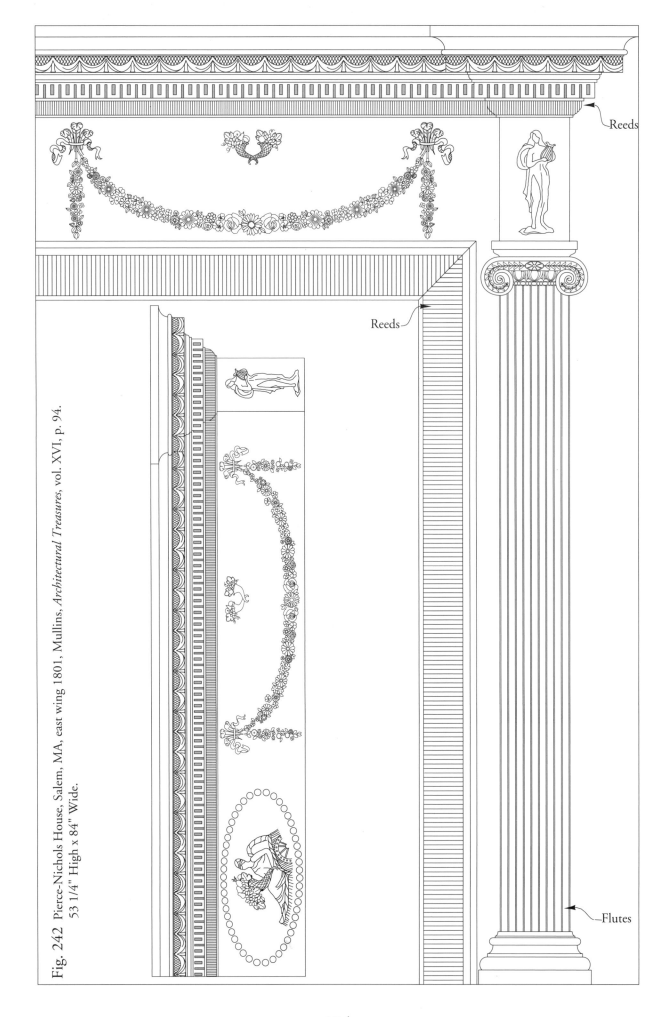

Reeds

Reeds

Flutes

Fig. 242 Pierce-Nichols House, Salem, MA, east wing 1801, Mullins, *Architectural Treasures*, vol. XVI, p. 94.
53 1/4" High x 84" Wide.

Flutes

Fig. 243 Marshal-Hancock House, Boston, MA, c. 18th century, *HABS*, MA-2-55-A, sheet 1.
51 1/8" High x 92 3/4" Wide.

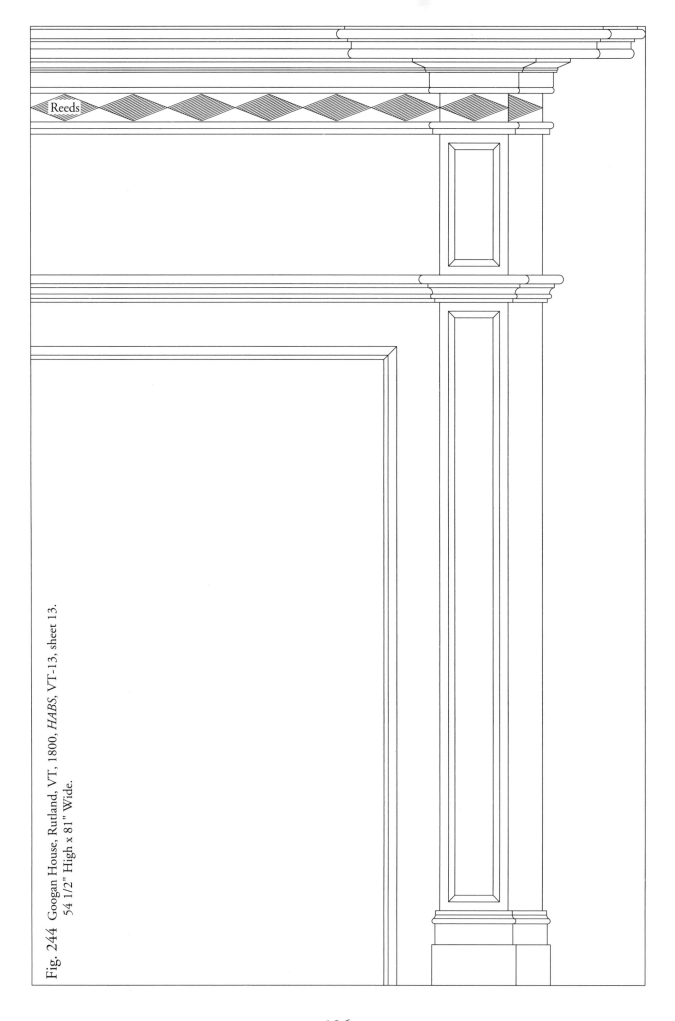

Reeds

Fig. 244 Googan House, Rutland, VT, 1800, *HABS*, VT-13, sheet 13.
54 1/2" High x 81" Wide.

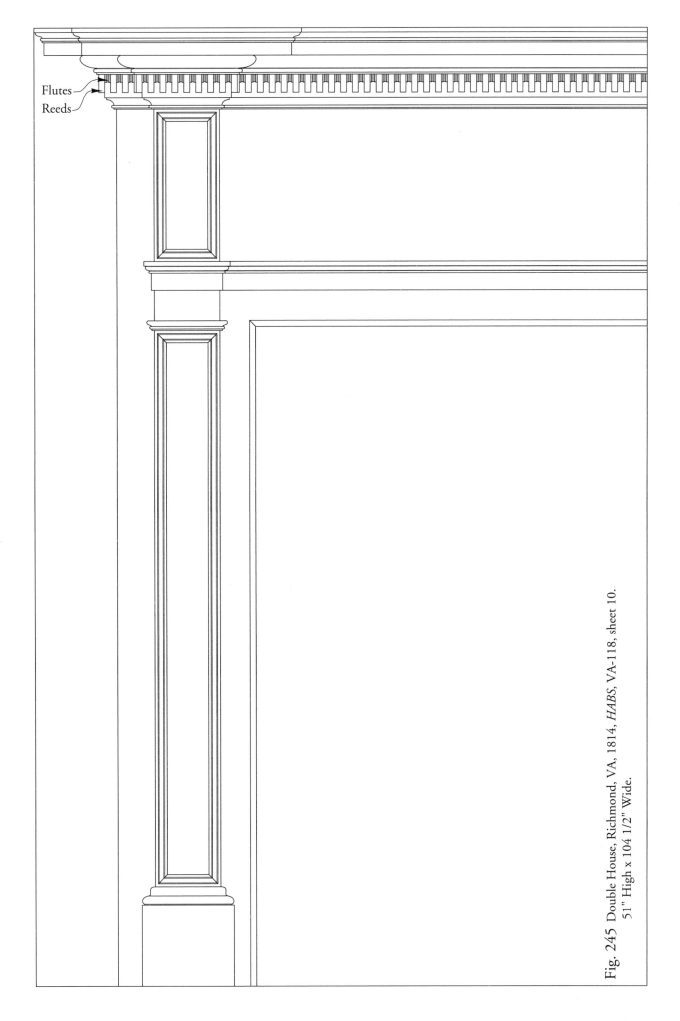

Flutes

Reeds

Fig. 245 Double House, Richmond, VA, 1814, *HABS*, VA-118, sheet 10.
51" High x 104 1/2" Wide.

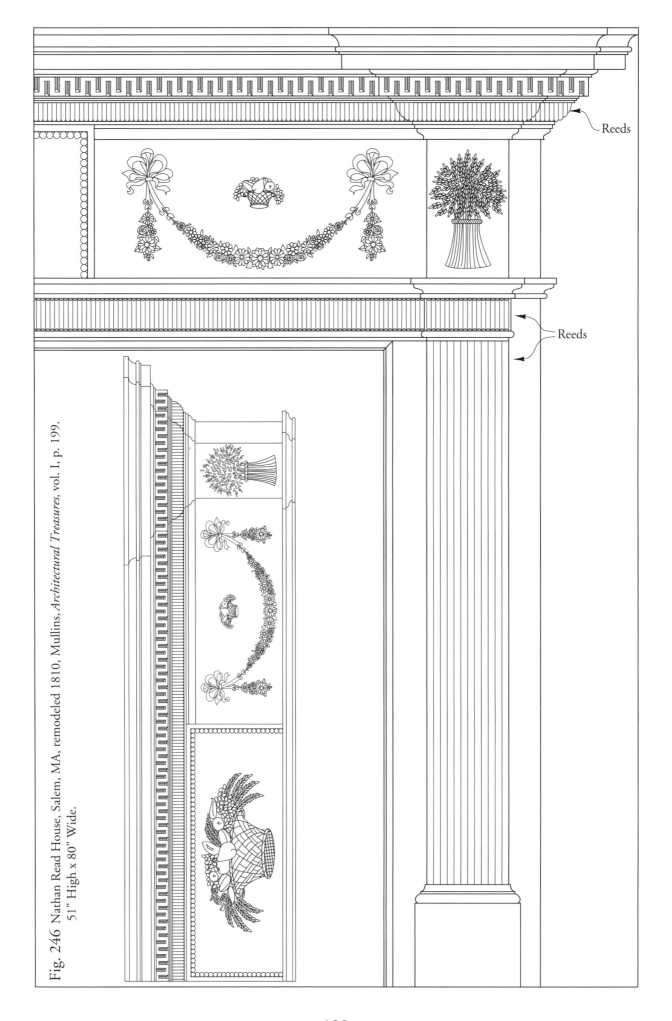

Reeds

Reeds

Fig. 246 Nathan Read House, Salem, MA, remodeled 1810, Mullins, *Architectural Treasures*, vol. I, p. 199.
51" High x 80" Wide.

Fig. 247 Amory-Ticknor House, Boston, MA, 1804, *HABS*, MA-175, sheet 17. 52 1/8" High x 64 5/8" Wide.

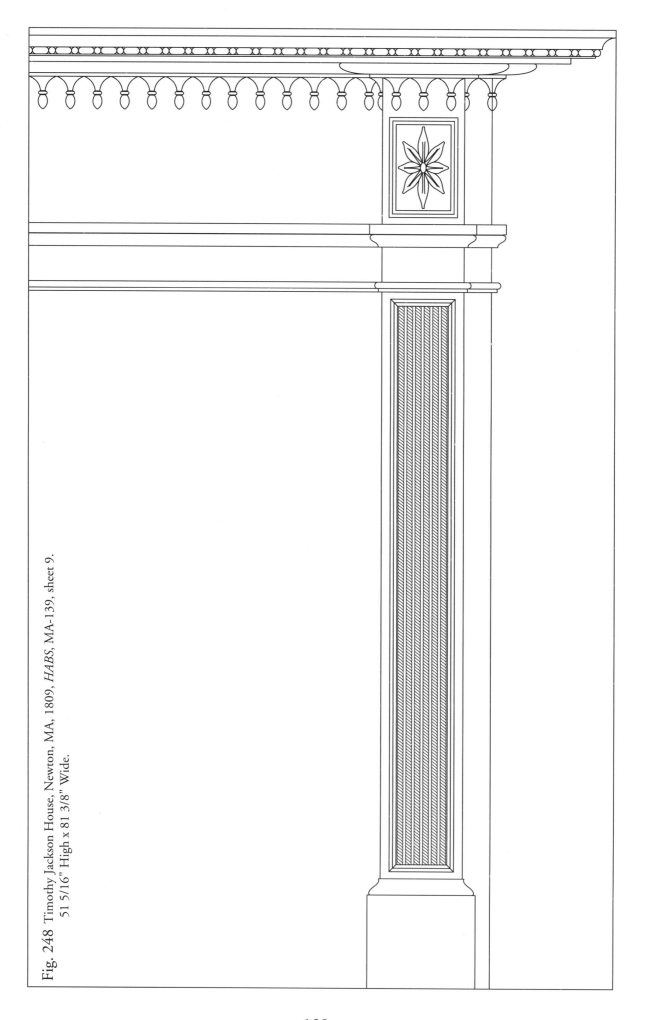

Fig. 248 Timothy Jackson House, Newton, MA, 1809, *HABS*, MA-139, sheet 9. 51 5/16" High x 81 3/8" Wide.

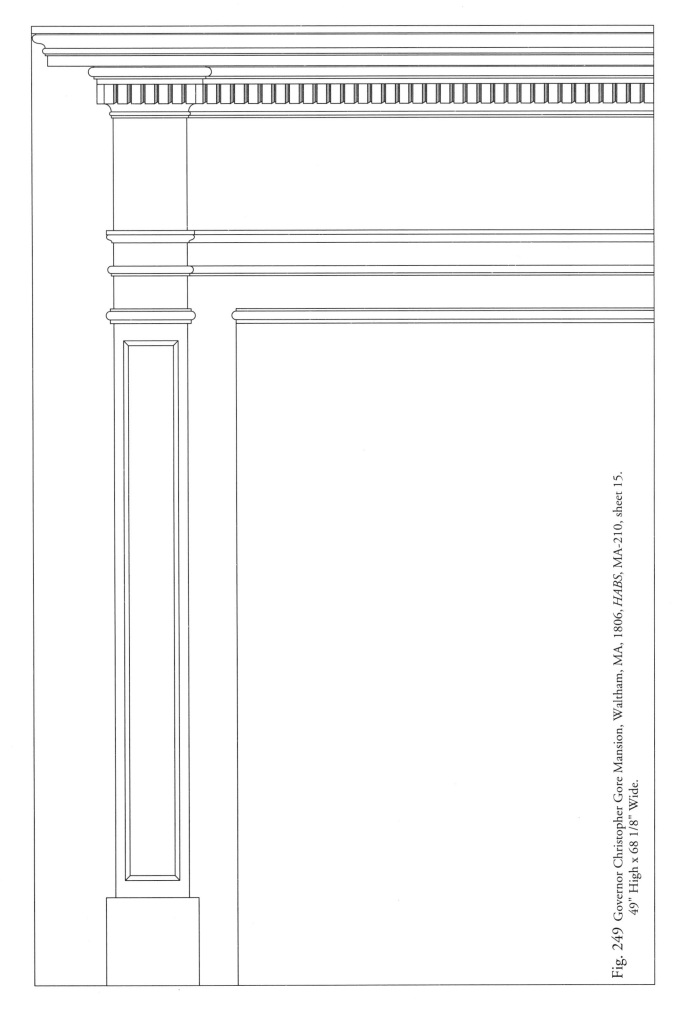

Fig. 249 Governor Christopher Gore Mansion, Waltham, MA, 1806, *HABS*, MA-210, sheet 15. 49" High x 68 1/8" Wide.

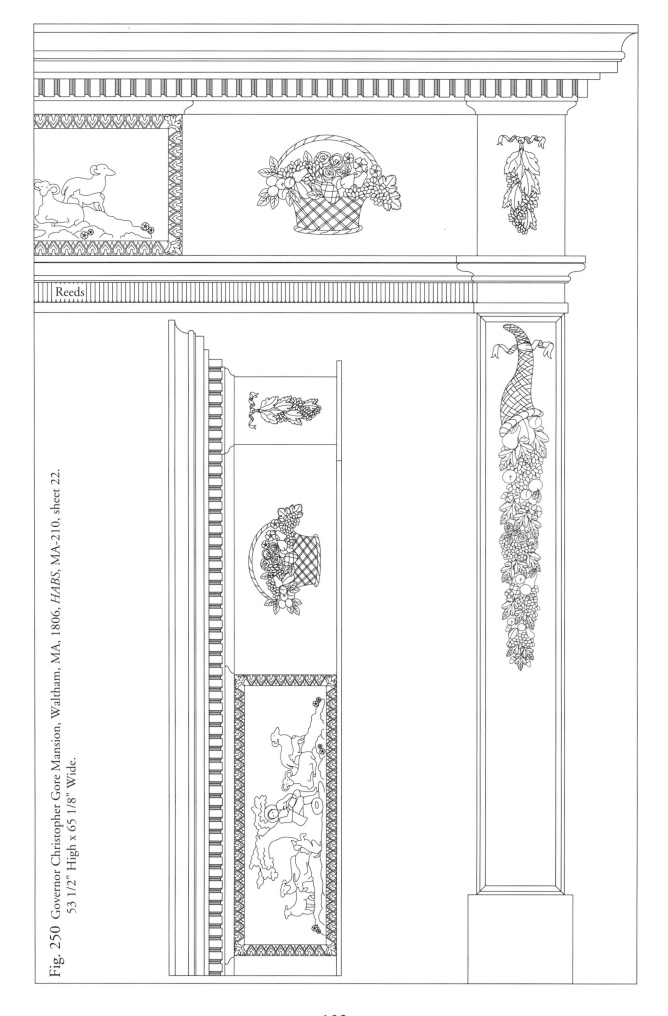

Reeds

Fig. 250 Governor Christopher Gore Mansion, Waltham, MA, 1806, *HABS*, MA-210, sheet 22.
53 1/2" High x 65 1/8" Wide.

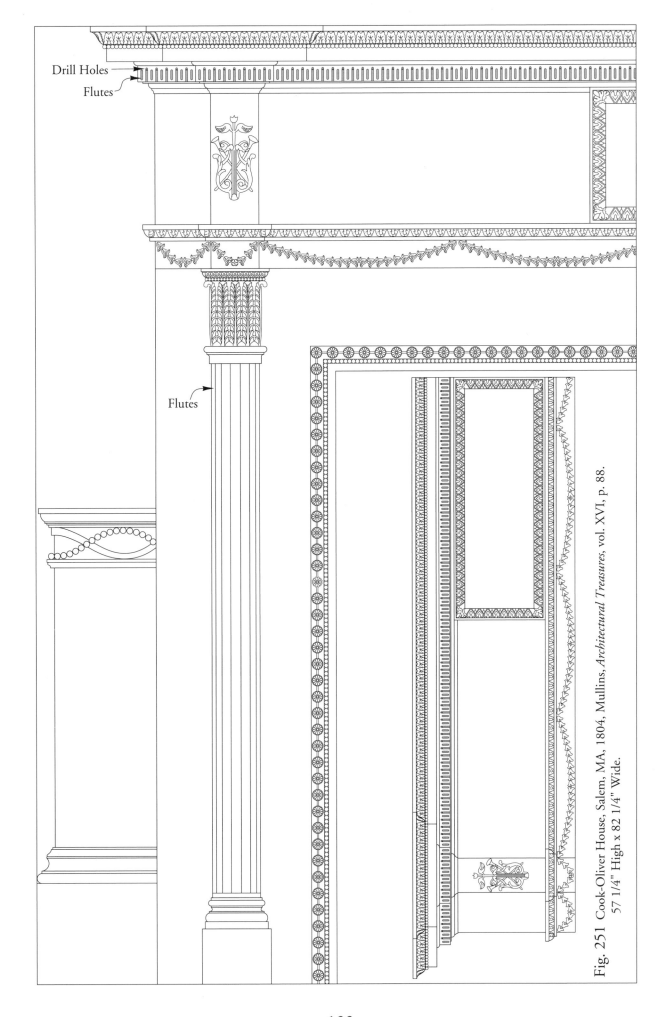

Drill Holes

Flutes

Flutes

Fig. 251 Cook-Oliver House, Salem, MA, 1804, Mullins, *Architectural Treasures*, vol. XVI, p. 88. 57 1/4" High x 82 1/4" Wide.

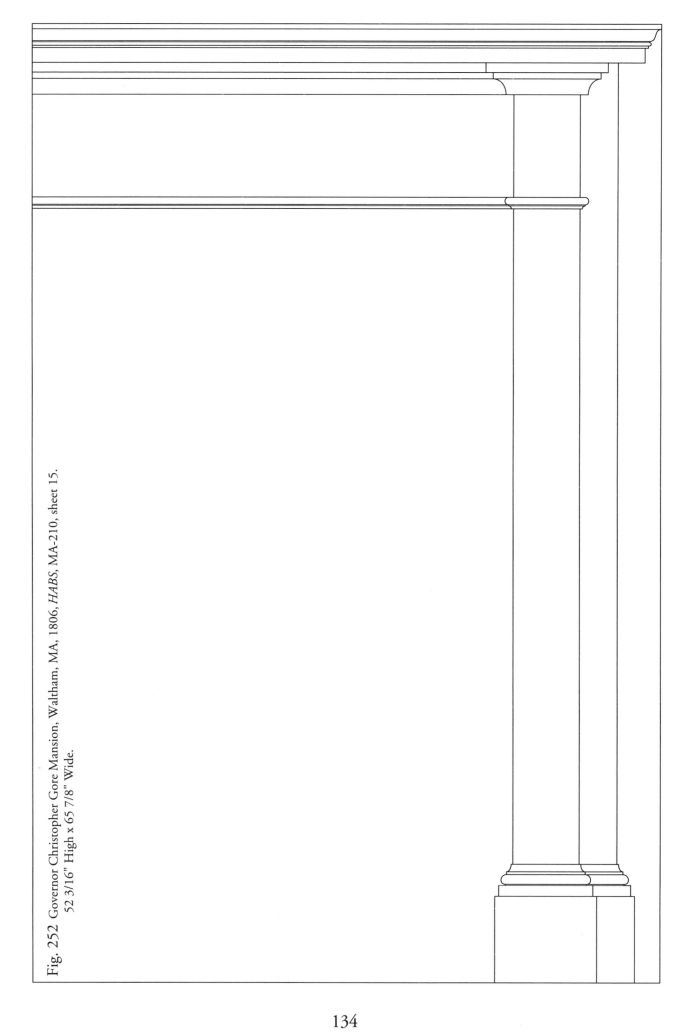

Fig. 252 Governor Christopher Gore Mansion, Waltham, MA, 1806, *HABS*, MA-210, sheet 15. 52 3/16" High x 65 7/8" Wide.

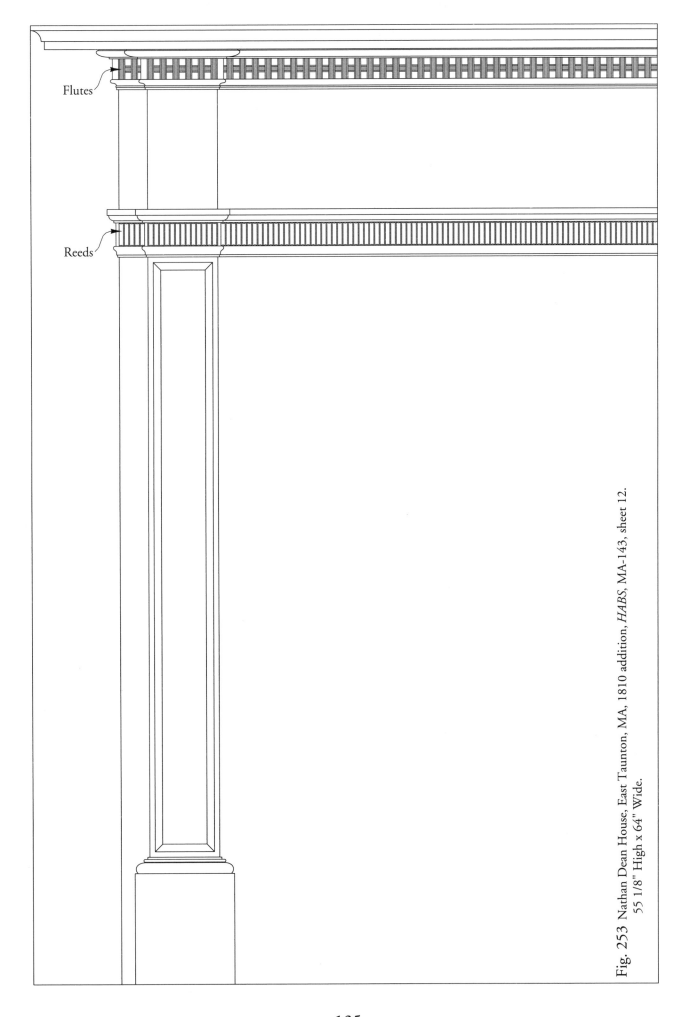

Flutes

Reeds

Fig. 253 Nathan Dean House, East Taunton, MA, 1810 addition, *HABS*, MA-143, sheet 12. 55 1/8" High x 64" Wide.

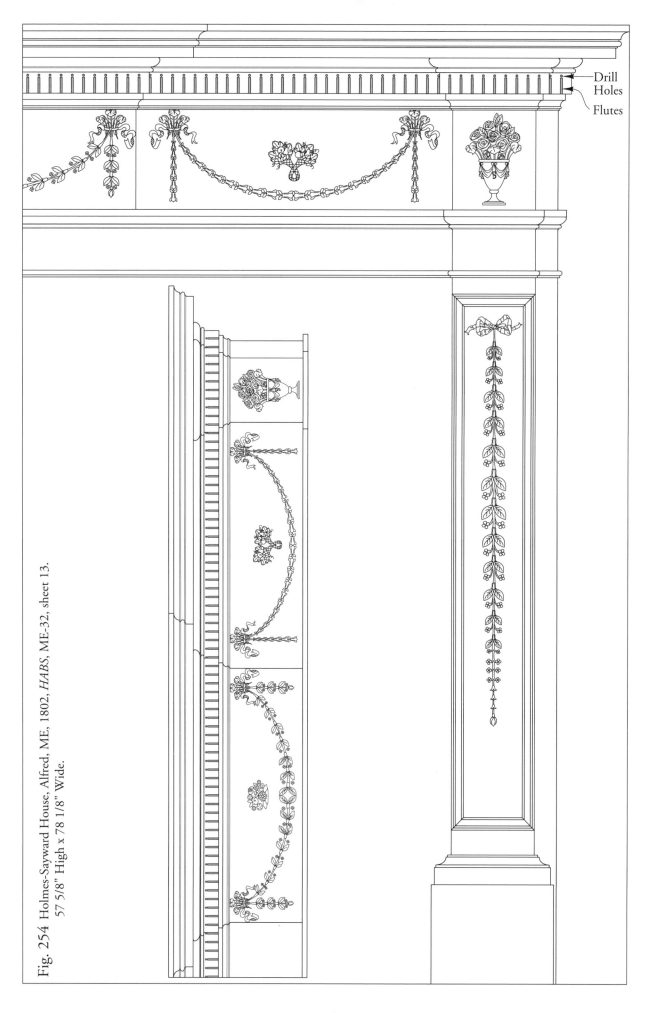

Drill
Holes

Flutes

Fig. 254 Holmes-Sayward House, Alfred, ME, 1802, *HABS*, ME-32, sheet 13.
57 5/8" High x 78 1/8" Wide.

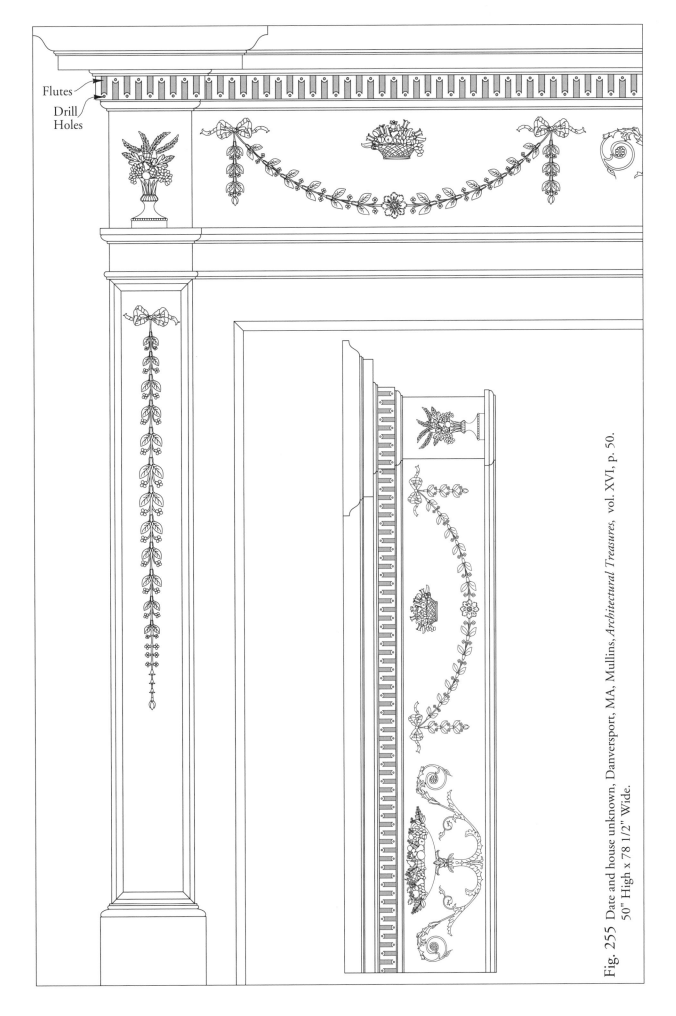

Flutes

Drill
Holes

Fig. 255 Date and house unknown, Danversport, MA, Mullins, *Architectural Treasures*, vol. XVI, p. 50.
50" High x 78 1/2" Wide.

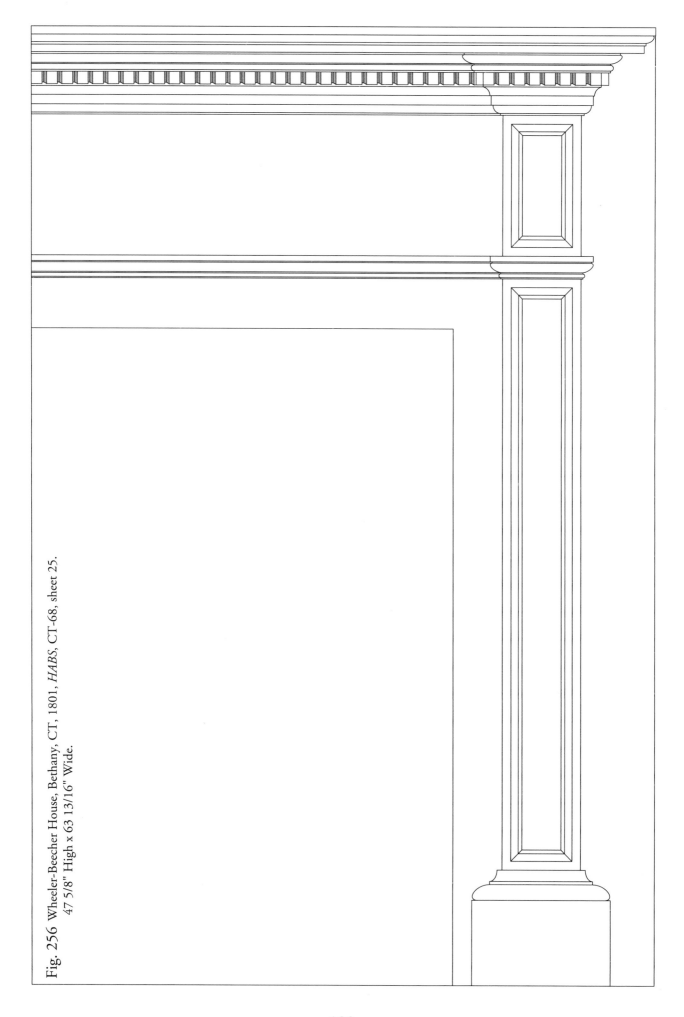

Fig. 256 Wheeler-Beecher House, Bethany, CT, 1801, *HABS*, CT-68, sheet 25. 47 5/8" High x 63 13/16" Wide.

Drill Holes
Flutes

Fig. 257 Henry Pettis House, Somerset, MA, 1800, *HABS*, MA-2-52, sheet 9.
56 1/2" High x 77 7/8" Wide.

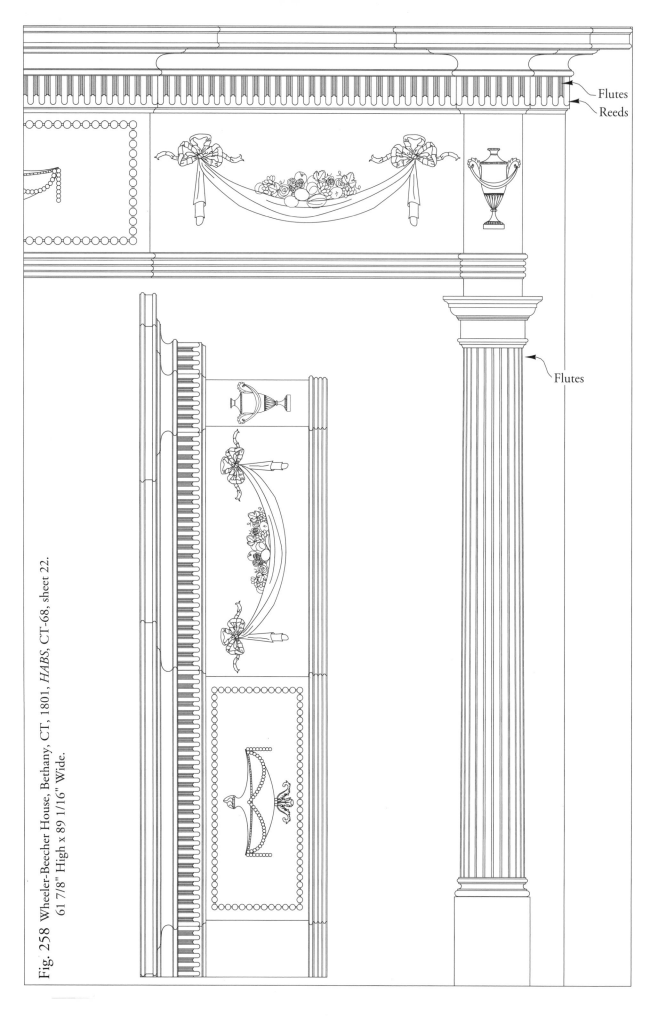

Flutes

Reeds

Flutes

Fig. 258 Wheeler-Beecher House, Bethany, CT, 1801, *HABS*, CT-68, sheet 22.
61 7/8" High x 89 1/16" Wide.

Reeds

Reeds

Fig. 259 Gardner-White-Pingree House, Salem, MA, 1804, Mullins, *Architectural Treasures, vol. XVI*, p. 104.
53" High x 85" Wide.

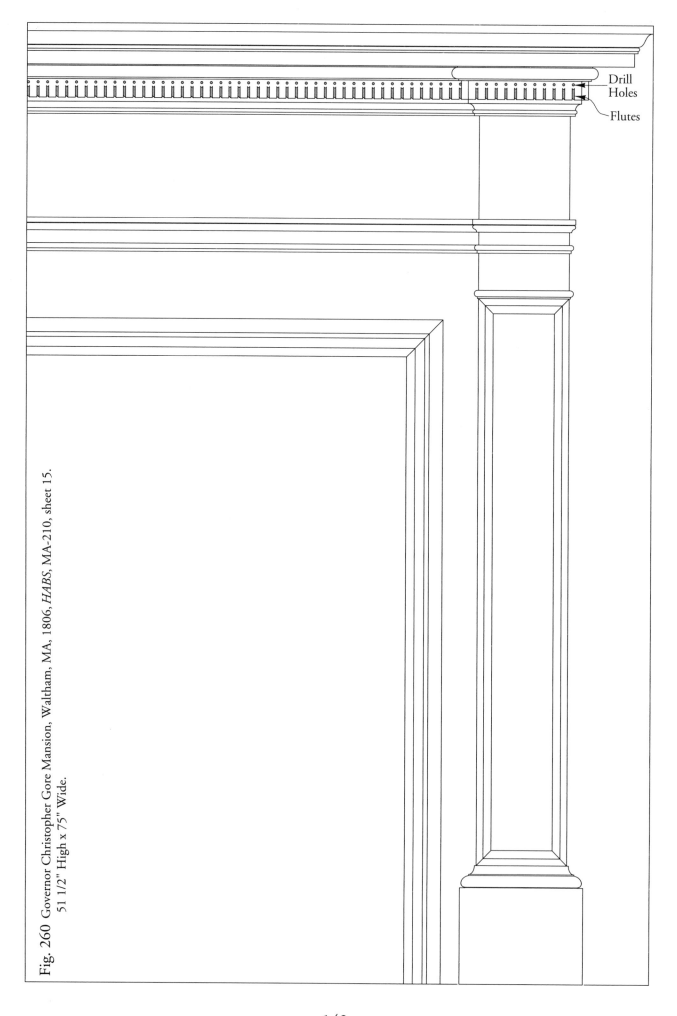

Drill
Holes

Flutes

Fig. 260 Governor Christopher Gore Mansion, Waltham, MA, 1806, *HABS*, MA-210, sheet 15.
51 1/2" High x 75" Wide.

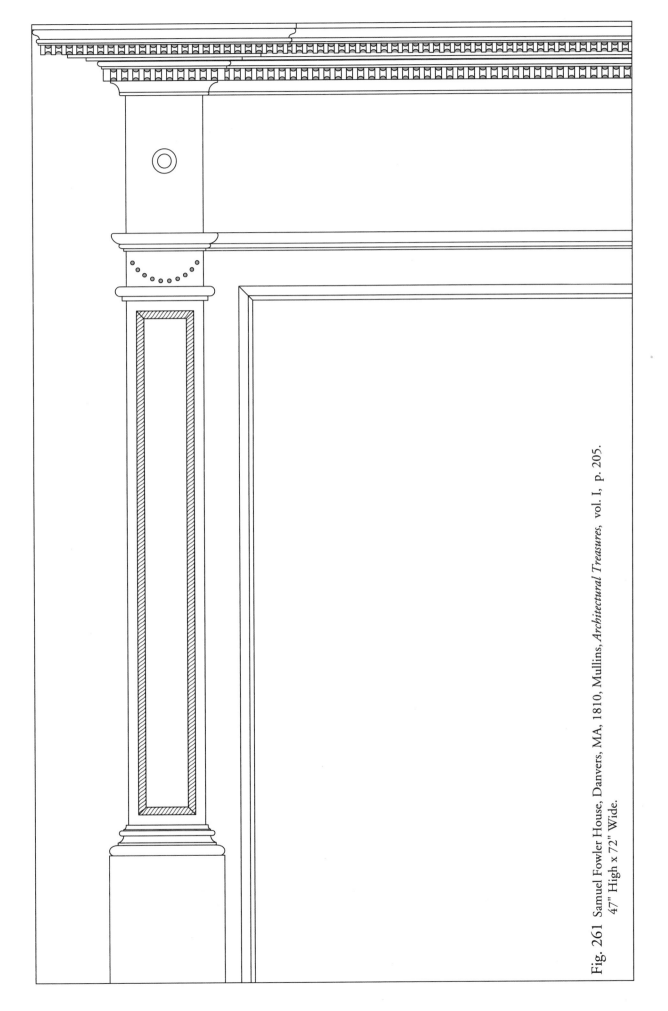

Fig. 261 Samuel Fowler House, Danvers, MA, 1810, Mullins, *Architectural Treasures*, vol. I, p. 205. 47" High x 72" Wide.

Fig. 262 Benjamin, *Country Builder's Assistant*, 1797, pl. XIX.
52 1/2" High x 66" Wide.

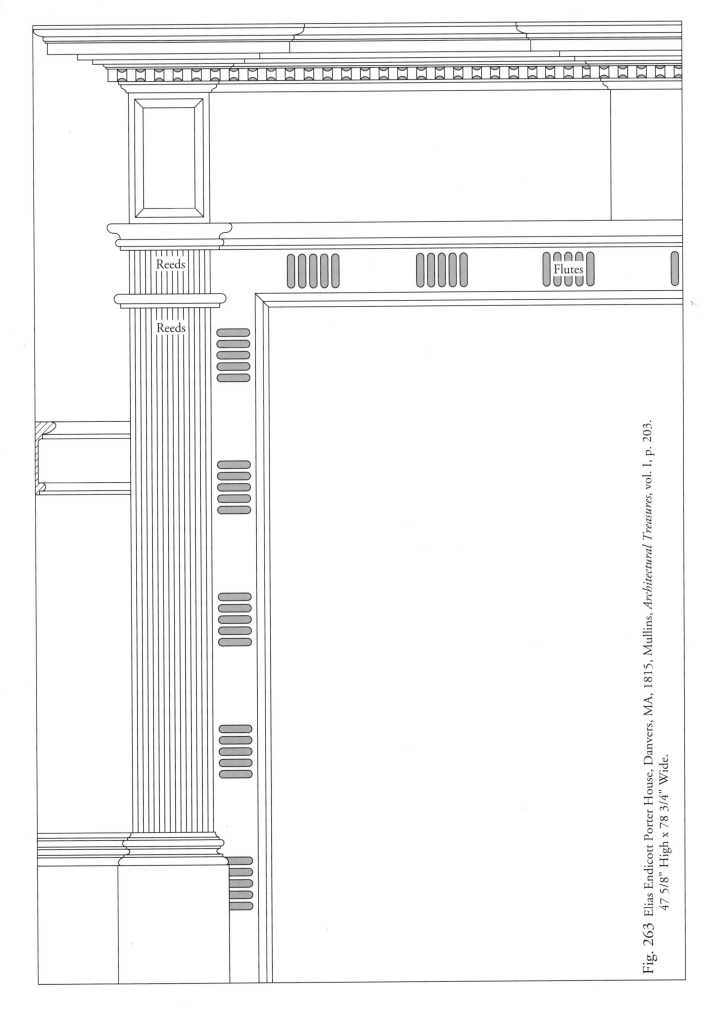

Reeds

Reeds

Flutes

Fig. 263 Elias Endicott Porter House, Danvers, MA, 1815, Mullins, *Architectural Treasures*, vol. I, p. 203. 47 5/8" High x 78 3/4" Wide.

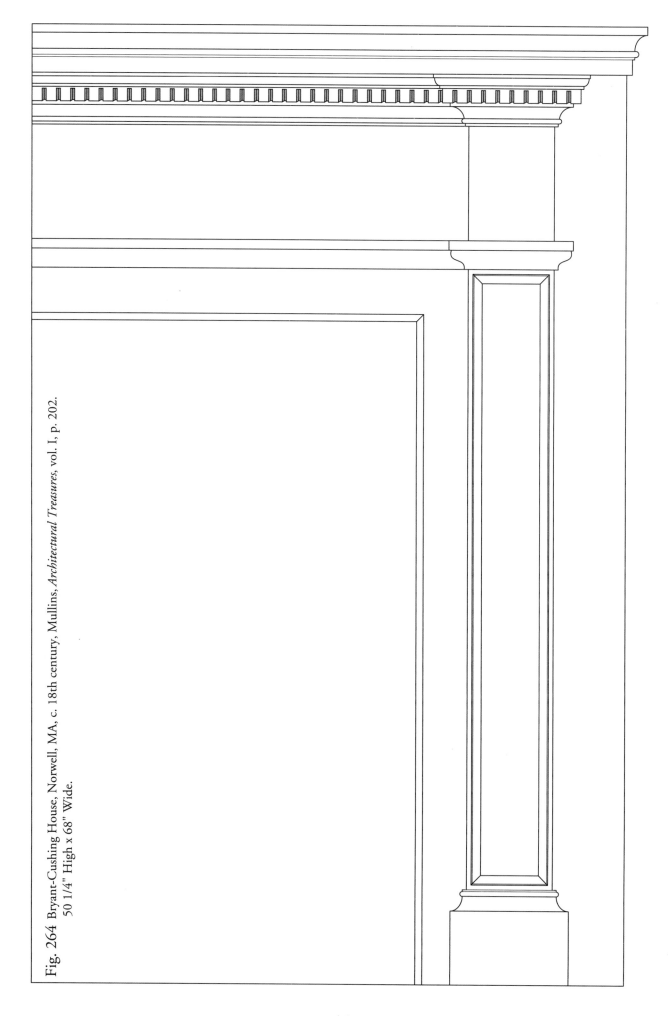

Fig. 264 Bryant-Cushing House, Norwell, MA, c. 18th century, Mullins, *Architectural Treasures*, vol. I, p. 202. 50 1/4" High x 68" Wide.

Flutes

Fig. 265 Bryant-Cushing House, Norwell, MA, c. 18th century, Mullins, *Architectural Treasures*, vol. 1, p. 202. 50 3/8" High x 56 3/4" Wide.

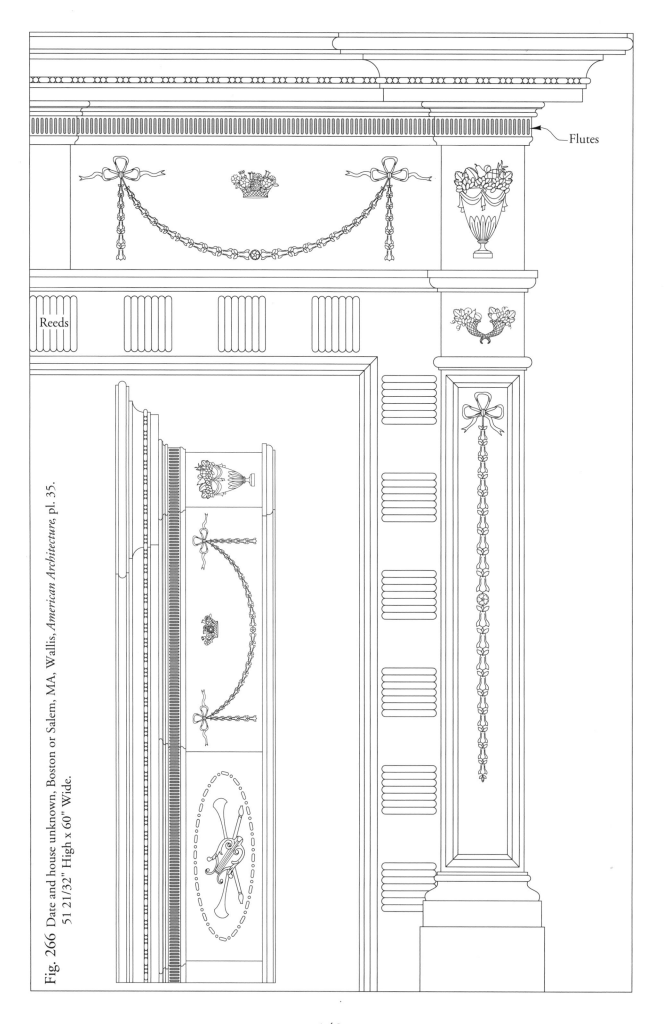

Flutes

Reeds

Fig. 266 Date and house unknown, Boston or Salem, MA, Wallis, *American Architecture*, pl. 35.
51 21/32" High x 60" Wide.

148

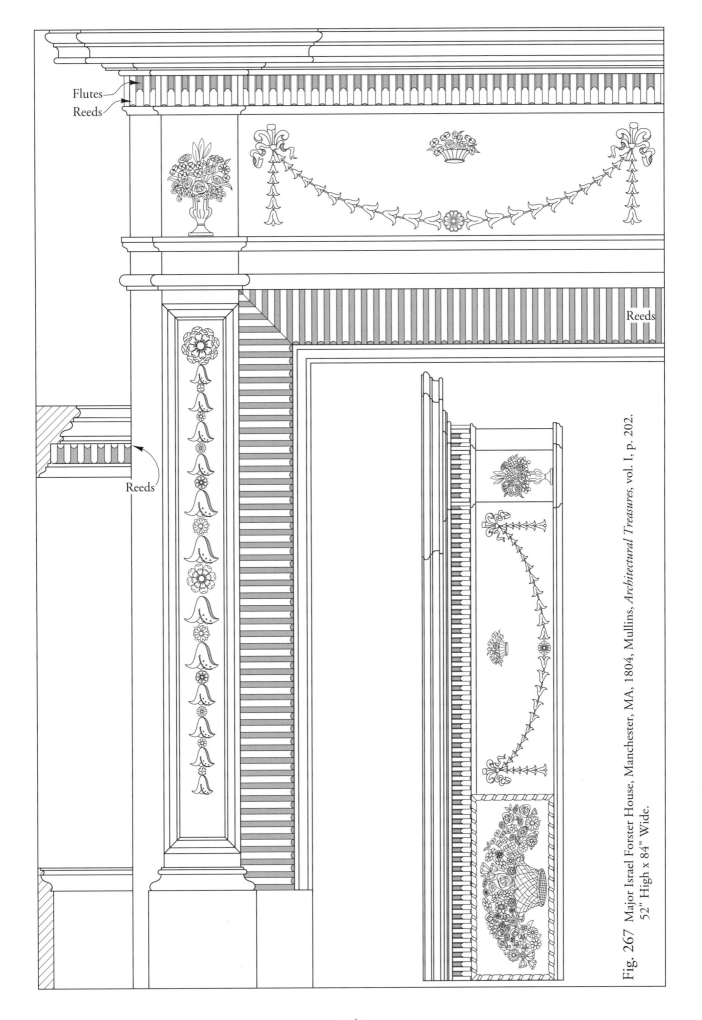

Flutes

Reeds

Reeds

Reeds

Fig. 267 Major Israel Forster House, Manchester, MA, 1804, Mullins, *Architectural Treasures*, vol. I, p. 202. 52" High x 84" Wide.

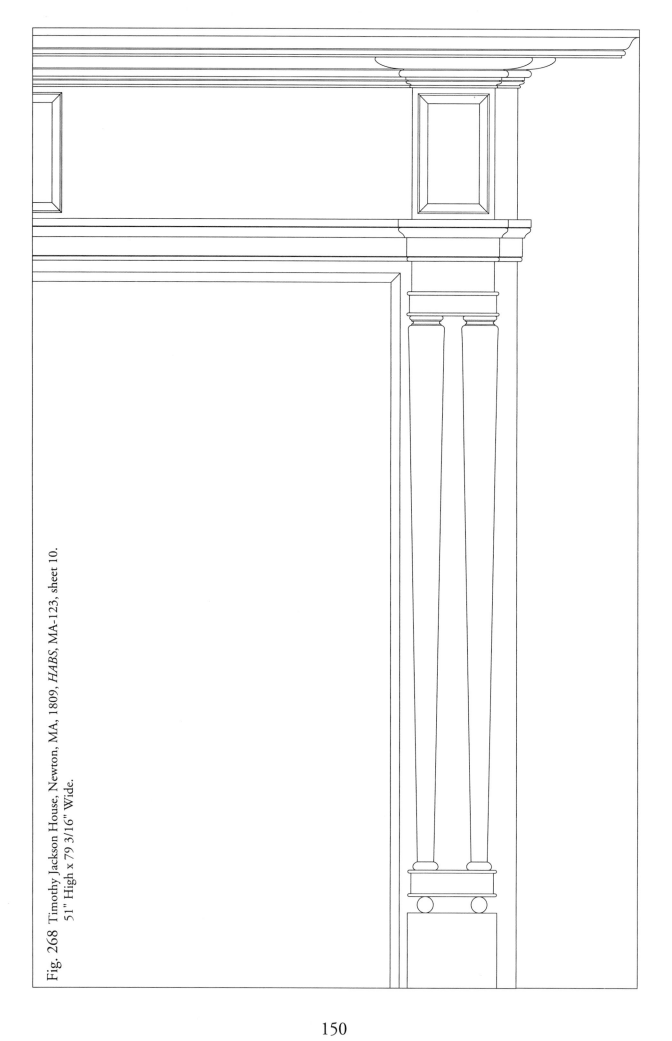

Fig. 268 Timothy Jackson House, Newton, MA, 1809, *HABS*, MA-123, sheet 10.
51" High x 79 3/16" Wide.

Reeds

Reeds

Reeds   Flutes

Fig. 269 Christopher Ryder House, Chathamport, MA, 1809, Mullins, *Architectural Treasures*, vol. I, p. 203. 49 7/8" High x 83 5/8" Wide.

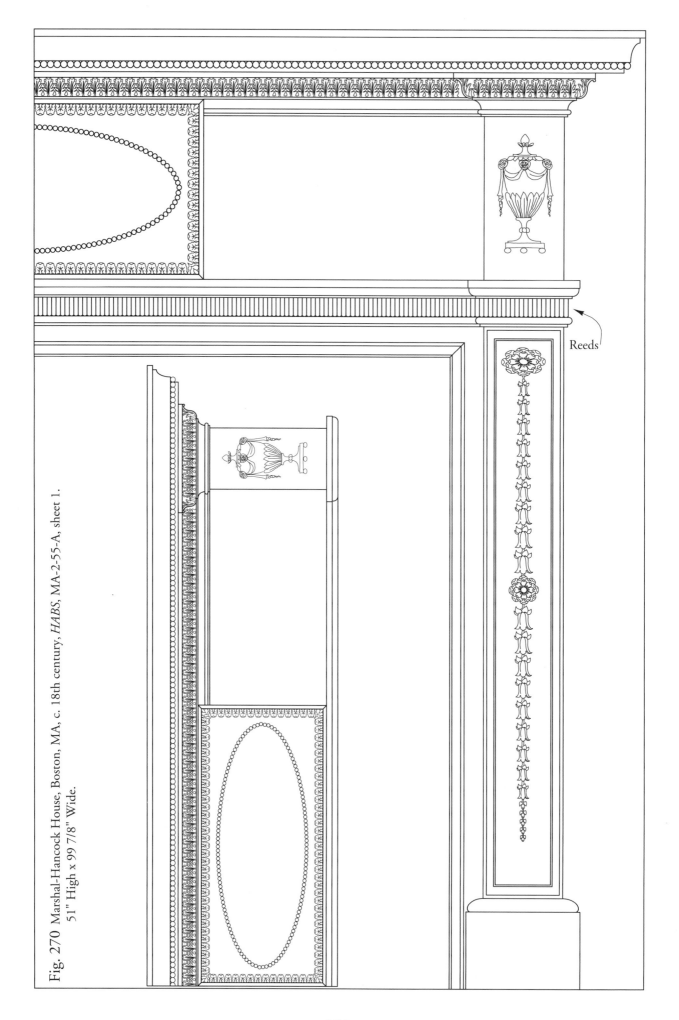

Reeds

Fig. 270 Marshal-Hancock House, Boston, MA, c. 18th century, *HABS*, MA-2-55-A, sheet 1.
51" High x 99 7/8" Wide.

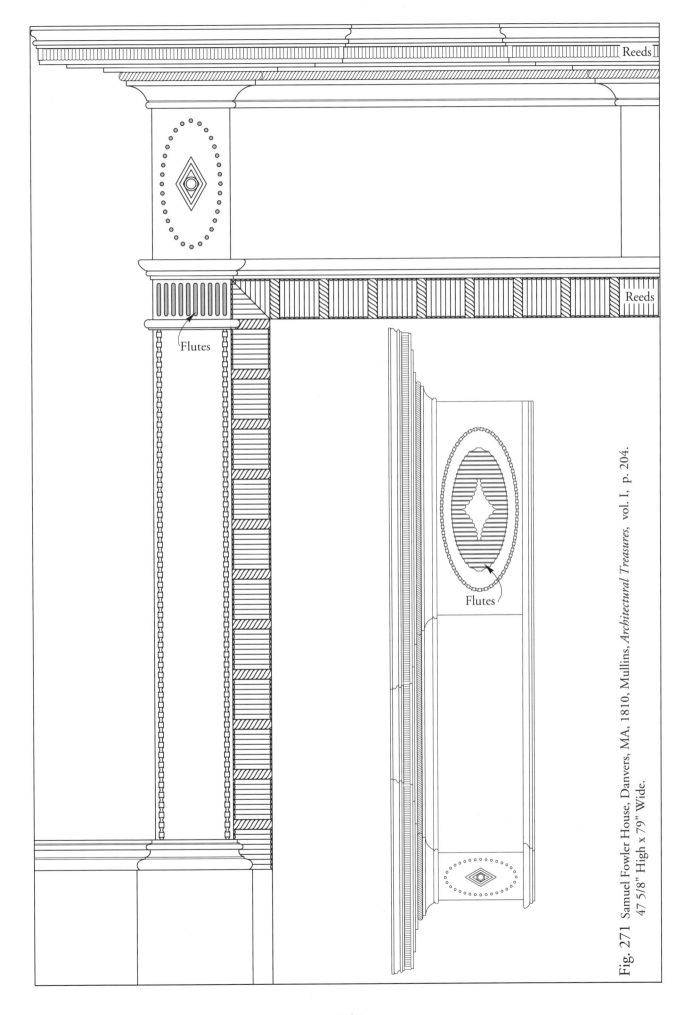

Reeds

Reeds

Flutes

Flutes

Fig. 271 Samuel Fowler House, Danvers, MA, 1810, Mullins, *Architectural Treasures*, vol. I, p. 204. 47 5/8" High x 79" Wide.

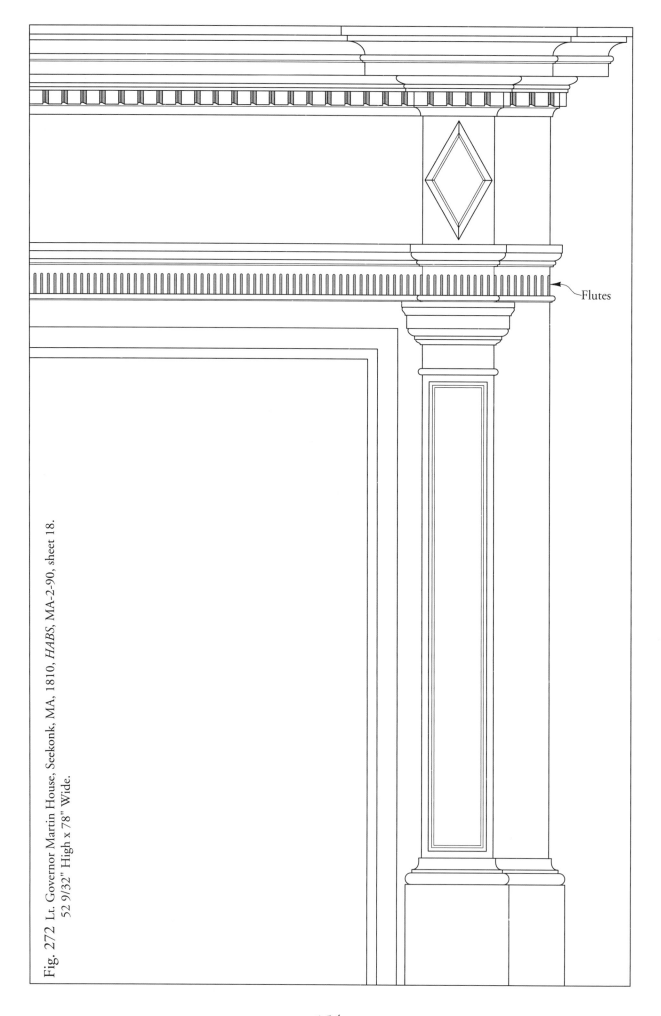

Flutes

Fig. 272 Lt. Governor Martin House, Seekonk, MA, 1810, *HABS*, MA-2-90, sheet 18. 52 9/32" High x 78" Wide.

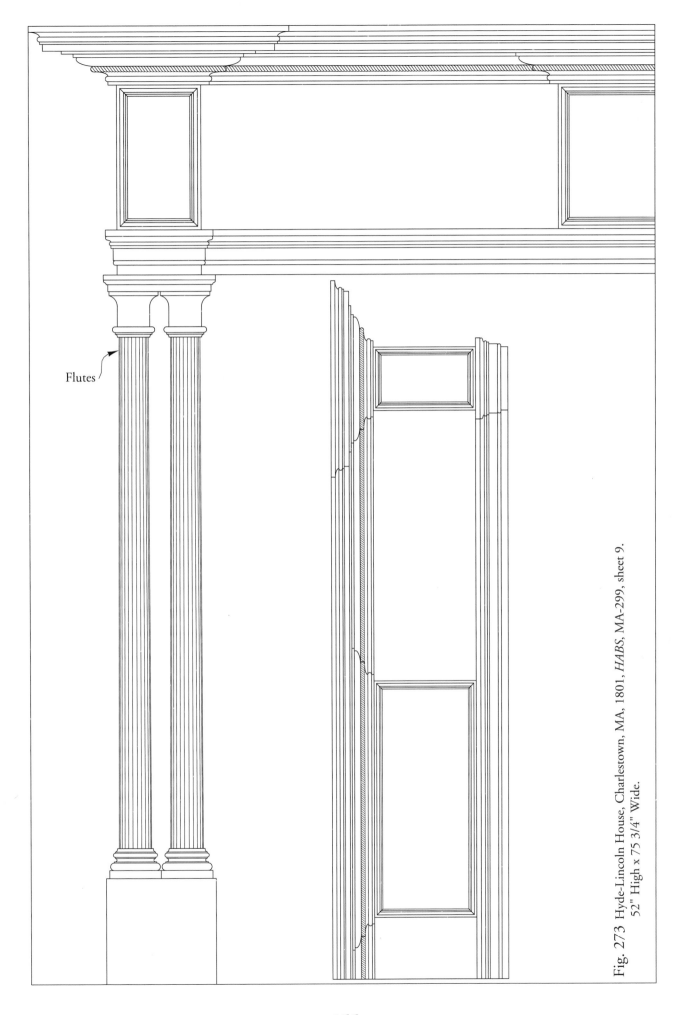

Flutes

Fig. 273 Hyde-Lincoln House, Charlestown, MA, 1801, *HABS*, MA-299, sheet 9. 52" High x 75 3/4" Wide.

Flutes

Reeds

Fig. 274 Benjamin, *Country Builder's Assistant*, 1797, pl. XX.
54 1/2" High x 70" Wide.

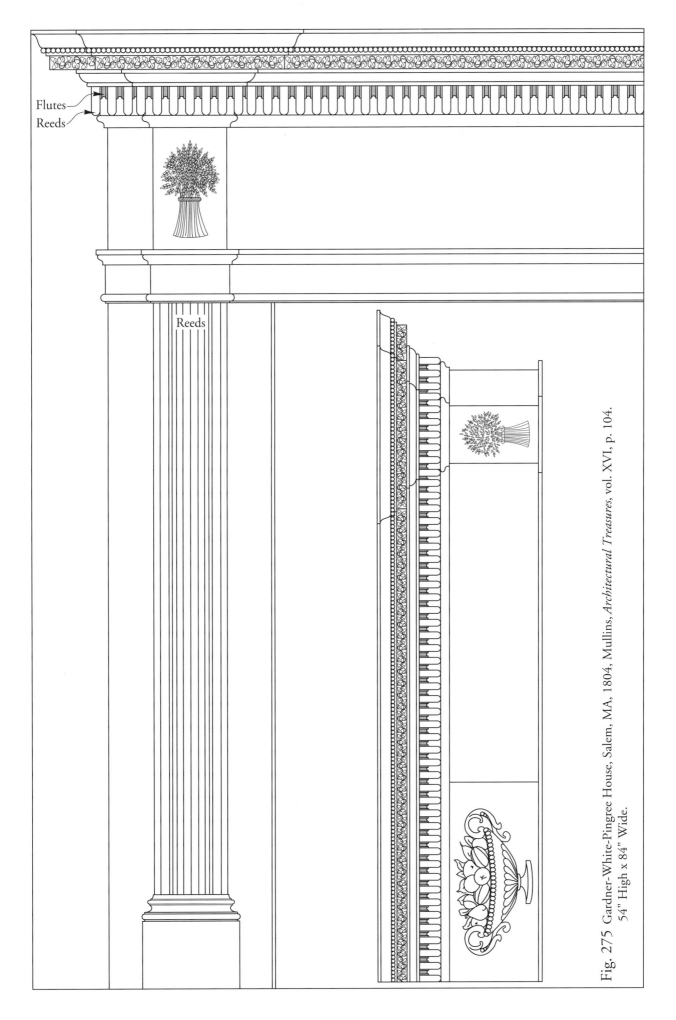

Flutes
Reeds

Reeds

Fig. 275 Gardner-White-Pingree House, Salem, MA, 1804, Mullins, *Architectural Treasures, vol. XVI, p. 104.*
54" High x 84" Wide.

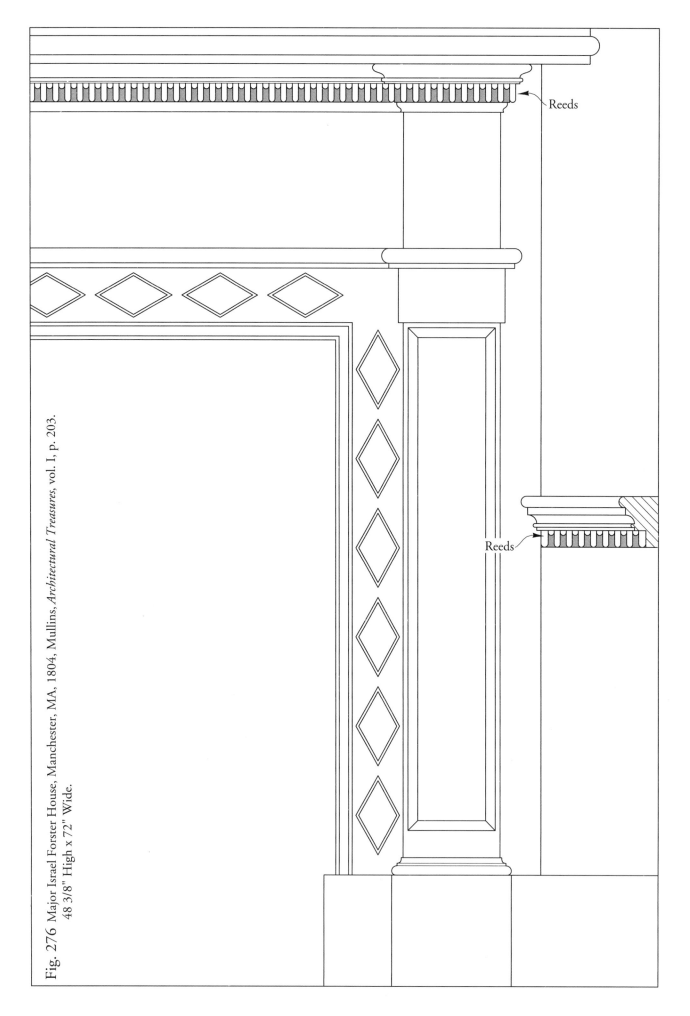

Reeds

Reeds

Fig. 276 Major Israel Forster House, Manchester, MA, 1804, Mullins, *Architectural Treasures*, vol. I, p. 203. 48 3/8" High x 72" Wide.

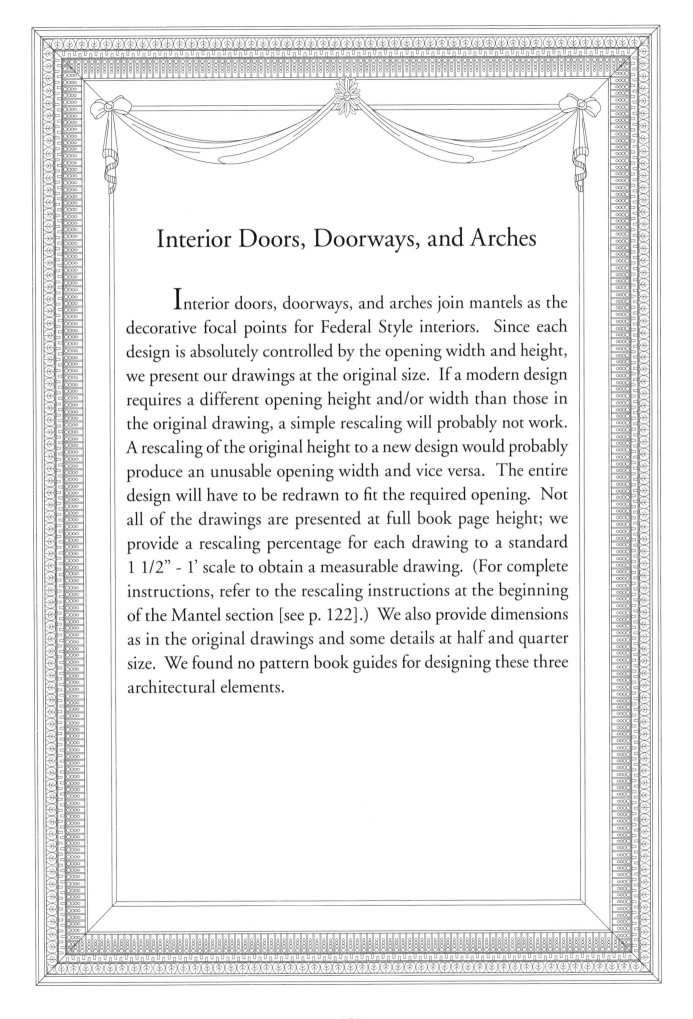

Interior Doors, Doorways, and Arches

Interior doors, doorways, and arches join mantels as the decorative focal points for Federal Style interiors. Since each design is absolutely controlled by the opening width and height, we present our drawings at the original size. If a modern design requires a different opening height and/or width than those in the original drawing, a simple rescaling will probably not work. A rescaling of the original height to a new design would probably produce an unusable opening width and vice versa. The entire design will have to be redrawn to fit the required opening. Not all of the drawings are presented at full book page height; we provide a rescaling percentage for each drawing to a standard 1 1/2" - 1' scale to obtain a measurable drawing. (For complete instructions, refer to the rescaling instructions at the beginning of the Mantel section [see p. 122].) We also provide dimensions as in the original drawings and some details at half and quarter size. We found no pattern book guides for designing these three architectural elements.

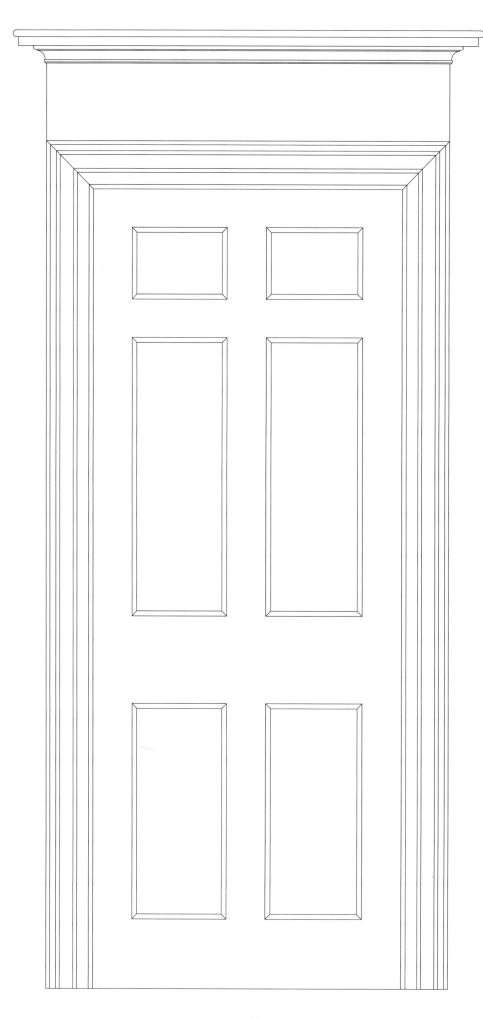

Fig. 277 Coleman-Hollister House, Greenfield, MA, 1796, HABS, MA-2-19, sheet 14. Outside - 106 9/16" High x 54" Wide. Door - 89" High x 35 1/2" Wide. Increase book drawing (10" H) by 33.2% to convert to 1 1/2" = 1' scale.

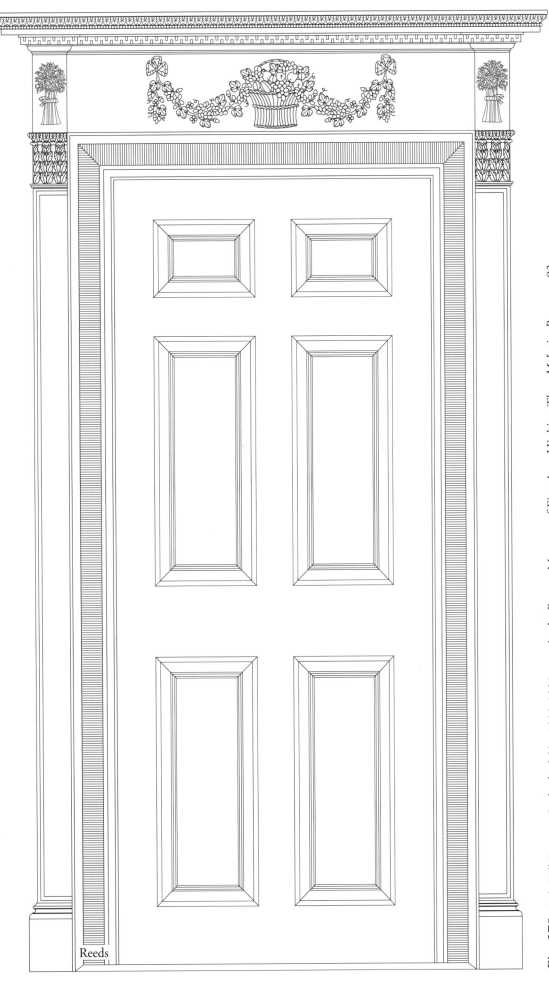

Reeds

Fig. 278 Oak Hill Rooms, Peabody, MA, 1800-1801, now in the Boston Museum of Fine Arts, Hipkiss, *Three McIntire Rooms*, p. 93. Outside - 106" High x 68 1/32" Wide. Door - 86 3/4" High x 36" Wide. Increase book drawing (10" H) by 32.5% to convert to 1 1/2" = 1' scale.

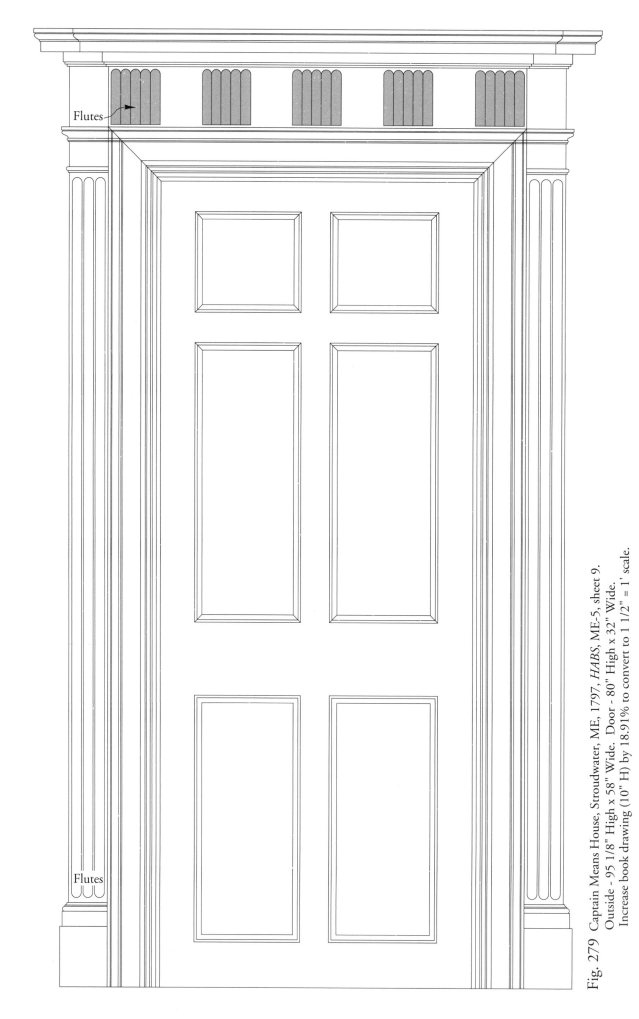

Flutes

Flutes

Fig. 279 Captain Means House, Stroudwater, ME, 1797, *HABS*, ME-5, sheet 9.
Outside - 95 1/8" High x 58" Wide. Door - 80" High x 32" Wide.
Increase book drawing (10" H) by 18.91% to convert to 1 1/2" = 1' scale.

162

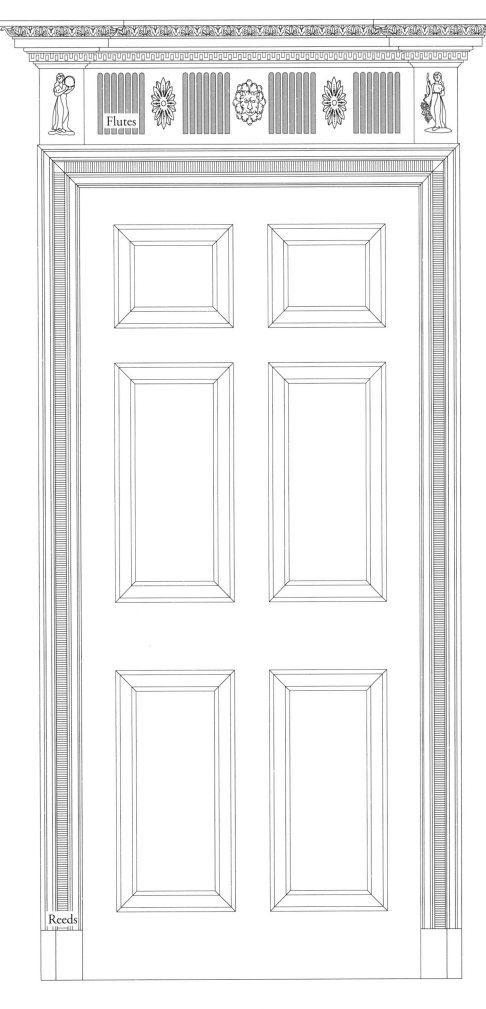

Flutes

Reeds

Fig. 280 Harrison Gray Otis House (first), Boston, MA, 1796, Mullins, *Architectural Treasures*, vol. I, p. 169. Outside - 109 1/4" High x 58 1/2" Wide. Door - 90 1/4" x 39 13/16" Wide. Increase book drawing (10"H) by 36.56% to convert to 1 1/2" = 1' scale.

Fig. 281 Hyde-Lincoln House, Charlestown, MA, 1801, *HABS*, MA-299, sheet 8. Outside - 97 5/32" High x 53 3/4" Wide. Door - 83" High x 35" Wide. Increase book drawing (10" H) by 21.445% to convert to 1 1/2" = 1' scale.

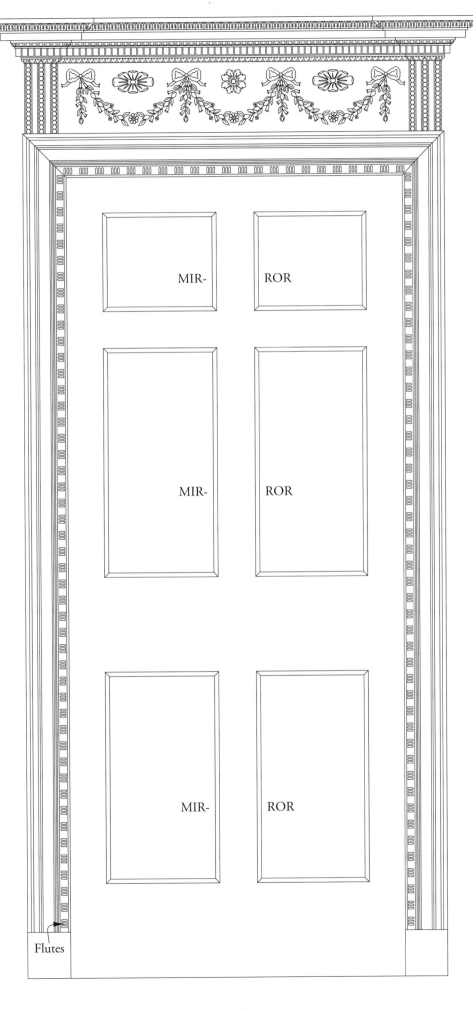

MIR-   ROR

MIR-   ROR

MIR-   ROR

Flutes

Fig. 282 Harrison Gray Otis House (first), Boston, MA, 1796, Mullins, *Architectural Treasures*, vol. I, p. 169. Outside - 109" High x 57 1/2" Wide. Door - 90 15/16" High x 39 3/8" Wide. Increase book drawing (10" H) by 36.25% to convert to 1 1/2" = 1' scale.

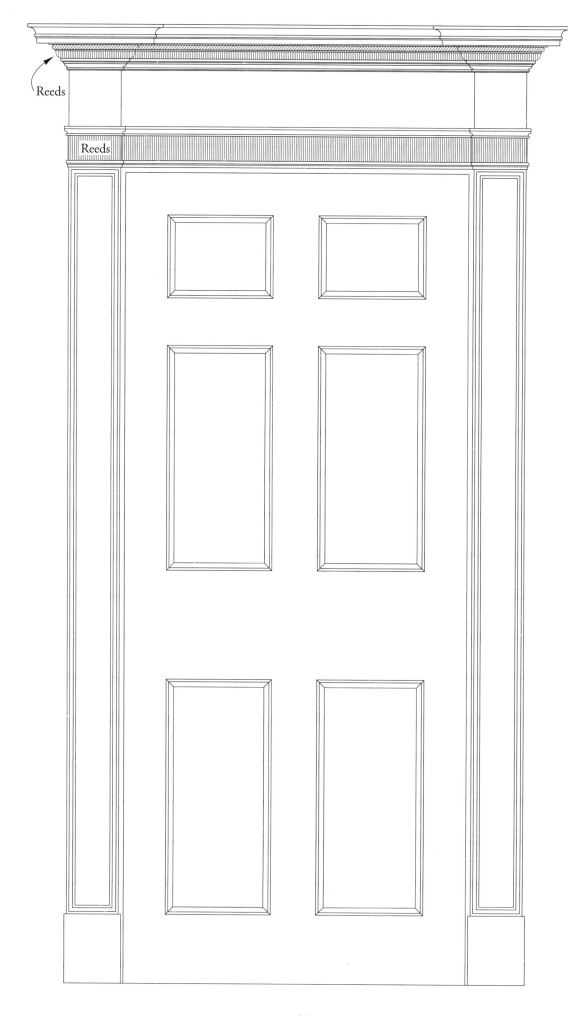

Reeds

Reeds

Fig. 283   Gideon Tucker House, Salem, MA, 1806, Mullins, *Architectural Treasures*, vol. I, p. 168. Outside - 93 3/4" High x 54 5/8" Wide. Door - 79 1/4" High x 34 5/8" Wide. Increase book drawing (10" H) by 17.18% to convert to 1 1/2" = 1' scale.

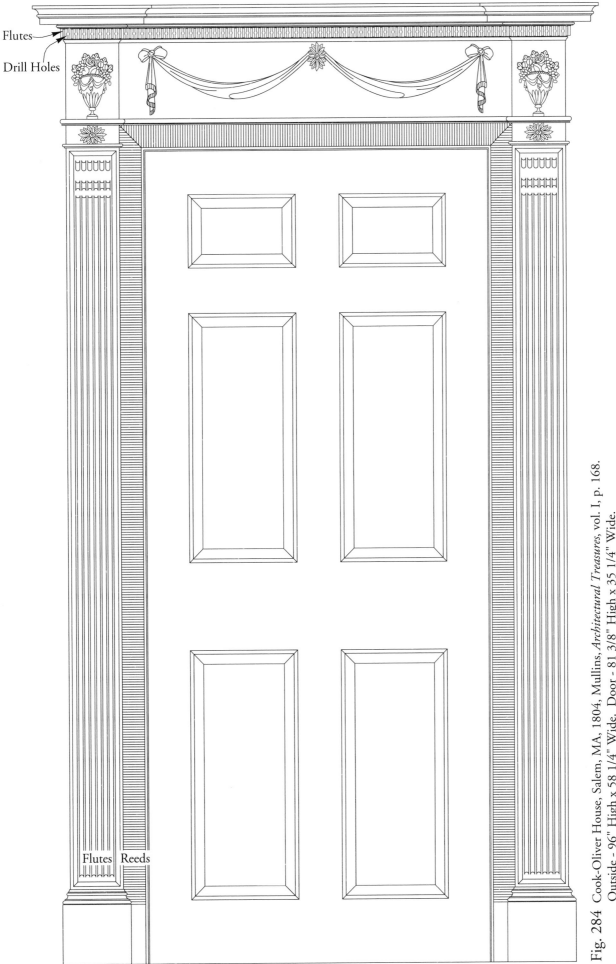

Flutes

Drill Holes

Flutes Reeds

Fig. 284 Cook-Oliver House, Salem, MA, 1804, Mullins, *Architectural Treasures*, vol. I, p. 168. Outside - 96" High x 58 1/4" Wide. Door - 81 3/8" High x 35 1/4" Wide. Increase book drawing (10" H) by 20% to convert to 1 1/2" = 1' scale.

Reeds

Fig. 285 Oak Hill Rooms, Peabody, MA, 1800-1801, now in the Boston Museum of Fine Arts, Hipkiss, *Three McIntire Rooms*, p. 83. Outside - 108" High x 69 11/32" Wide. Inside - 87 7/16" High x 39" Wide. Increase book drawing (10" H) by 35% to convert to 1 1/2" = 1' scale.

Flutes

Reeds

Fig. 286 Oak Hill Rooms, Peabody, MA, 1800-1801, now in the Boston Museum of Fine Arts, Hipkiss, *Three McIntire Rooms*, p. 87.
Outside - 95" High x 40" Wide. Inside - 75 3/4" High x 67 27/32" Wide. Increase book drawing (9 13/32" H) by 26.245% to convert to 1 1/2" = 1' scale.

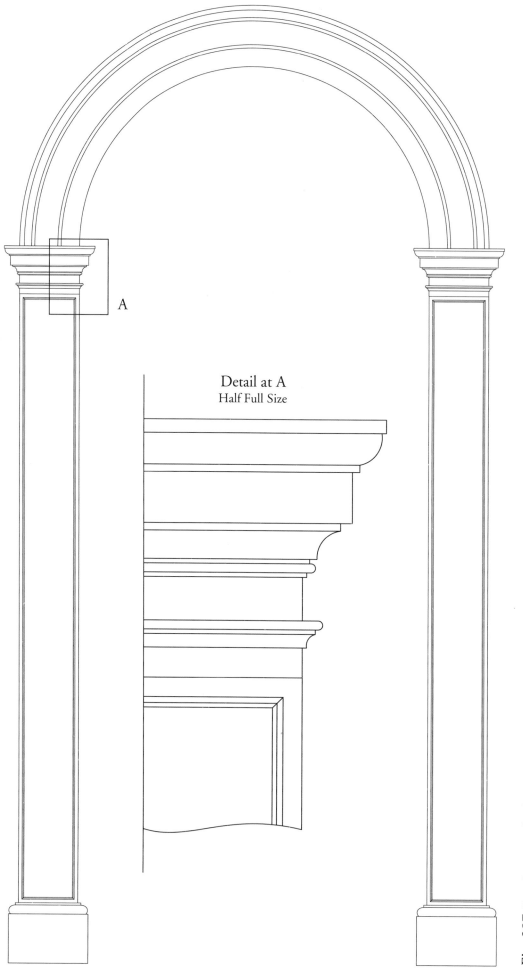

Detail at A
Half Full Size

Fig. 287 Jonathan Woodbridge House, Worthington, MA, 1806, *HABS*, MA-124, sheet 14.
Outside - 107 11/32" High x 54 1/8" Wide. Inside - 100 13/32" High x 40 3/8" Wide.
Scale up Arch book drawing (10" H) by 34.179% to convert to 1 1/2" = 1' scale.

A

170

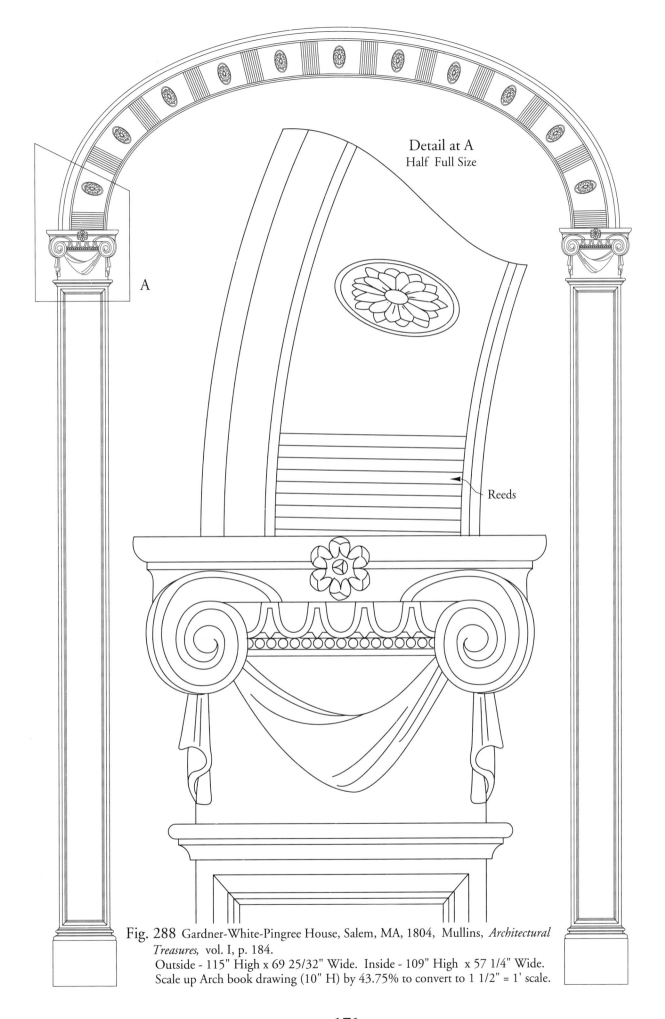

Detail at A
Half Full Size

A

Reeds

Fig. 288 Gardner-White-Pingree House, Salem, MA, 1804, Mullins, *Architectural Treasures*, vol. I, p. 184.
Outside - 115" High x 69 25/32" Wide. Inside - 109" High x 57 1/4" Wide.
Scale up Arch book drawing (10" H) by 43.75% to convert to 1 1/2" = 1' scale.

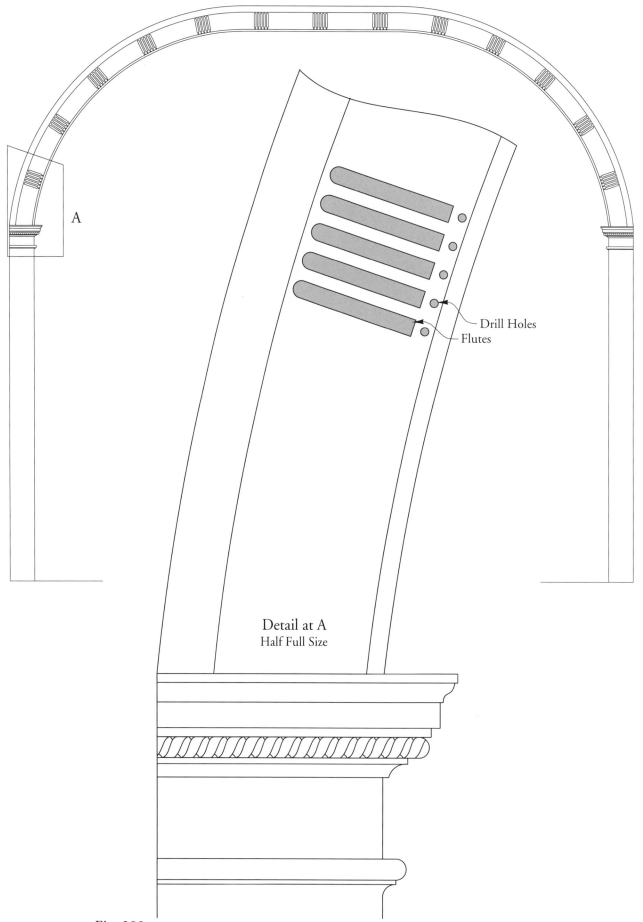

A

Drill Holes
Flutes

Detail at A
Half Full Size

Fig. 289 Captain Leonard House, Agawam, MA, 1807, *HABS*, MA-2-50, sheets 13, 14.
Outside - 110" High x 123" Wide. Inside - 105 18" High x 113 1/4" Wide.
Scale up Arch book drawing (6" H) by 129.166% to convert to 1 1/2" = 1' scale.

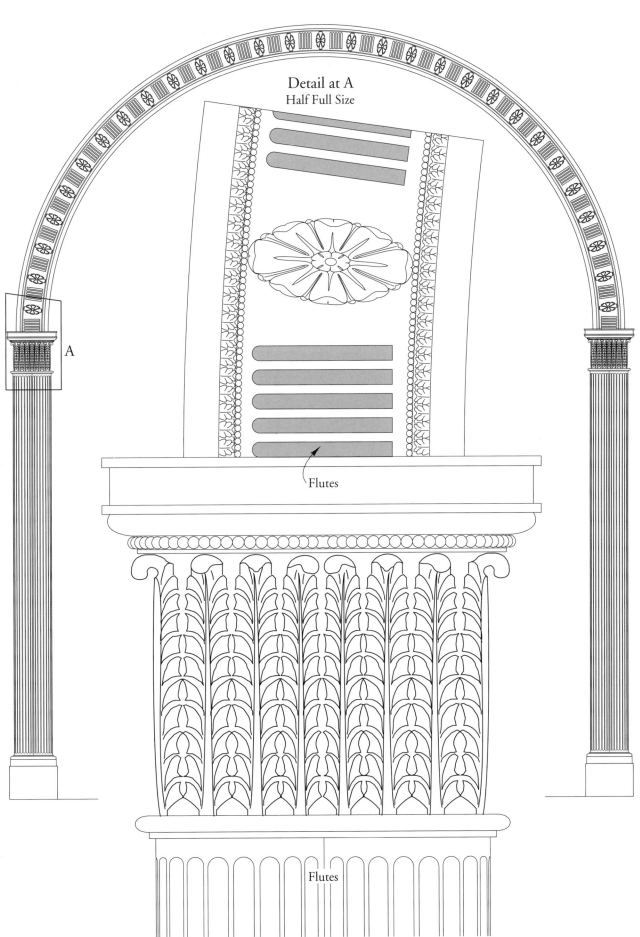

Detail at A
Half Full Size

A

Flutes

Flutes

Fig. 290 Amory-Ticknor House, Boston, MA, 1804, *HABS*, MA-175, sheet 14.
Outside - 144 5/8" High x 115 13/16" Wide. Inside - 138 11/16" High x 101 7/16" Wide.
Scale up Arch book drawing (8 1/16" H) by 124.418% to convert to 1 1/2" = 1' scale.

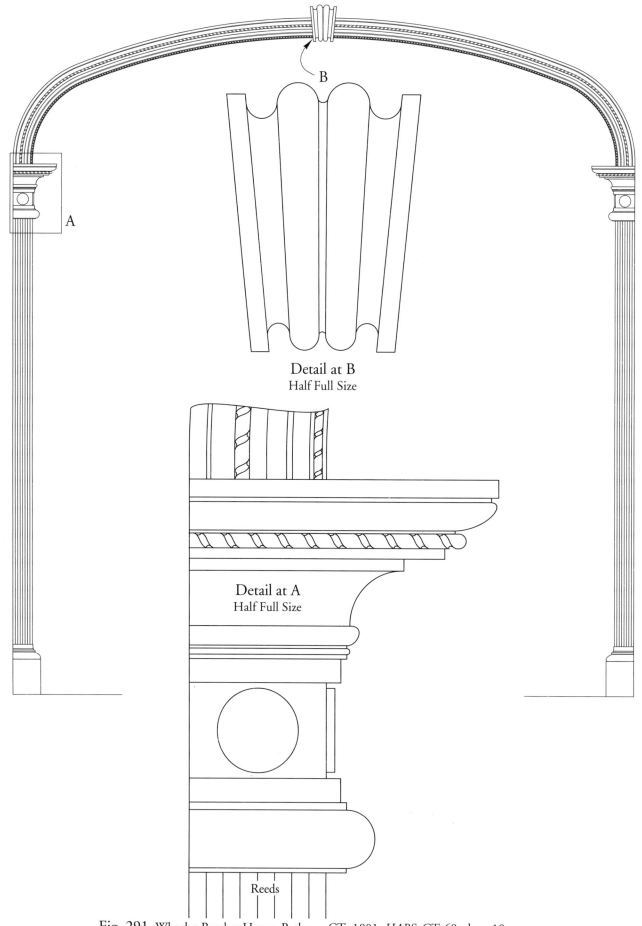

Detail at B
Half Full Size

Detail at A
Half Full Size

Reeds

Fig. 291 Wheeler-Beecher House, Bethany, CT, 1801, *HABS*, CT-68, sheet 18.
Outside - 103 1/2" High x 96 1/8" Wide. Inside - 98" High x 90" Wide.
Scale up Arch book drawing (7 3/16" H) by 80% to convert to 1 1/2" = 1' scale.

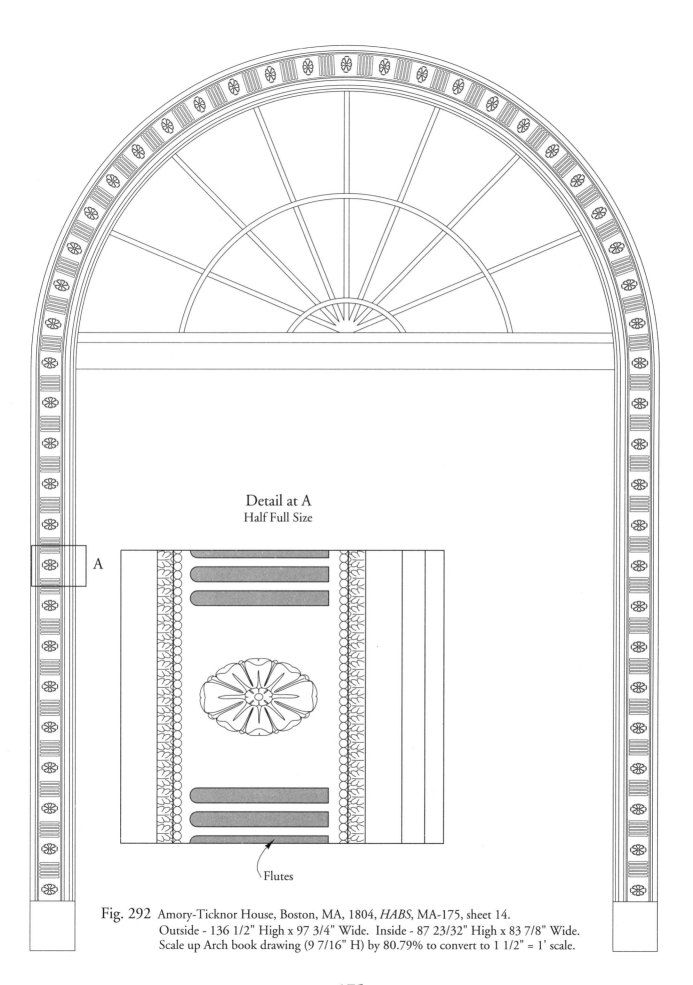

Detail at A
Half Full Size

A

Flutes

Fig. 292 Amory-Ticknor House, Boston, MA, 1804, *HABS*, MA-175, sheet 14.
Outside - 136 1/2" High x 97 3/4" Wide. Inside - 87 23/32" High x 83 7/8" Wide.
Scale up Arch book drawing (9 7/16" H) by 80.79% to convert to 1 1/2" = 1' scale.

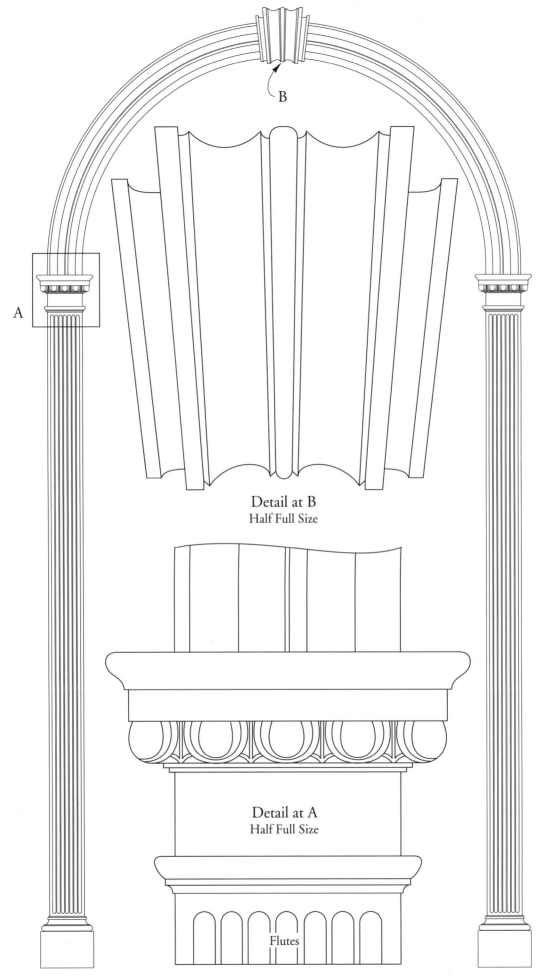

Detail at B
Half Full Size

Detail at A
Half Full Size

Flutes

A

B

Fig. 293 Amory-Ticknor House, Boston, MA, 1804, HABS, MA-175, sheet 15. Outside - 130 1/16" High x 66 1/4" Wide. Inside - 122 15/32" High x 56 1/2" Wide. Scale up Arch book drawing (10" H) by 62.578% to convert to 1 1/2" = 1' scale.

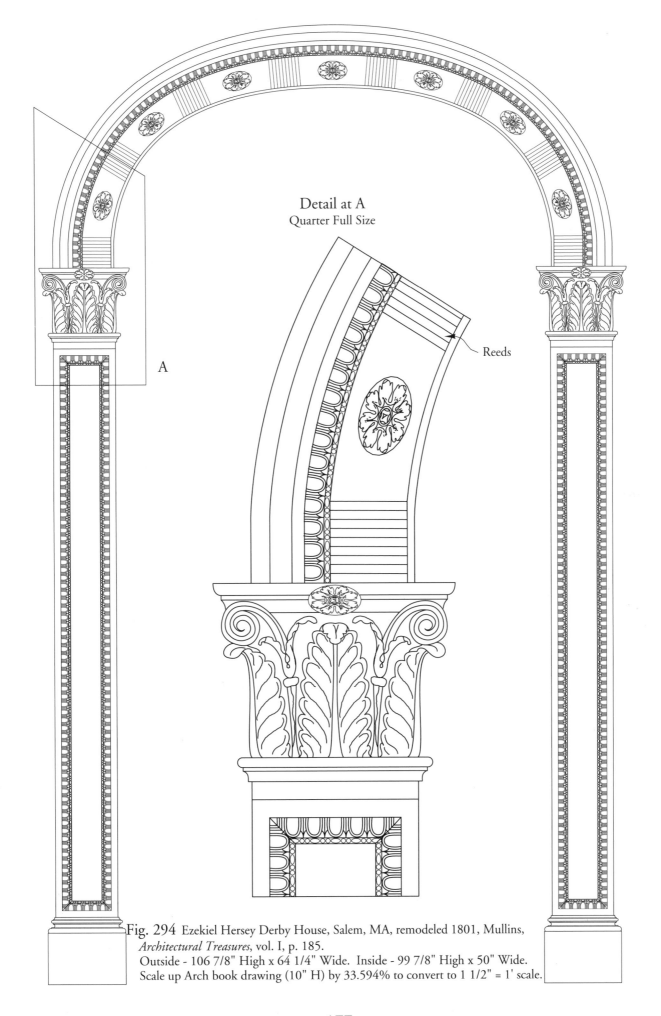

Detail at A
Quarter Full Size

A

Reeds

Fig. 294 Ezekiel Hersey Derby House, Salem, MA, remodeled 1801, Mullins,
Architectural Treasures, vol. I, p. 185.
Outside - 106 7/8" High x 64 1/4" Wide. Inside - 99 7/8" High x 50" Wide.
Scale up Arch book drawing (10" H) by 33.594% to convert to 1 1/2" = 1' scale.

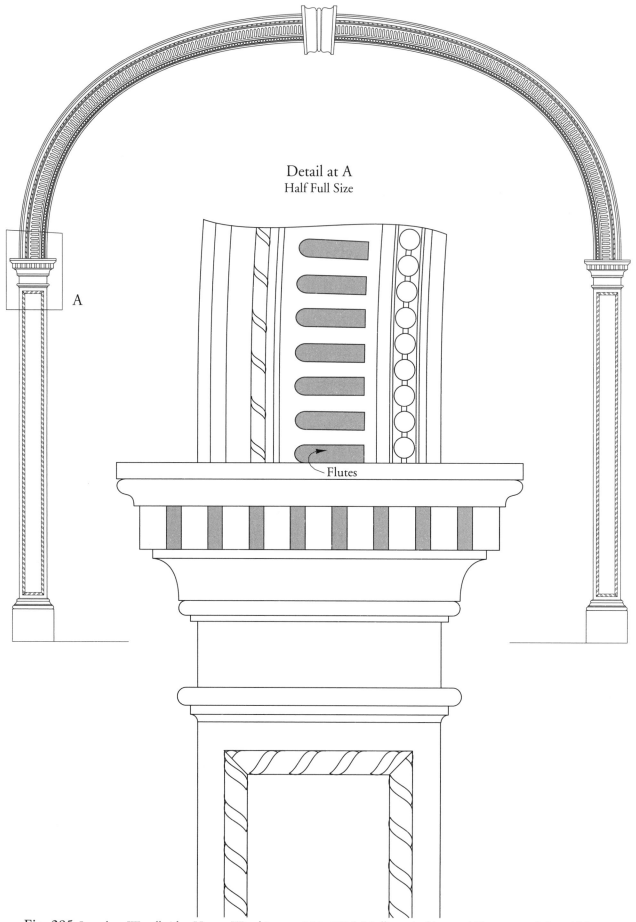

Detail at A
Half Full Size

A

Flutes

Fig. 295 Jonathan Woodbridge House, Worthington, MA, 1806, Mullins, *Architectural Treasures*, vol. I, p. 184.
Outside - 117 1/2" High x 118 1/4" Wide. Inside - 108 17/32" High x 104 1/4" Wide.
Scale up Arch book drawing (6 5/8" H) by 121.698% to convert to 1 1/2" = 1' scale.

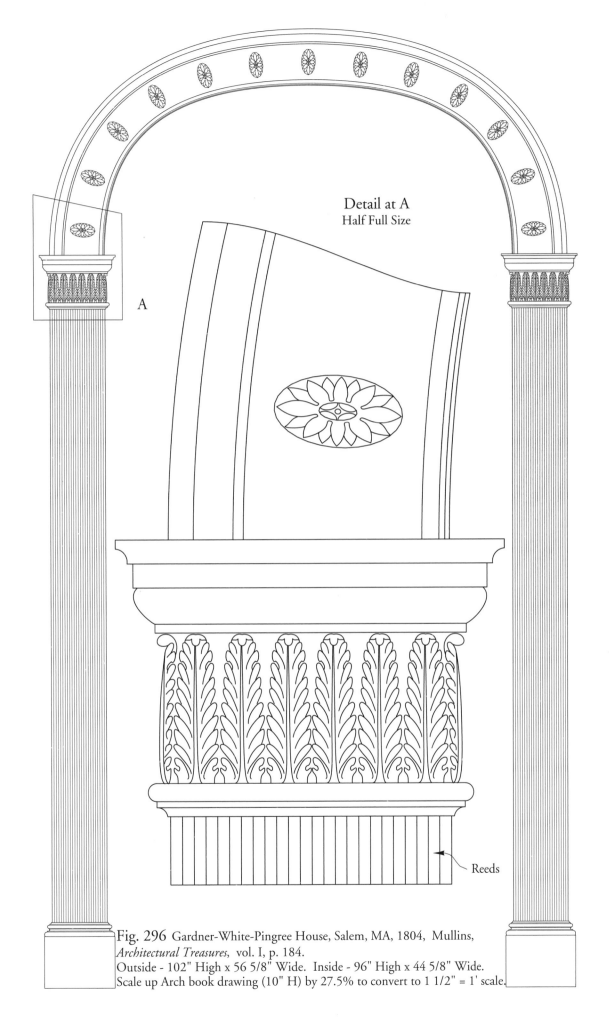

Detail at A
Half Full Size

A

Reeds

Fig. 296 Gardner-White-Pingree House, Salem, MA, 1804, Mullins,
Architectural Treasures, vol. I, p. 184.
Outside - 102" High x 56 5/8" Wide. Inside - 96" High x 44 5/8" Wide.
Scale up Arch book drawing (10" H) by 27.5% to convert to 1 1/2" = 1' scale.

Reeds

A

Detail at A
Half Full Size

Reeds

Fig. 297 Benjamin Pickman House, Salem, MA, remodeled 1800, Mullins, *Architectural Treasures*, vol. I, p. 185.
Outside - 116 7/8" High x 77" Wide. Inside - 112" High x 63 1/2" Wide.
Scale up Arch book drawing (9 27/32" H) by 48.413% to convert to 1 1/2" = 1' scale.

Designs for Historic and Contemporary Rooms

In this section, the historic room elevations have the original house dimensions given, and the contemporary room elevations have dimensions given for an 8' room height. A rescaling percentage to a standard scale is provided for each drawing in this section. (For complete instructions, refer to the rescaling instructions at the beginning of the Mantel section [see p. 122].)

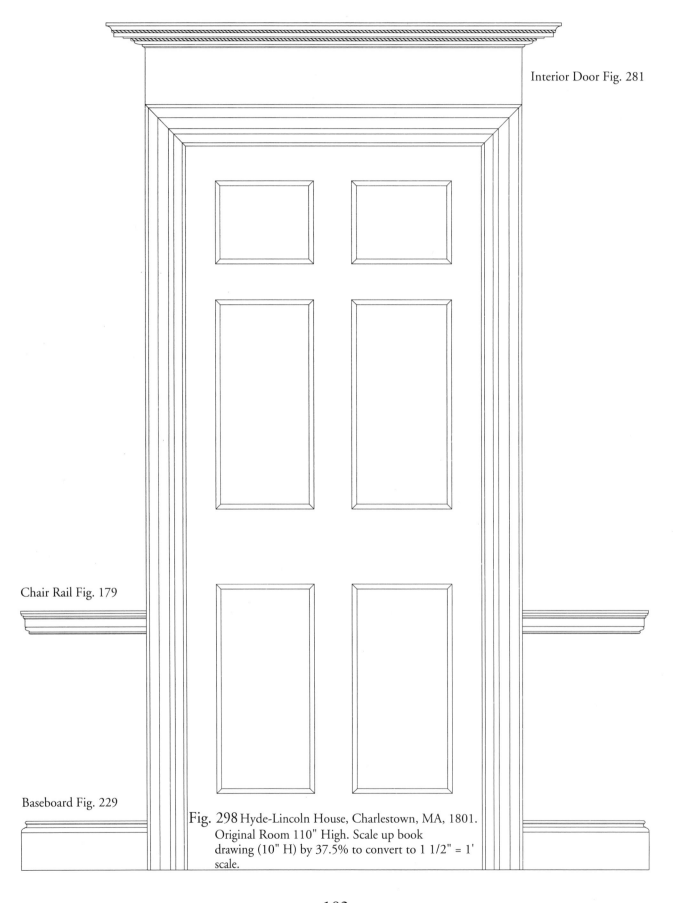

Cornice Type C Fig. 78

Interior Door Fig. 281

Chair Rail Fig. 179

Baseboard Fig. 229

Fig. 298 Hyde-Lincoln House, Charlestown, MA, 1801. Original Room 110" High. Scale up book drawing (10" H) by 37.5% to convert to 1 1/2" = 1' scale.

Cornice Type A Fig. 1

Drill Holes
and Flutes

Interior Door Fig. 284

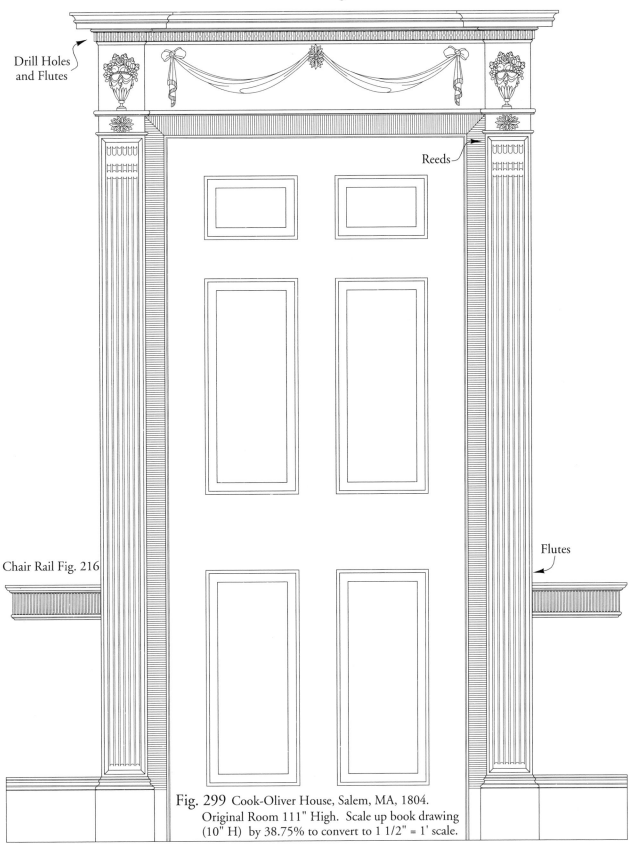

Drill Holes
and Flutes

Reeds

Chair Rail Fig. 216

Flutes

Fig. 299 Cook-Oliver House, Salem, MA, 1804.
Original Room 111" High. Scale up book drawing
(10" H) by 38.75% to convert to 1 1/2" = 1' scale.

Cornice Type C Fig. 81

Mantel Fig. 269

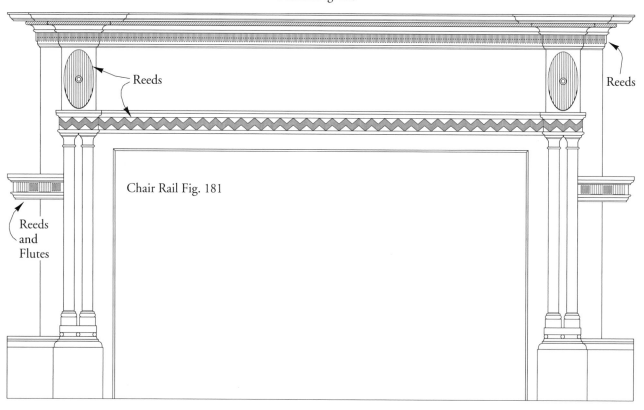

Reeds

Reeds

Chair Rail Fig. 181

Reeds
and
Flutes

Fig. 300 Christopher Ryder House, Chathamport, MA, 1809. Original Room 96" High.
Scale up book drawing (7 3/4" H) by 55% to convert to 1 1/2" = 1' scale.

Cornice Type B Fig. 63

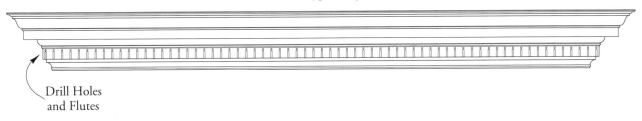

Drill Holes
and Flutes

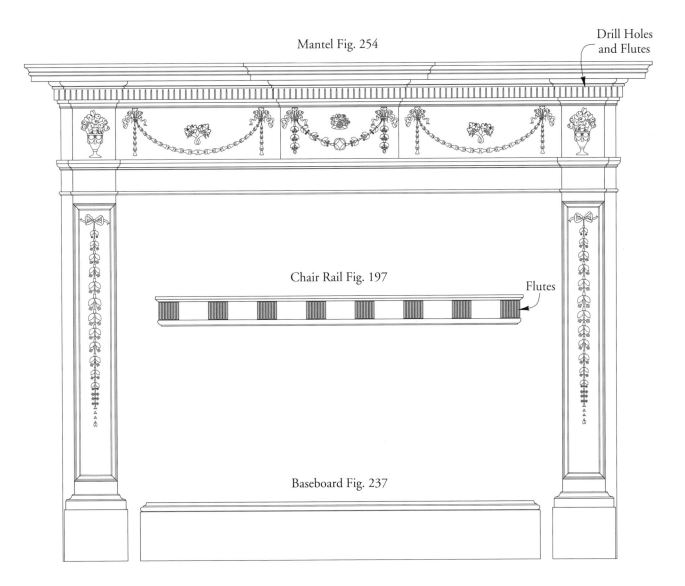

Drill Holes
and Flutes

Mantel Fig. 254

Chair Rail Fig. 197

Flutes

Baseboard Fig. 237

Fig. 301 Holmes-Sayward House, Alfred, ME, 1802. Original Room 96 1/2" High.
Scale up book drawing (8 11/16" H) by 38.85% to convert to 1 1/2" = 1' scale.

185

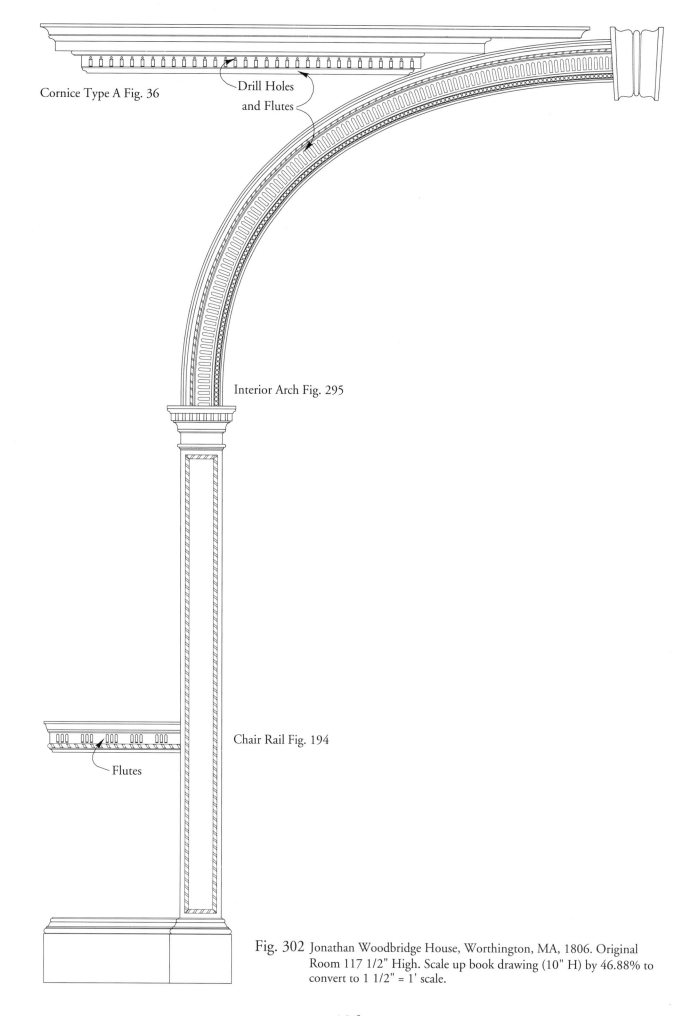

Cornice Type A Fig. 36

Drill Holes
and Flutes

Interior Arch Fig. 295

Chair Rail Fig. 194

Flutes

Fig. 302 Jonathan Woodbridge House, Worthington, MA, 1806. Original
Room 117 1/2" High. Scale up book drawing (10" H) by 46.88% to
convert to 1 1/2" = 1' scale.

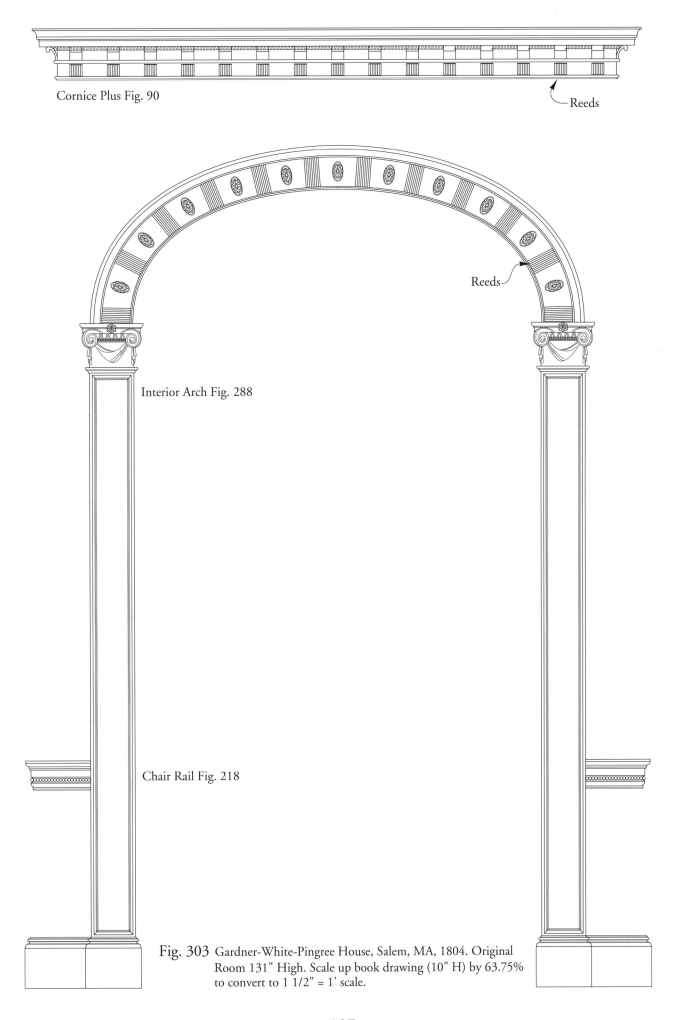

Cornice Plus Fig. 90

Reeds

Reeds

Interior Arch Fig. 288

Chair Rail Fig. 218

Fig. 303 Gardner-White-Pingree House, Salem, MA, 1804. Original
Room 131" High. Scale up book drawing (10" H) by 63.75%
to convert to 1 1/2" = 1' scale.

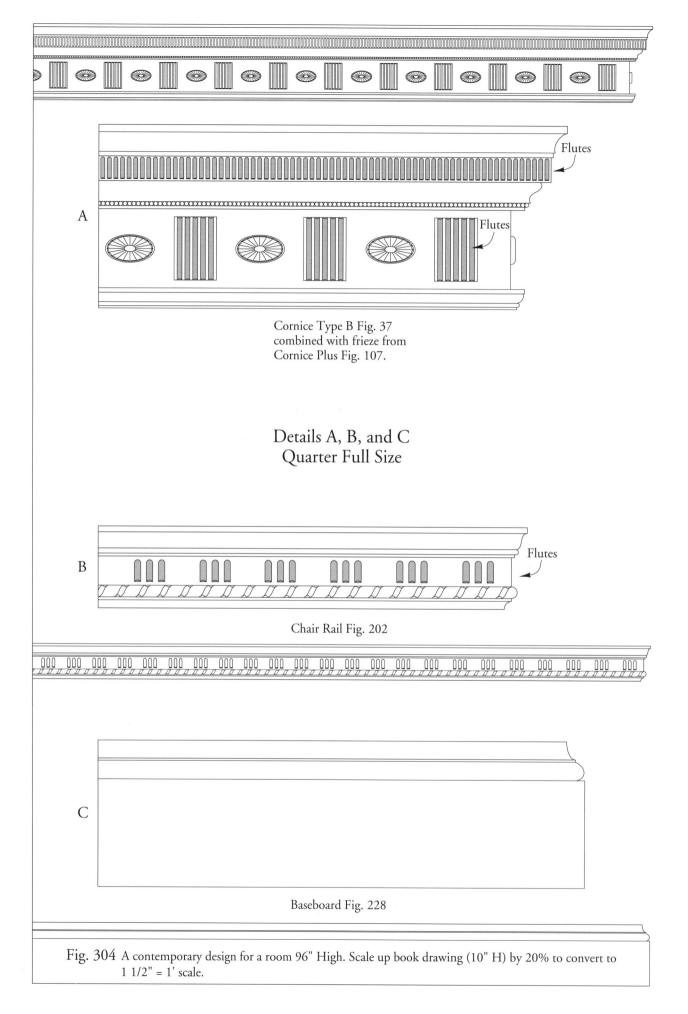

A

Cornice Type B Fig. 37
combined with frieze from
Cornice Plus Fig. 107.

Details A, B, and C
Quarter Full Size

B

Chair Rail Fig. 202

C

Baseboard Fig. 228

Fig. 304 A contemporary design for a room 96" High. Scale up book drawing (10" H) by 20% to convert to
1 1/2" = 1' scale.

188

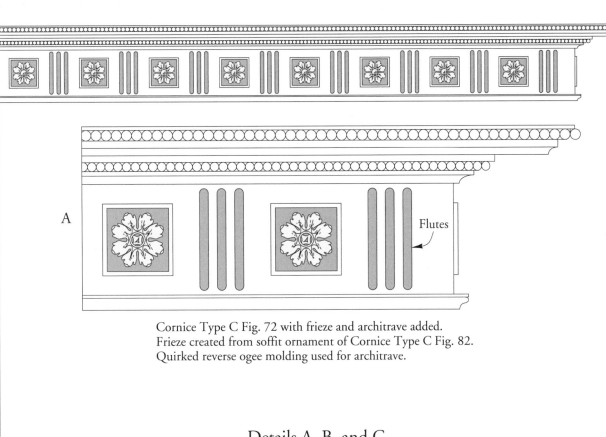

A

Flutes

Cornice Type C Fig. 72 with frieze and architrave added.
Frieze created from soffit ornament of Cornice Type C Fig. 82.
Quirked reverse ogee molding used for architrave.

Details A, B, and C
Quarter Full Size

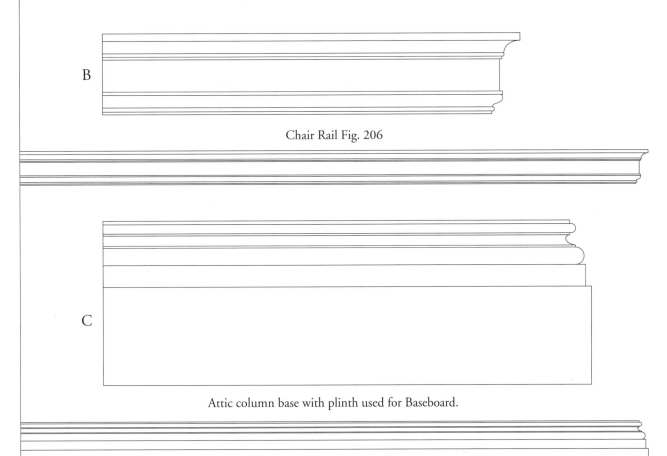

B

Chair Rail Fig. 206

C

Attic column base with plinth used for Baseboard.

Fig. 305 A contemporary design for a room 96" High. Scale up book drawing (10" H) by 20% to convert to 1 1/2" = 1' scale.

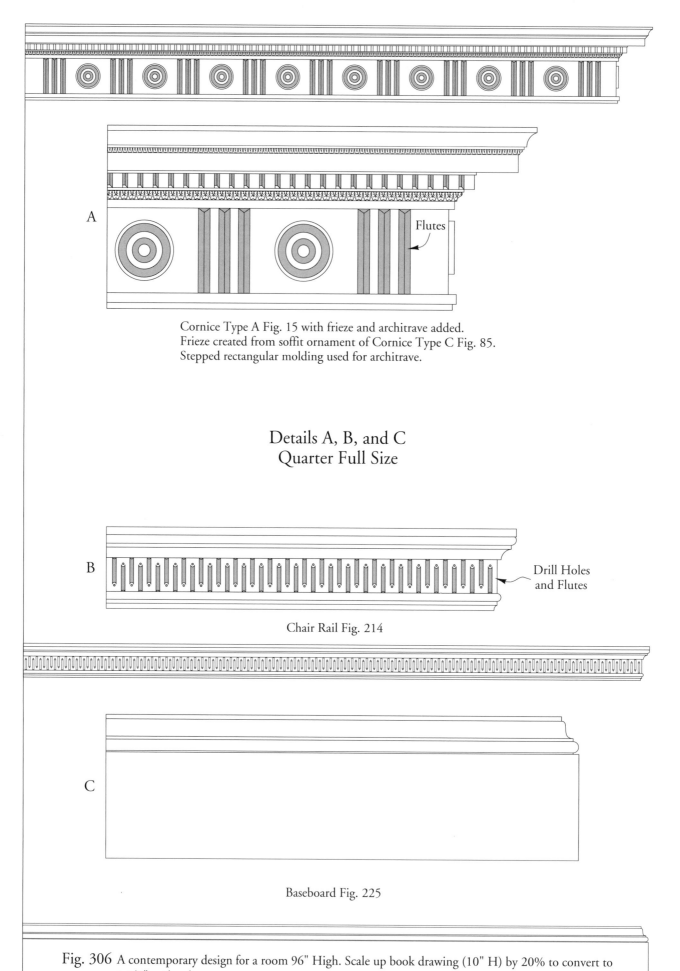

A

Cornice Type A Fig. 15 with frieze and architrave added.
Frieze created from soffit ornament of Cornice Type C Fig. 85.
Stepped rectangular molding used for architrave.

Details A, B, and C
Quarter Full Size

Flutes

B

Drill Holes
and Flutes

Chair Rail Fig. 214

C

Baseboard Fig. 225

Fig. 306 A contemporary design for a room 96" High. Scale up book drawing (10" H) by 20% to convert to 1 1/2" = 1' scale.

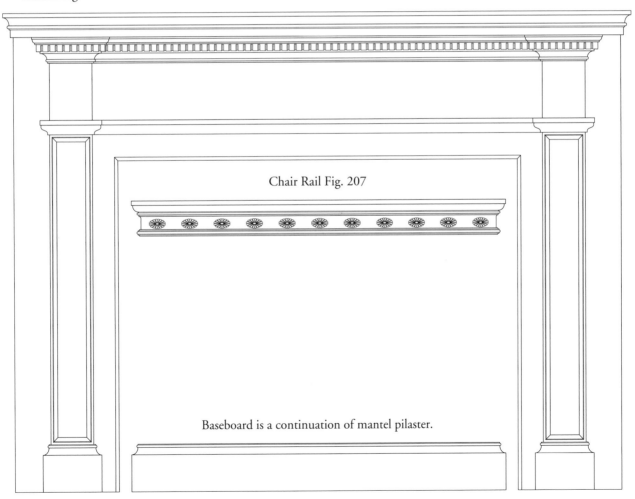

Cornice Type B Fig. 45

Mantel Fig. 264

Chair Rail Fig. 207

Baseboard is a continuation of mantel pilaster.

Fig. 307 A contemporary design for a room 96" High. Scale up book drawing (9 17/32" H) by 25.9% to convert to 1 1/2" = 1' scale.

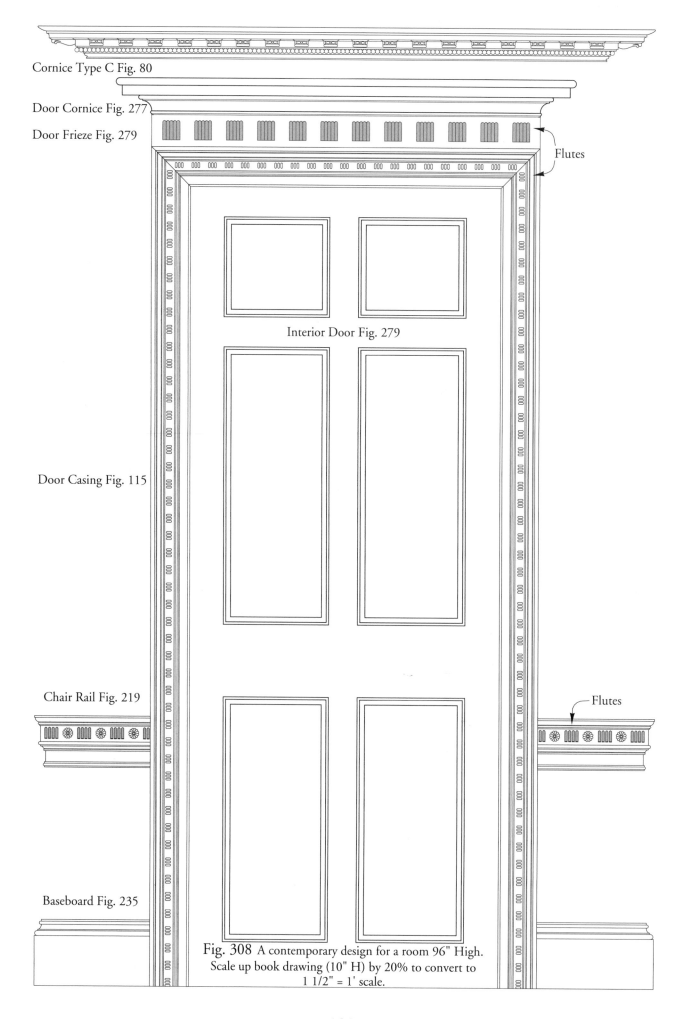

Cornice Type C Fig. 80

Door Cornice Fig. 277

Door Frieze Fig. 279

Flutes

Interior Door Fig. 279

Door Casing Fig. 115

Chair Rail Fig. 219

Flutes

Baseboard Fig. 235

Fig. 308 A contemporary design for a room 96" High.
Scale up book drawing (10" H) by 20% to convert to
1 1/2" = 1' scale.

192

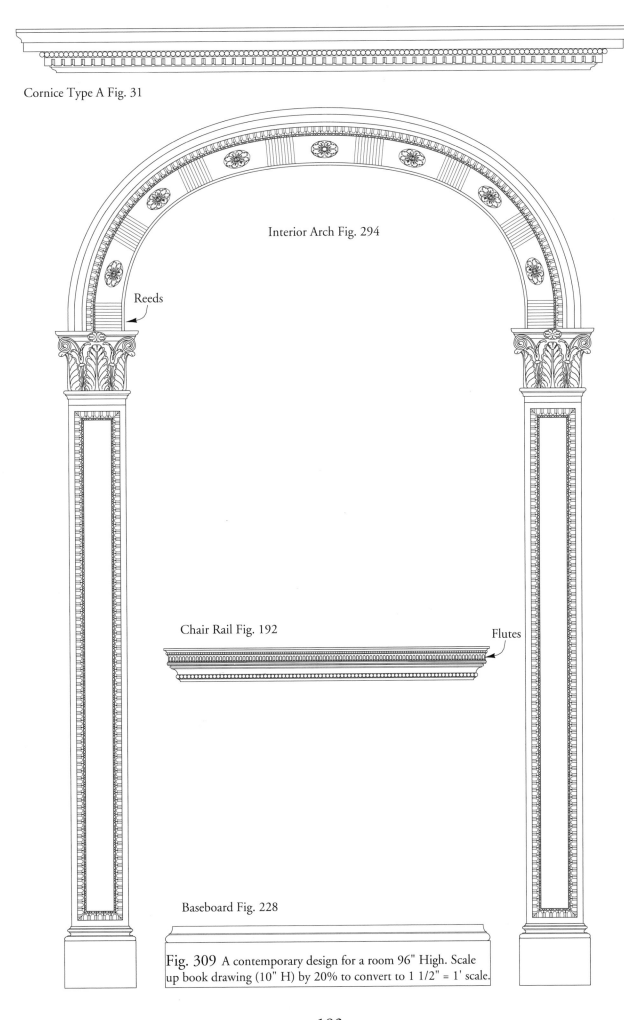

Cornice Type A Fig. 31

Interior Arch Fig. 294

Reeds

Chair Rail Fig. 192

Flutes

Baseboard Fig. 228

Fig. 309 A contemporary design for a room 96" High. Scale up book drawing (10" H) by 20% to convert to 1 1/2" = 1' scale.

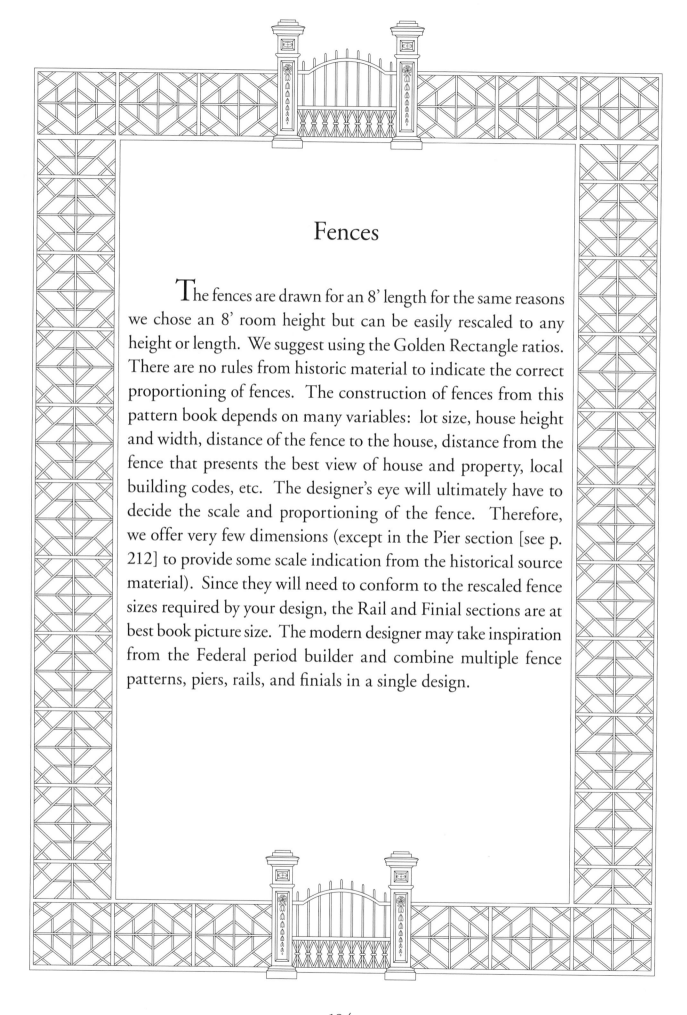

Fences

The fences are drawn for an 8' length for the same reasons we chose an 8' room height but can be easily rescaled to any height or length. We suggest using the Golden Rectangle ratios. There are no rules from historic material to indicate the correct proportioning of fences. The construction of fences from this pattern book depends on many variables: lot size, house height and width, distance of the fence to the house, distance from the fence that presents the best view of house and property, local building codes, etc. The designer's eye will ultimately have to decide the scale and proportioning of the fence. Therefore, we offer very few dimensions (except in the Pier section [see p. 212] to provide some scale indication from the historical source material). Since they will need to conform to the rescaled fence sizes required by your design, the Rail and Finial sections are at best book picture size. The modern designer may take inspiration from the Federal period builder and combine multiple fence patterns, piers, rails, and finials in a single design.

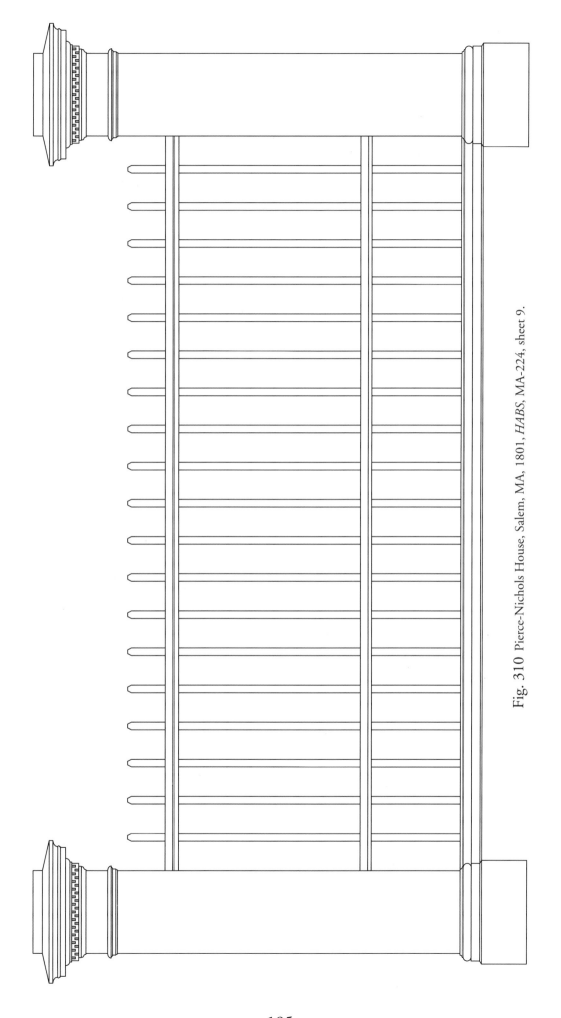

Fig. 310 Pierce-Nichols House, Salem, MA, 1801, *HABS*, MA-224, sheet 9.

Fig. 311 DeWolf-Middleton House, Bristol, RI, 1808, roof balustrade, *HABS*, RI-3-12, sheet 13.

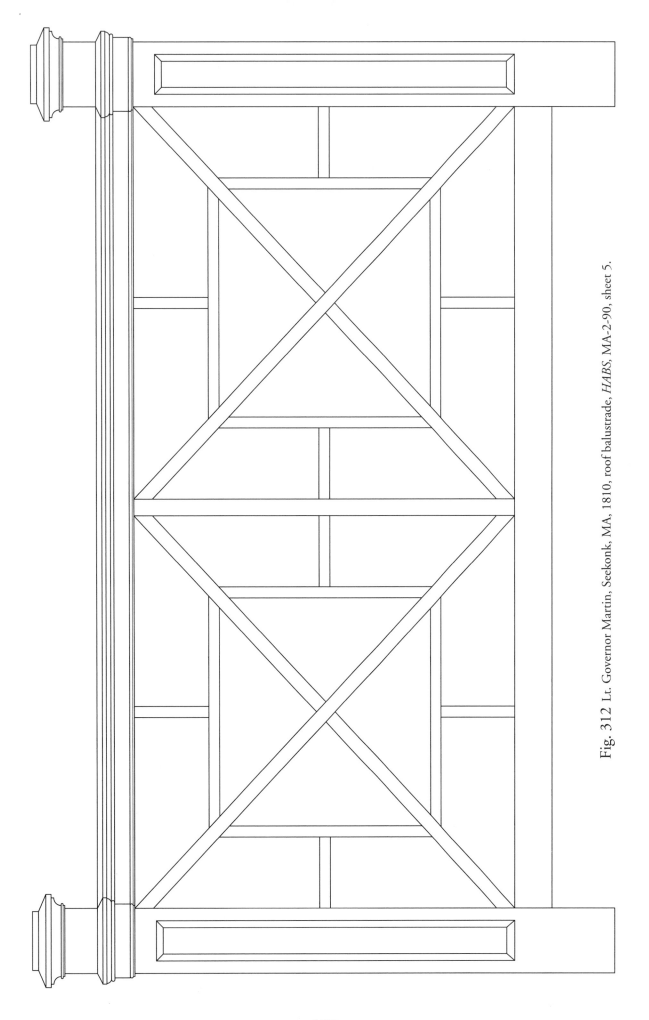

Fig. 312 Lt. Governor Martin, Seekonk, MA, 1810, roof balustrade, *HABS*, MA-2-90, sheet 5.

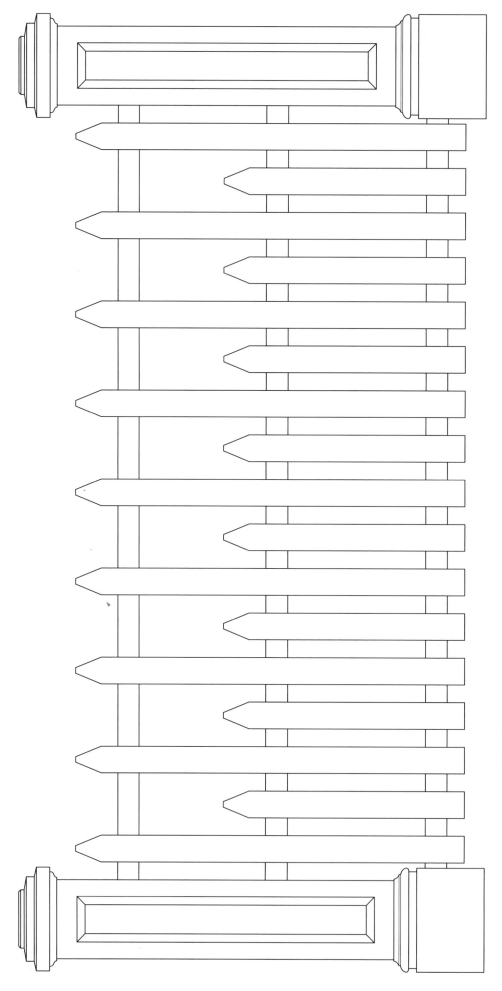

Fig. 313 Board-Zabriskie House, Paramus, NJ, c. 1800, Mullins, *Architectural Treasures*, vol. IV, p. 17.

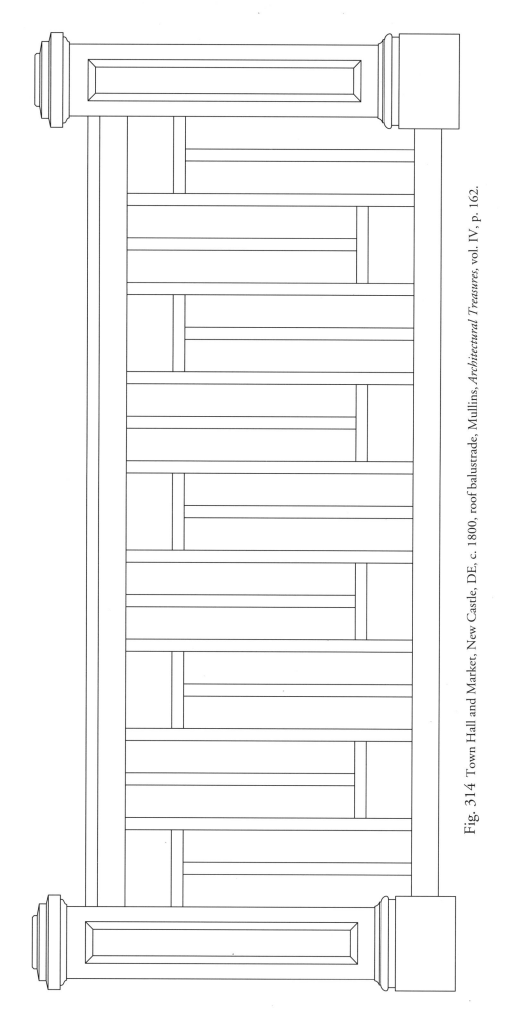

Fig. 314 Town Hall and Market, New Castle, DE, c. 1800, roof balustrade, Mullins, *Architectural Treasures*, vol. IV, p. 162.

Fig. 315 Gracie Mansion, New York, NY, c. 1800, roof balustrade, *HABS*, NY-461, photo 2.

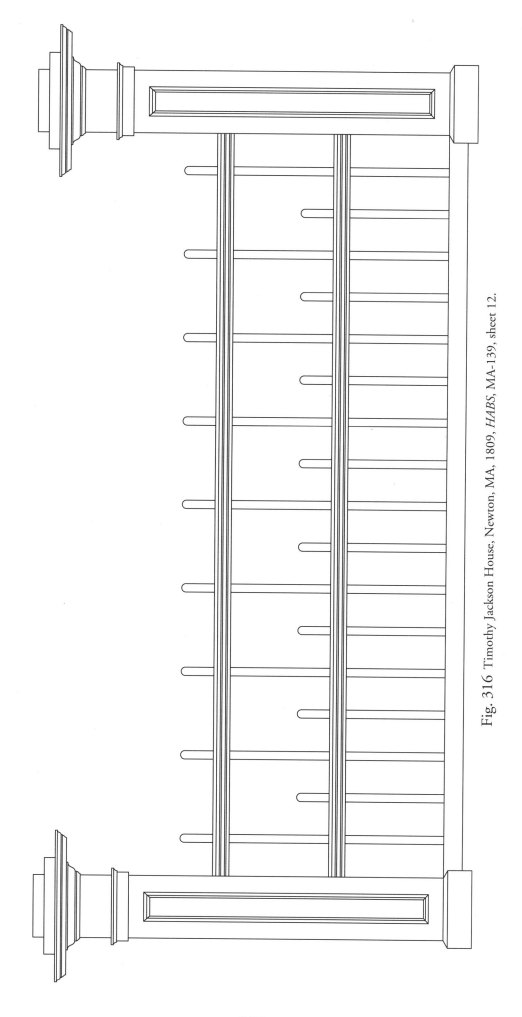

Fig. 316 Timothy Jackson House, Newton, MA, 1809, *HABS*, MA-139, sheet 12.

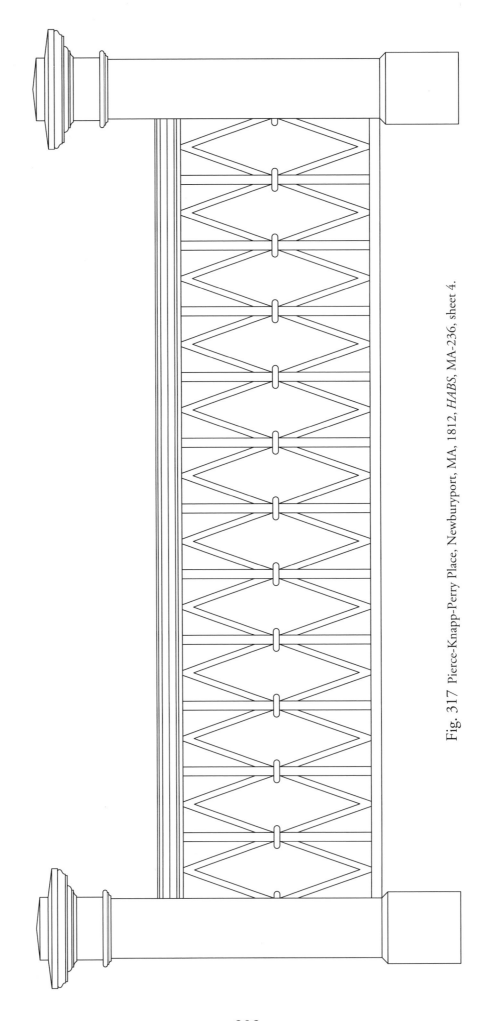

Fig. 317 Pierce-Knapp-Perry Place, Newburyport, MA, 1812, *HABS*, MA-236, sheet 4.

Fig. 318 Major Israel Forster House, Manchester, MA, 1804, roof balustrade, *HABS*, MA-373, photos 1-3.

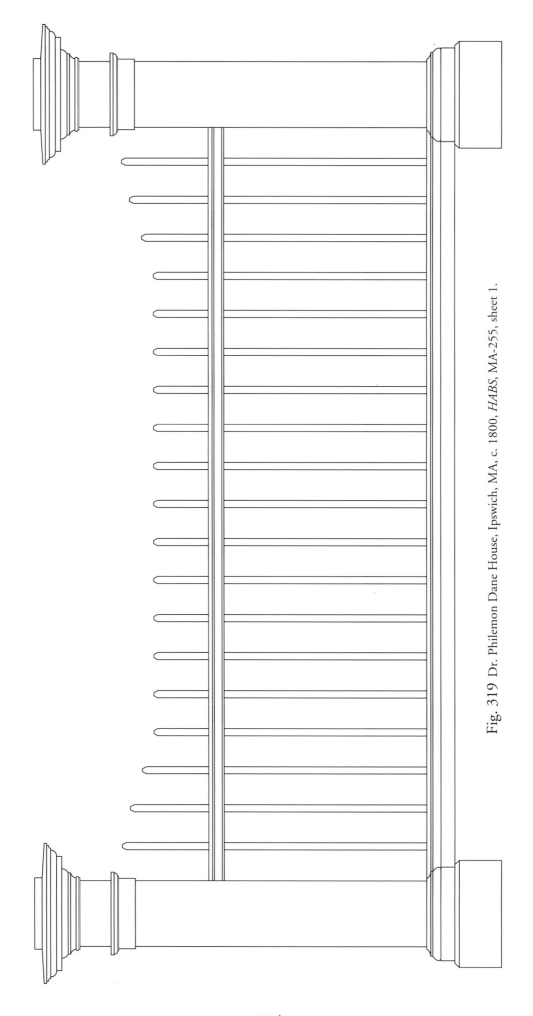

Fig. 319 Dr. Philemon Dane House, Ipswich, MA, c. 1800, *HABS*, MA-255, sheet 1.

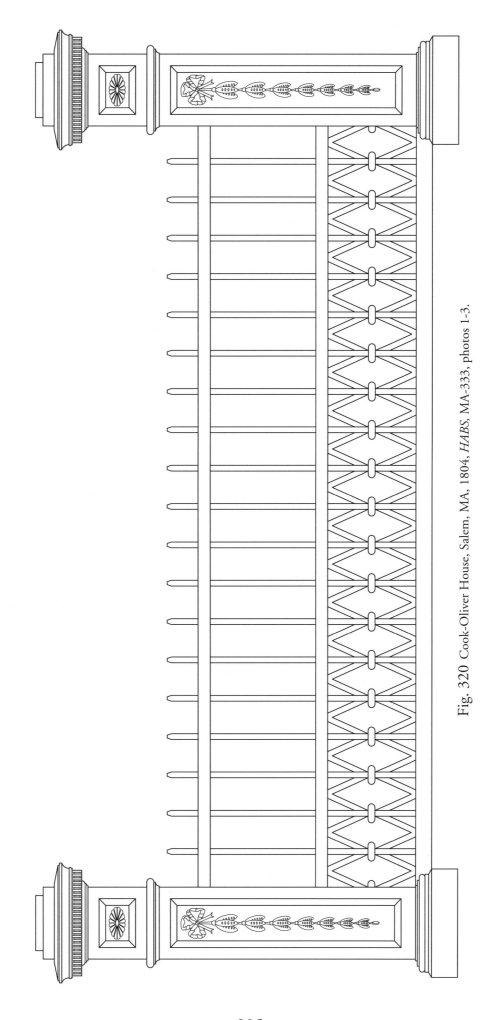

Fig. 320 Cook-Oliver House, Salem, MA, 1804, *HABS*, MA-333, photos 1-3.

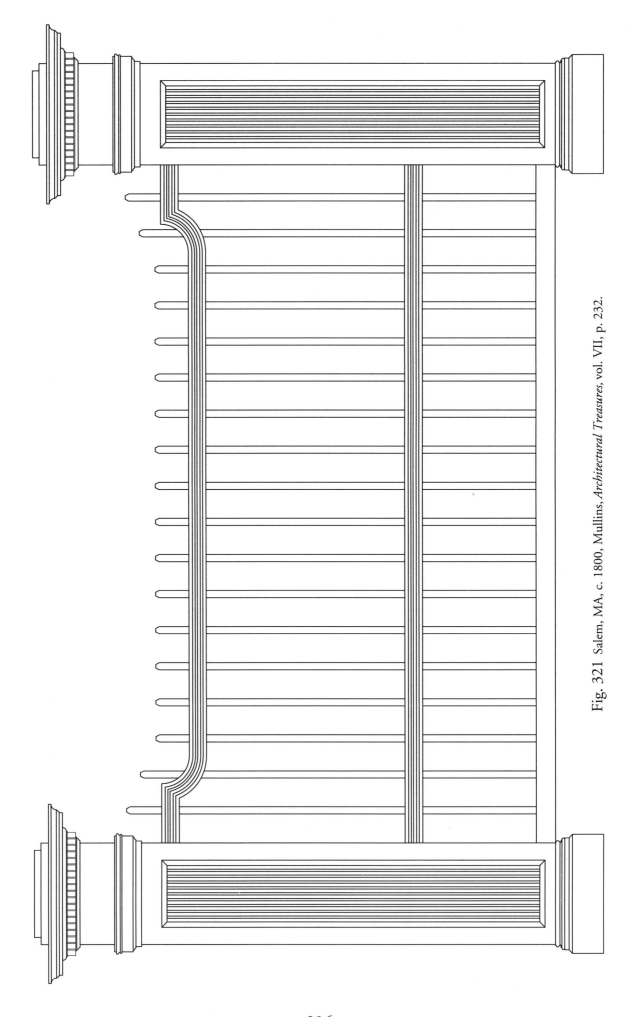

Fig. 321 Salem, MA, c. 1800, Mullins, *Architectural Treasures*, vol. VII, p. 232.

Fig. 322 Colonel Josiah Quincy House, Quincy, MA, c. 1800, backrest of front porch seat, *HABS*, MA-2-42, sheet 5.

Fig. 323 Gracie Mansion, New York, NY, c. 1800, roof balustrade, *HABS*, NY-461, photo 1.

Fig. 324 Gracie Mansion, New York, NY, c. 1800, roof balustrade, *HABS*, NY-461, photo 1.

Fig. 325 Colony House, Newport, RI, c. 1800, roof balustrade, *HABS*, RI-33, photo 39.

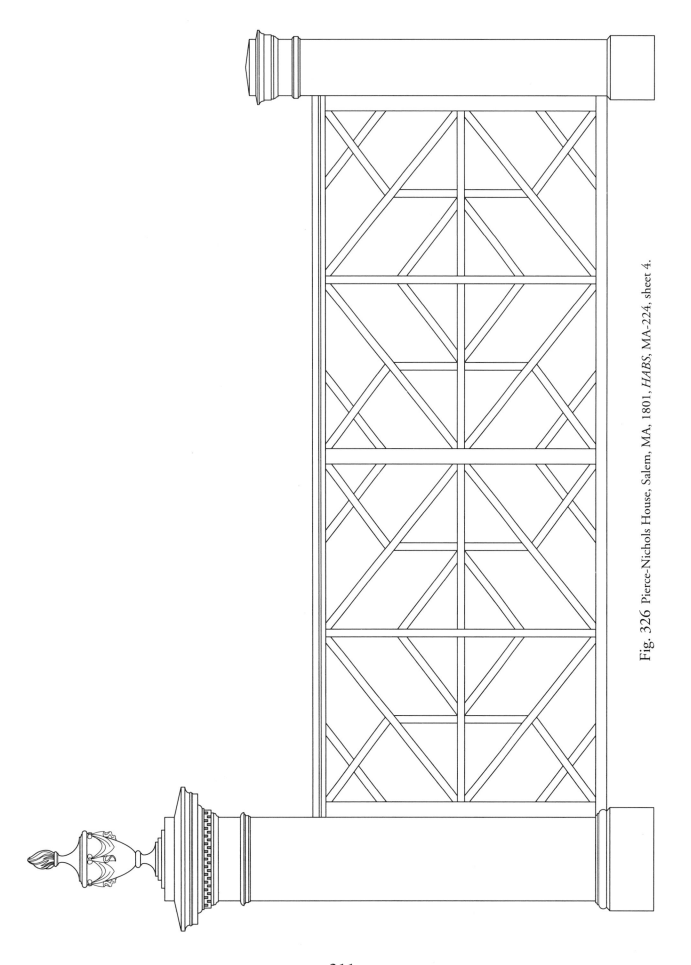

Fig. 326 Pierce-Nichols House, Salem, MA, 1801, *HABS*, MA-224, sheet 4.

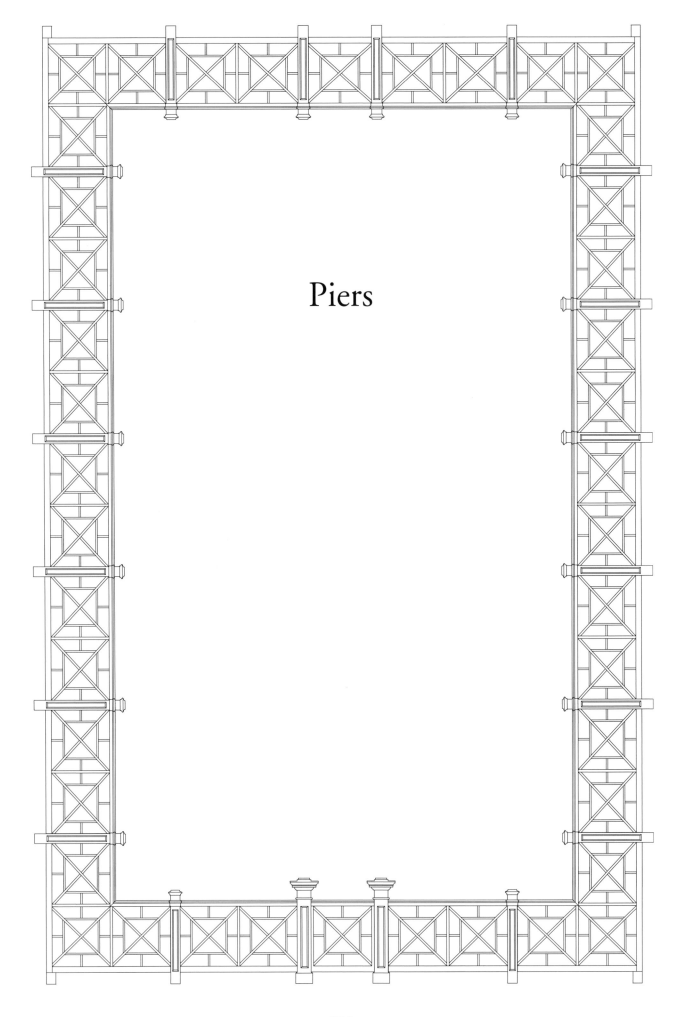

Piers

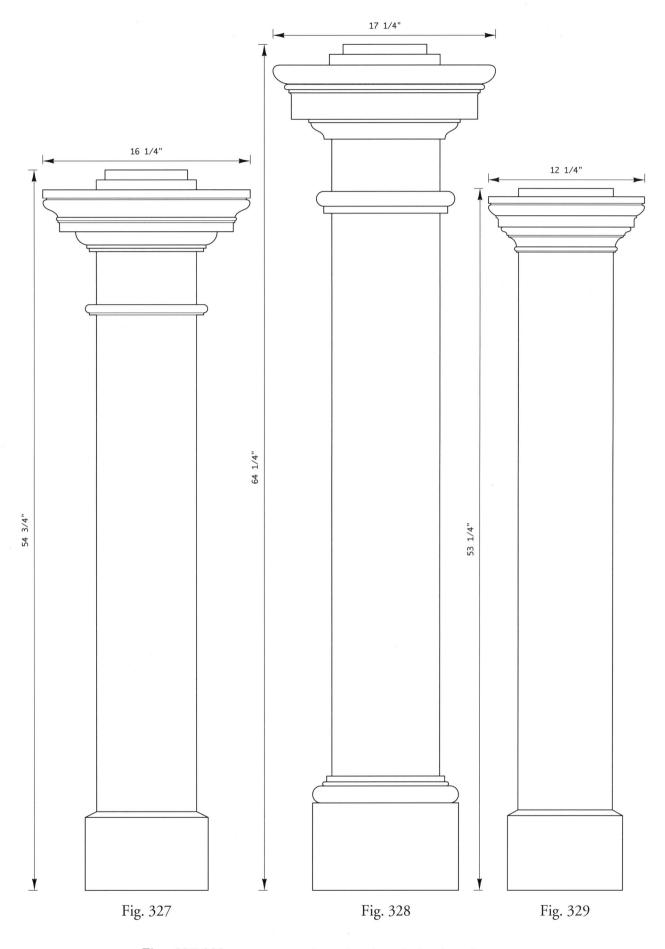

17 1/4"

16 1/4"

12 1/4"

64 1/4"

54 3/4"

53 1/4"

Fig. 327

Fig. 328

Fig. 329

Figs. 327-329 Contemporary designs by The Federal Style Orders, 2003.

213

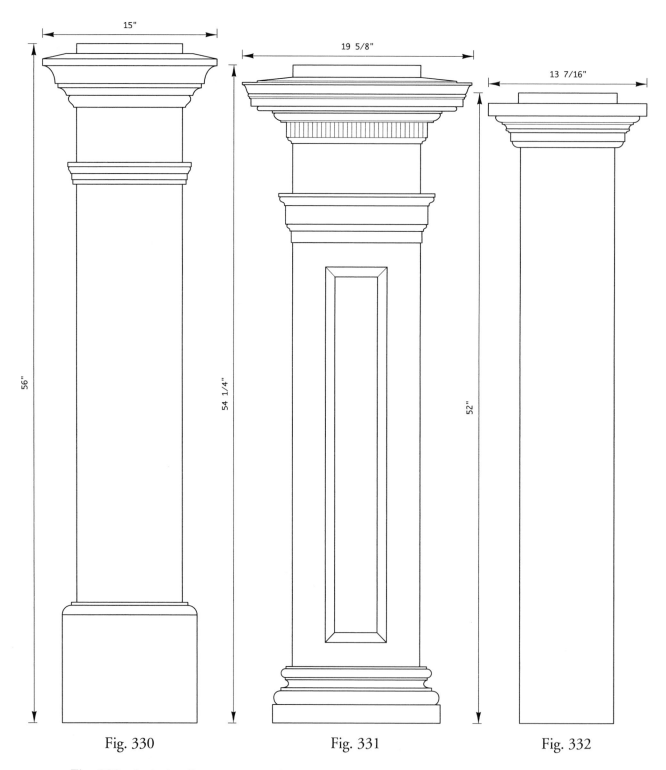

Fig. 330   Fig. 331   Fig. 332

Fig. 330 Elizabeth Billings House, Rowley, MA, c. 1800, *HABS*, MA-277, sheet 2.
Fig. 331 Chestnut Street, Salem, MA, c. 18th century, Mullins, *Architectural Treasures,* vol. XVI, p. 107.
Fig. 332 Boardman-Bowen House, Salem, MA, 1785, *HABS*, MA-490, photo 2.

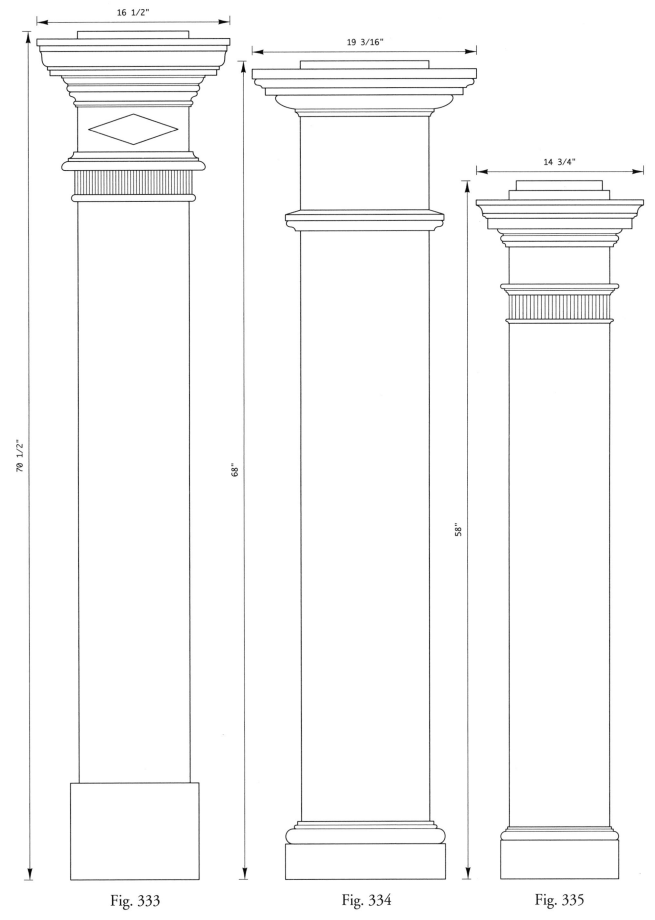

16 1/2"

70 1/2"

19 3/16"

68"

14 3/4"

58"

Fig. 333

Fig. 334

Fig. 335

Fig. 333 Baldwin-Lyman House, Salem, MA, 1818, *HABS,* MA-485, photo 1.
Fig. 334 Lindall-Barnard-Andrews House, Salem, MA, c. 18th century, *HABS*, MA-484, photo 1.
Fig. 335 Dr. Phippen House, Salem, MA, c. 18th century, *HABS*, MA-486, photo 3.

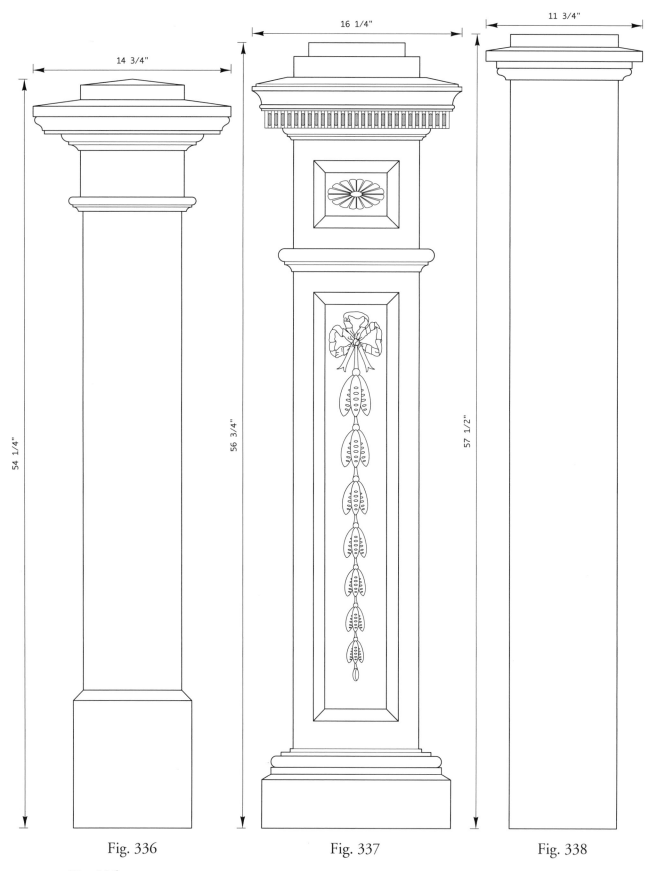

Fig. 336   Fig. 337   Fig. 338

Fig. 336 Pierce-Knapp-Perry Place, Newburyport, MA, 1815, *HABS*, MA-236, sheet 5.
Fig. 337 Cook-Oliver House, Salem, MA, 1804, Mullins, *Architectural Treasures*, vol. XVI, p. 81.
Fig. 338 De-Wolf Middleton House, Bristol, RI, 1808, roof balustrade, *HABS*, RI-3-12, sheet 6.

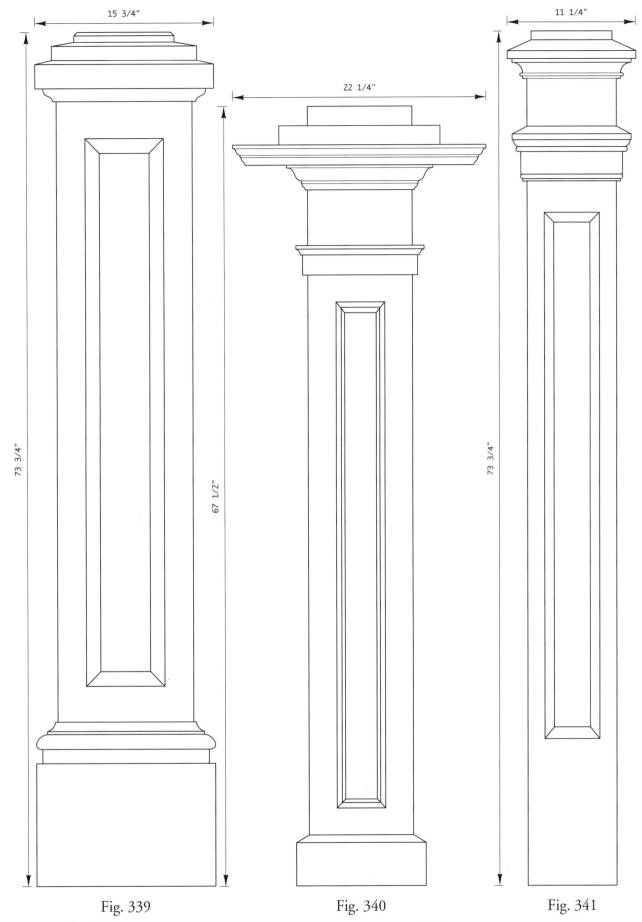

15 3/4"

73 3/4"

Fig. 339

22 1/4"

67 1/2"

Fig. 340

11 1/4"

73 3/4"

Fig. 341

Fig. 339 Forrester-Peabody House, Salem, MA, 1818, *HABS*, MA-264, sheet 2.
Fig. 340 Timothy Jackson House, Newton, MA, 1809, *HABS*, MA-139, sheet 12.
Fig. 341 Lt. Governor Martin House, Seekonk, MA, 1810, roof balustrade, *HABS*, MA-2-90, sheet 6.

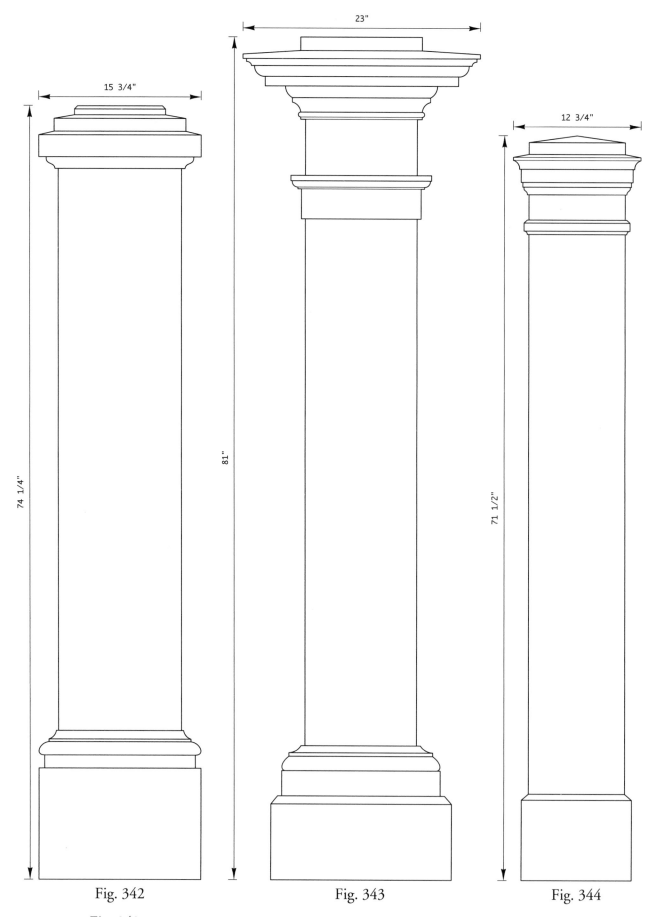

Fig. 342

Fig. 343

Fig. 344

Fig. 342 Forrester-Peabody House, Salem, MA, 1818, *HABS*, MA-264, sheet 2.
Fig. 343 Dr. Philemon Dane House, Ipswich, MA, date unknown, *HABS*, MA-256, sheet 1.
Fig. 344 Pierce-Nichols House, Salem, MA, 1801, *HABS*, MA-224, sheet 5.

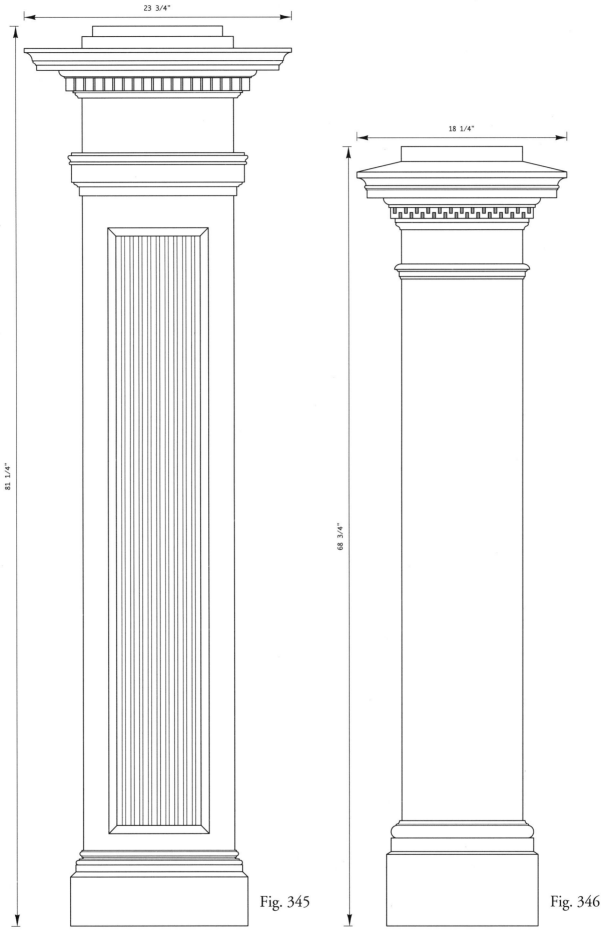

23 3/4"

81 1/4"

18 1/4"

68 3/4"

Fig. 345

Fig. 346

Fig. 345 Salem, MA, c. 1800, Mullins, *Architectural Treasures*, vol. XVI, p. 107.
Fig. 346 Pierce-Nichols House, Salem, MA, 1801, *HABS*, MA-224, sheet 5.

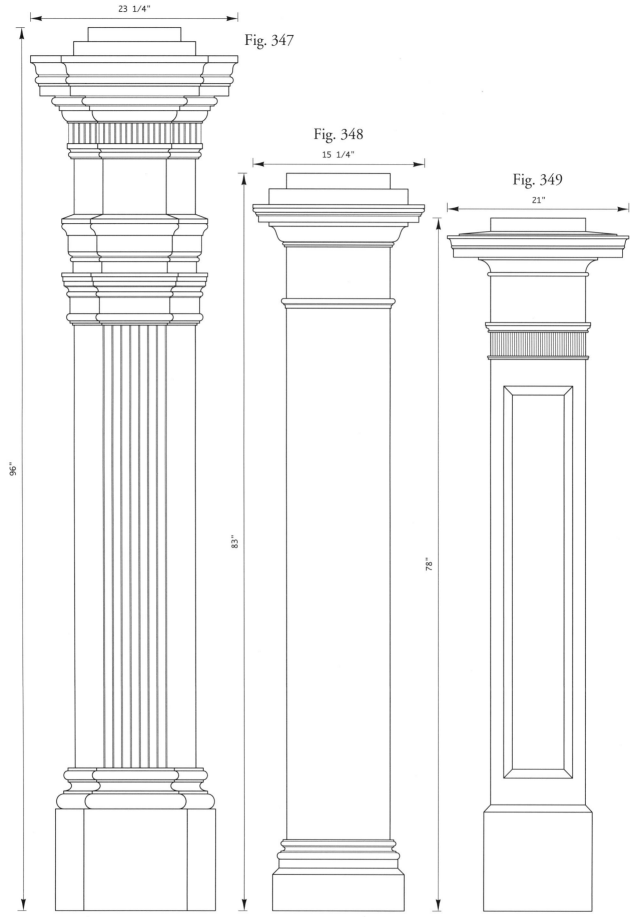

Fig. 347

Fig. 348

Fig. 349

23 1/4"

15 1/4"

21"

96"

83"

78"

Fig. 347 Phillips House, Salem, MA, c. 18th century, Mullins, *Architectural Treasures*, vol. XVI, p. 107.
Fig. 348 Isaac Royal House, Medford, MA, c. 18th century, *HABS*, MA-130-A, sheet 1.
Fig. 349 Lafayette Street, Salem, MA, c. 18th century, Mullins, *Architectural Treasures,* vol. XVI, p. 107.

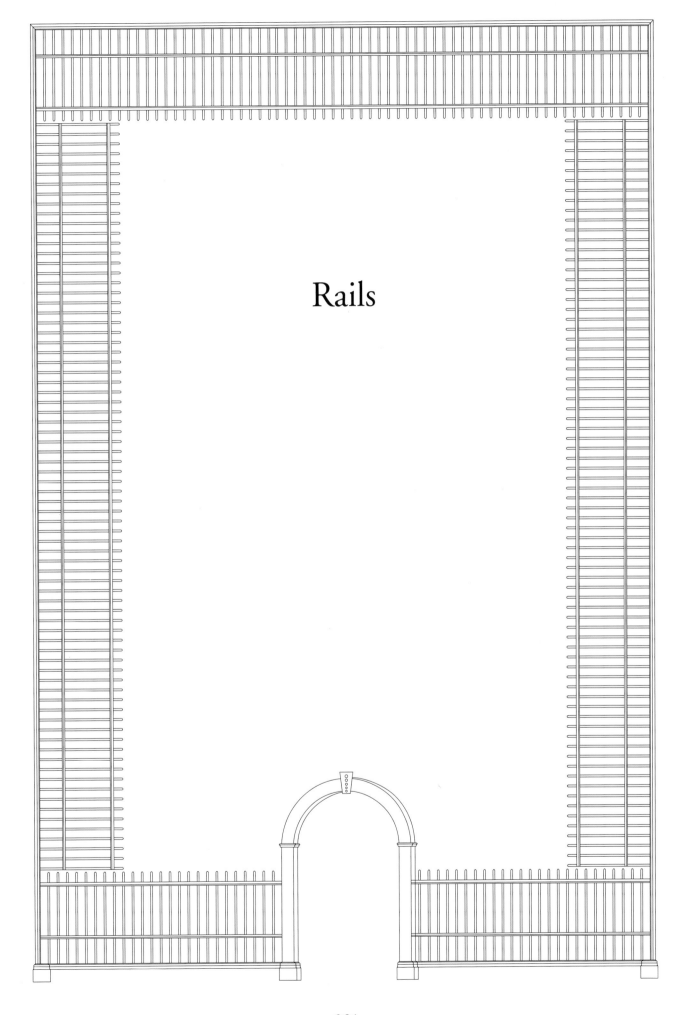

Rails

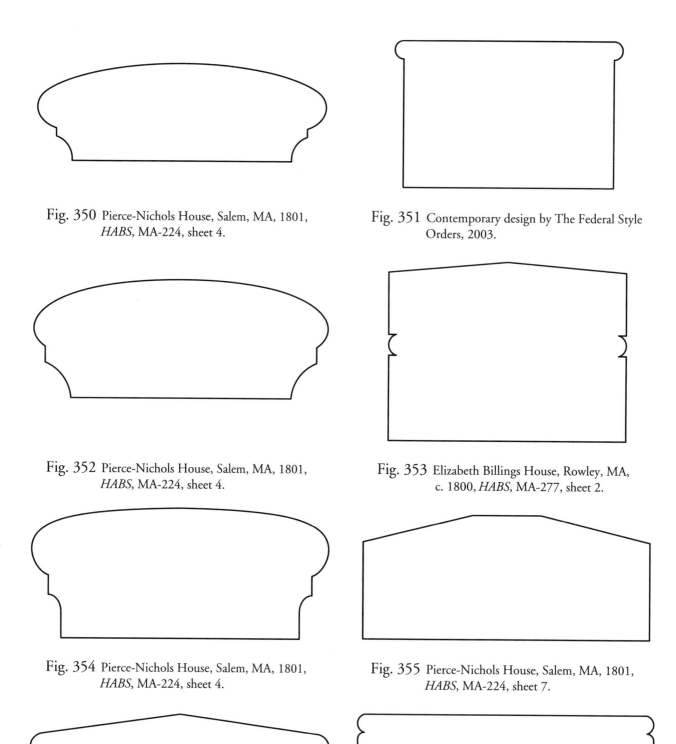

Fig. 350 Pierce-Nichols House, Salem, MA, 1801, *HABS*, MA-224, sheet 4.

Fig. 351 Contemporary design by The Federal Style Orders, 2003.

Fig. 352 Pierce-Nichols House, Salem, MA, 1801, *HABS*, MA-224, sheet 4.

Fig. 353 Elizabeth Billings House, Rowley, MA, c. 1800, *HABS*, MA-277, sheet 2.

Fig. 354 Pierce-Nichols House, Salem, MA, 1801, *HABS*, MA-224, sheet 4.

Fig. 355 Pierce-Nichols House, Salem, MA, 1801, *HABS*, MA-224, sheet 7.

Fig. 356 Pierce-Nichols House, Salem, MA, 1801, *HABS*, MA-224, sheet 4.

Fig. 357 Dr. Philemon Dane House, Ipswich, MA, date unknown, *HABS*, MA-256, sheet 2.

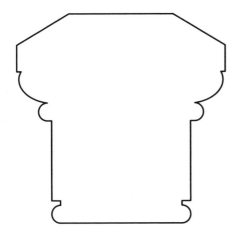

Fig. 358 Lt. Governor Martin House, Seekonk, MA, 1810, roof balustrade, *HABS*, MA-2-90, sheet 6.

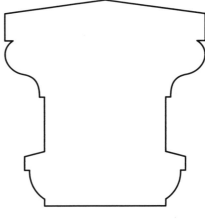

Fig. 359 Pierce-Knapp-Perry Place, Newburyport, MA, 1815, *HABS*, MA-236, sheet 5.

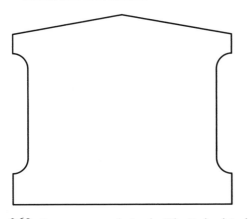

Fig. 360 Elizabeth Billings House, Rowley, MA, c. 1800, *HABS*, MA-277, sheet 2.

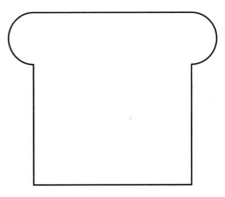

Fig. 361 Pierce-Nichols House, Salem, MA, 1801, *HABS*, MA-224, sheet 4.

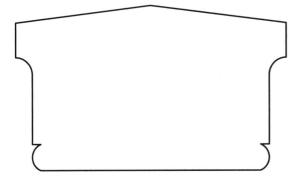

Fig. 362 Contemporary design by The Federal Style Orders, 2003.

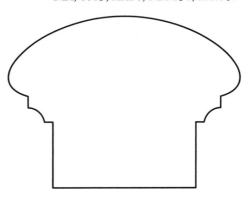

Fig. 363 Contemporary design by The Federal Style Orders, 2003.

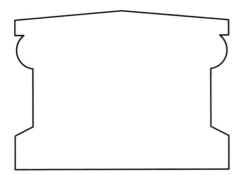

Fig. 364 Contemporary design by The Federal Style Orders, 2003.

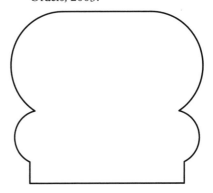

Fig. 365 Contemporary design by The Federal Style Orders, 2003.

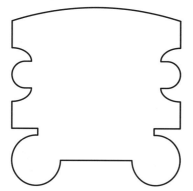

Fig. 366 Timothy Jackson House, Newton, MA, 1809, *HABS*, MA-139, sheet 12.

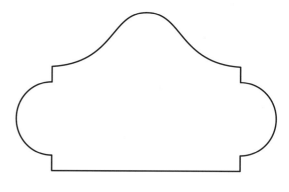

Fig. 367 Elizabeth Billings House, Rowley, MA, c. 1800, *HABS*, MA-277, sheet 3.

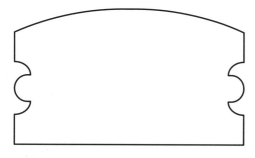

Fig. 368 Timothy Jackson House, Newton, MA, 1809, *HABS*, MA-139, sheet 12.

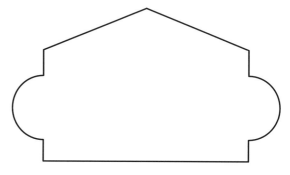

Fig. 369 Dr. Philemon Dane House, Ipswich, MA, date unknown, *HABS*, MA-256, sheet 2.

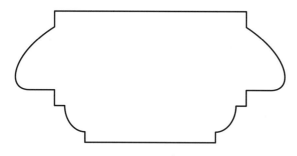

Fig. 370 De-Wolf Middleton House, Bristol, RI, 1808, roof balustrade, *HABS*, RI-3-12, sheet 6.

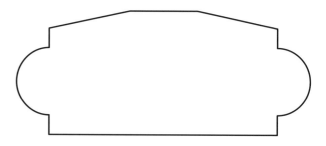

Fig. 371 Pierce-Nichols House, Salem, MA, 1801, *HABS*, MA-224, sheet 7.

Fig. 372 De-Wolf Middleton House, Bristol, RI, 1808, roof balustrade, *HABS*, RI-3-12, sheet 6.

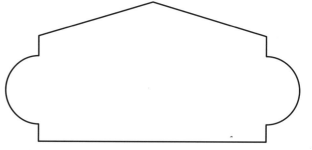

Fig. 373 Dr. Philemon Dane House, Ipswich, MA, date unknown, *HABS*, MA-256, sheet 2.

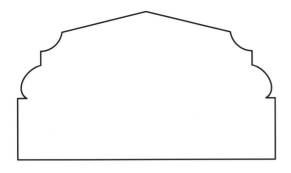

Fig. 374 Dr. Philemon Dane House, Ipswich, MA,
date unknown, *HABS*, MA-256, sheet 2.

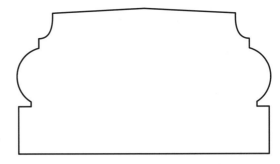

Fig. 375 Pierce-Nichols House, Salem, MA,
1801, *HABS*, MA-224, sheet 4.

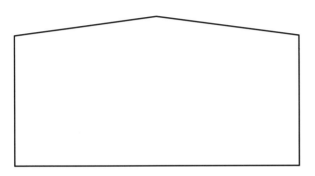

Fig. 376 Elizabeth Billings House, Rowley, MA,
c. 1800, *HABS*, MA-277, sheet 2.

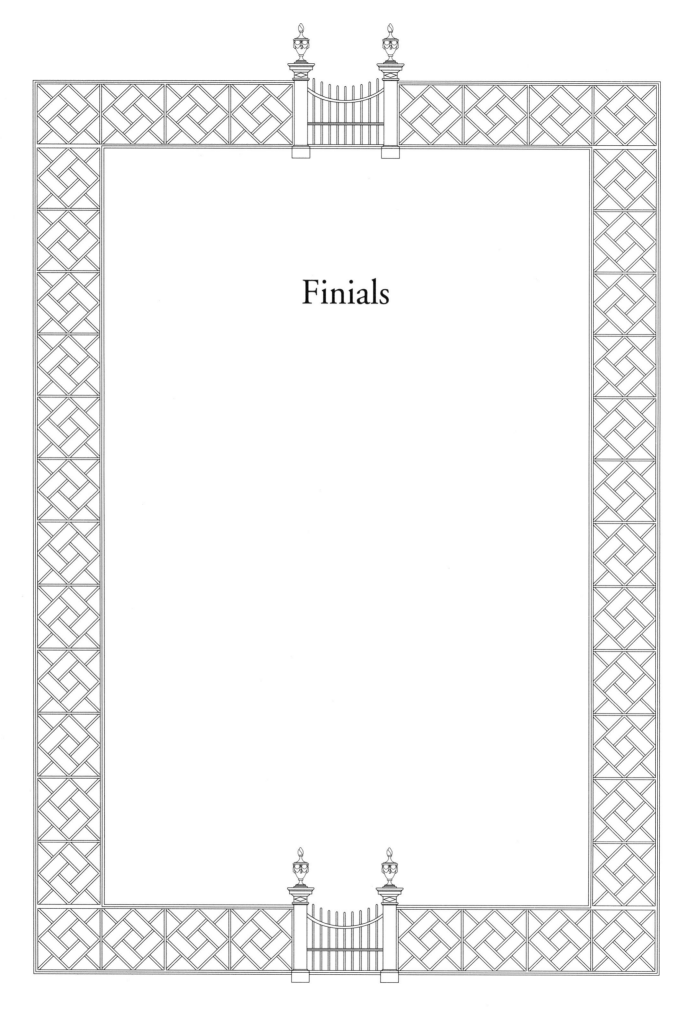

Finials

Fig. 377 Lafayette Street, Salem, MA, c. 1800, Mullins, *Architectural Treasures*, vol. XVI, p. 107.

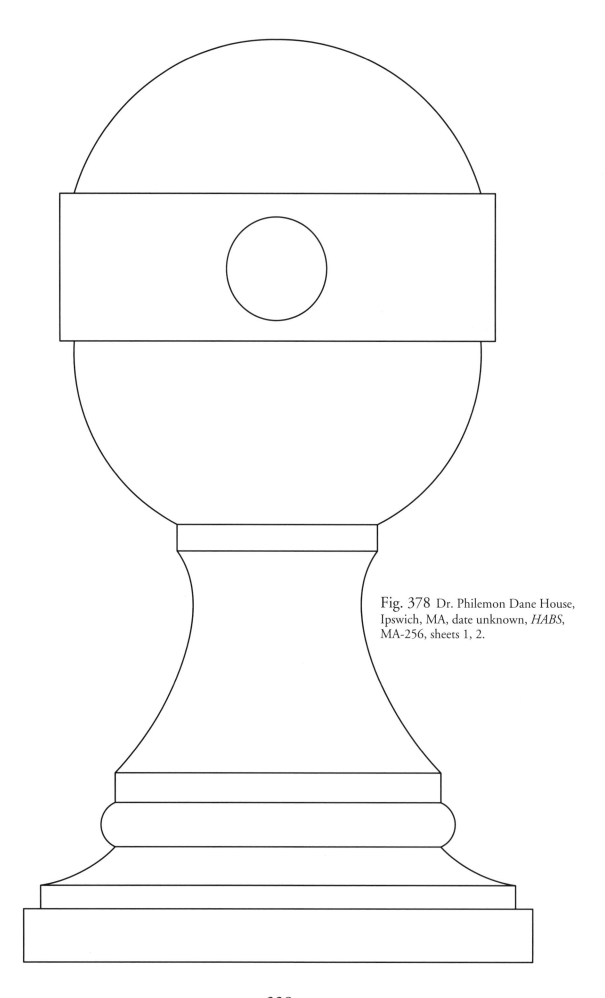

Fig. 378 Dr. Philemon Dane House, Ipswich, MA, date unknown, *HABS*, MA-256, sheets 1, 2.

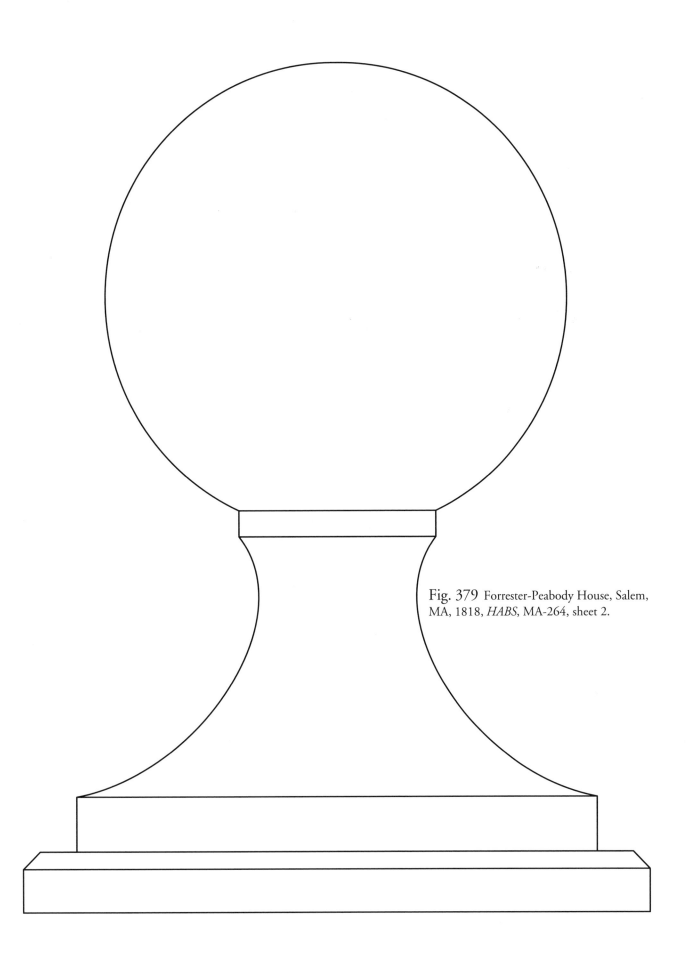

Fig. 379 Forrester-Peabody House, Salem, MA, 1818, *HABS*, MA-264, sheet 2.

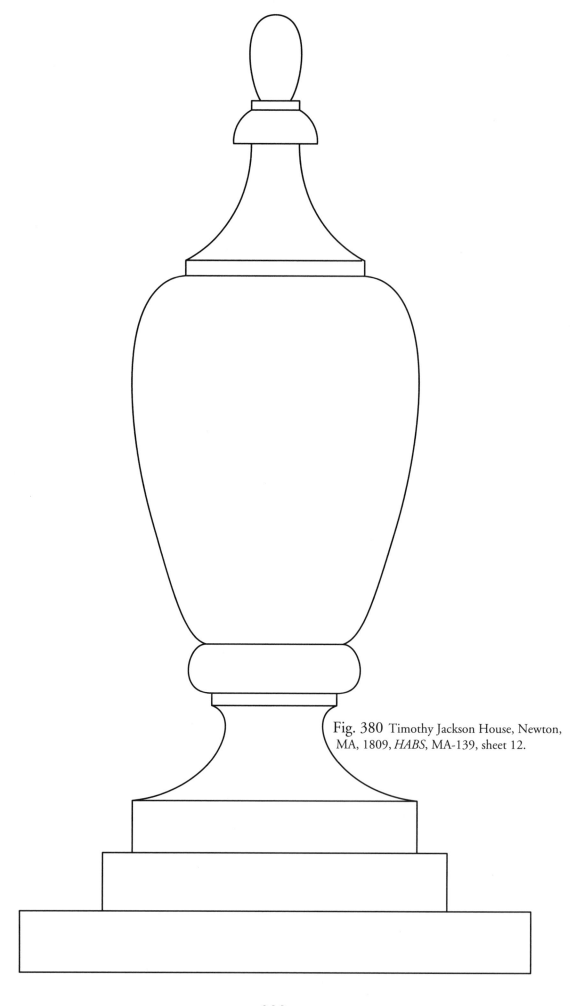

Fig. 380 Timothy Jackson House, Newton,
MA, 1809, *HABS*, MA-139, sheet 12.

Fig. 381 34 Chestnut Street, Salem, MA, c. 1800,
Mullins, *Architectural Treasures*, vol. XVI, p. 107.

Fig. 382 25 Chestnut Street, Salem, MA, c. 1800,
Mullins, *Architectural Treasures*, vol. XVI, p. 107.

Fig. 383 Elizabeth Billings House, Rowley, MA, c. 1800, *HABS*, MA-277, sheets 1, 2.

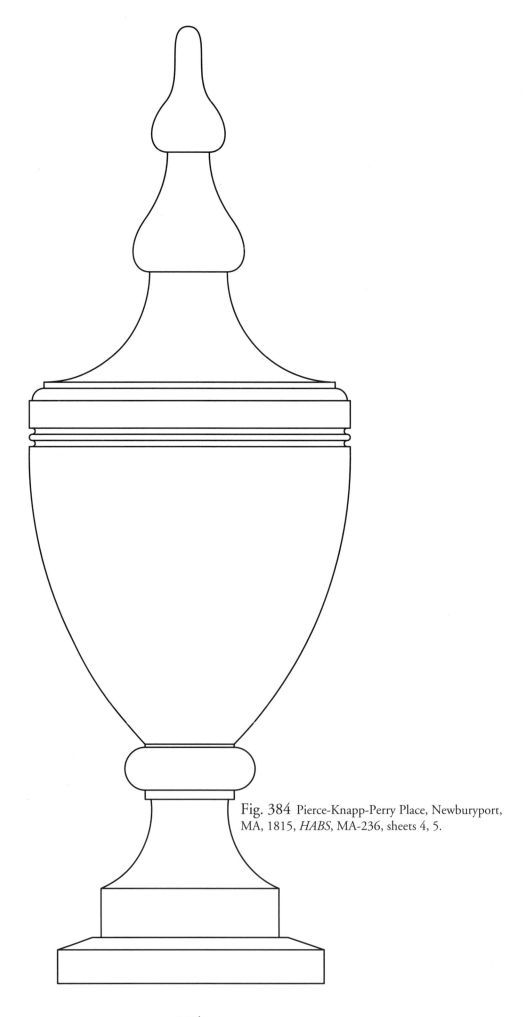

Fig. 384 Pierce-Knapp-Perry Place, Newburyport, MA, 1815, *HABS*, MA-236, sheets 4, 5.

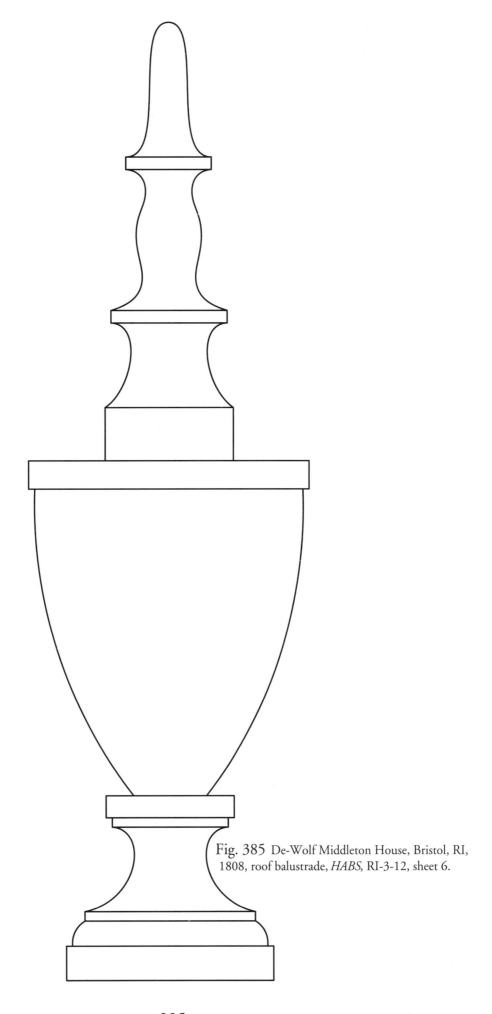

Fig. 385 De-Wolf Middleton House, Bristol, RI, 1808, roof balustrade, *HABS*, RI-3-12, sheet 6.

Fig. 386 Lt. Governor Martin House, Seekonk, MA, 1810, roof balustrade, *HABS*, MA-2-90, sheet 6.

Fig. 387 Pierce-Nichols House, Salem, MA, 1801, *HABS*, MA-224, sheet 5.

Index to the Figures

Type A Cornices (cont'd.)

Type B Cornices

Type B Cornices (cont'd.)

52.-p. 37   Kenwood, Middlesex, England, remodeled by Robert Adam 1767-1769, Adam, *Works,* 1975 reprint, p. 93, vol. I, no. II, pl. IV.

53.-p. 37   Contemporary design by The Federal Style Orders, 2003, based on a design for a cornice by Benjamin, *Country Builder's Assistant,* 1797, pl. XVI.

54.-p. 37   Coleman-Hollister House, Greenfield, MA, 1795, *HABS,* MA-2-19, sheet 20.

55.-p. 38   Luton Park, Beds, England, built by Robert Adam 1767-1775, Adam, *Works,* 1975 reprint, p. 138, vol. I, no. III, pl. IV.

56.-p. 38   Shelburne House, London, England, built by Robert Adam 1762-1768, Adam, *Works,* 1975 reprint, p. 130, vol. III, no. III, pl. V.

57.-p. 38   South Yarmouth, MA, date of original house source unknown, Howe and Fuller, *Details,* pl. XVII.

58.-p. 39   Contemporary design by The Federal Style Orders, 2003, based on a design for a cornice by Benjamin, *Country Builder's Assistant,* 1797, pl. XVI.

59.-p. 39   Sion House, Middlesex, England, remodeled by Robert Adam 1762-1769 and 1773, Adam, *Works,* 1975 reprint, p. 77, vol. I, no. I, pl. VII.

60.-p. 39   Contemporary design by The Federal Style Orders, 2003, based on a design for a cornice by Benjamin, *Country Builder's Assistant,* 1797, pl. XVI.

61.-p. 40   Contemporary design by The Federal Style Orders, 2003, based on a design for a cornice by Benjamin, *Country Builder's Assistant,* 1797, pl. XVI.

62.-p. 40   General Salem Towne House, Charlton, MA, 1796, Mullins, *Architectural Treasures,* vol. X, p. 156.

63.-p. 40   Sayward-Holmes House, Alfred, ME, 1802, *HABS,* ME-32, sheet 13.

Type C Cornices

64.-p. 42   Captain Barnes House, Portsmouth, NH, 1807, *HABS,* NH-26, sheet 45.

65.-p. 42   Christopher Ryder House, Chathamport, MA, 1809, *HABS,* MA-118, sheet 13.

66.-p. 42   Edward Carrington House, Providence, RI, 1812, *HABS,* RI-19, sheet 51.

67.-p. 42   Benjamin, *Builder's Companion,* 1806, pl. XII.

68.-p. 43   Benjamin, *Builder's Companion,* 1806, pl. XII.

69.-p. 43   Benjamin, *Builder's Companion,* 1806, pl. XII.

70.-p. 43   Benjamin, *Builder's Companion,* 1806, pl. XIII.

71.-p. 43   Edward Carrington House, 1812, Providence, RI, *HABS,* RI-19, sheet 53.

72.-p. 43   Benjamin, *Builder's Companion,* 1806, pl. XIII.

73.-p. 44   Benjamin, *Builder's Companion,* 1806, pl. XII.

74.-p. 44   Governor Woodbury Mansion, Portsmouth, NH, 1809, *HABS,* NH-20, sheet 33.

75.-p. 44   Captain Barnes House, Portsmouth, NH, 1807, *HABS,* NH-26, sheet 46.

76.-p. 44   Edward Carrington House, Providence, RI, 1812, *HABS,* RI-19, sheet 53.

77.-p. 45   Edward Carrington House, Providence, RI, 1812, *HABS,* RI-19, sheet 52.

78.-p. 45   Hyde-Lincoln House, Charlestown, MA, 1801, *HABS,* MA-299, sheet 8.

79.-p. 45   Edward Carrington House, Providence, RI, 1812, *HABS,* RI-19, sheet 53.

Type C Cornices (cont'd.)

Cornice Plus Cornices

Palace of Diocletian Cornices

Window and Door Casings (cont'd.)

Window Sills and Aprons

Window Sills and Aprons (cont'd.)

Chair Rails

Chair Rails (cont'd.)

Baseboards

Mantels

Mantels (cont'd.)

Interior Doors, Doorways, and Arches

Rails (cont'd.)

Finials

BIBLIOGRAPHY

I. GENERAL FEDERAL STYLE ARCHITECTURE

Architects' Emergency Committee. *Great Georgian Houses of America*, volume 1, Dover Publications, NY, 1970. Reprint of original title, *The Editorial Committee of The Great Georgian Houses of America for the benefit of The Architects' Emergency Committee.* Published by The Kaklhoff Press, Inc., NY, 1933.

Architects' Emergency Committee. *Great Georgian Houses of America*, volume 2, Dover Publications, NY, 1970. Reprint of original title, *The Editorial Committee of The Great Georgian Houses of America for the benefit of The Architects' Emergency Committee.* Published by The Scribner Press, NY, 1937.

Boyd, Sterling M. *The Adam Style in America, 1770-1820,* Garland Publishing, Inc., NY and London. 1985. A dissertation presented to the faculty of Princeton University in candidacy for the degree of Doctor of Philosophy. September 1966.

Calloway, Stephen, and Cromely, Elizabeth. *The Elements of Style*, Simon and Schuster, NY, 1996.

Chamberlain, Samuel. *Beyond New England Thresholds*, Hastings House, NY, 1937.

Chamberlain, Samuel. *Boston Landmarks,* Hastings House, NY, 1946.

Chamberlain, Samuel and Narcissa. *Charleston Interiors,* Dover Publications, NY, 2002. Reprint of the 1956 edition.

Chamberlain, Samuel. *Historic Boston in Four Seasons,* Hastings House, NY, 1938.

Chamberlain, Samuel. *Historic Salem in Four Seasons,* Golden Hind Press, Madison, NJ, 1938.

Chamberlain, Samuel. *New England Doorways,* Hastings House, NY, 1939.

Chamberlain, Samuel. *New England Rooms, 1639-1843,* Architectural Book Publishing Company, Inc., CT, 1993.

Chamberlain, Samuel. *Open House in New England,* Stephen Daye Press, Brattleboro, VT, 1937.

Chamberlain, Samuel. *Salem Interiors,* Hastings House, NY, 1950.

Cousins, Frank, and Riley, Phil M. *The Colonial Architecture of Salem,* Dover Publications, NY, 2000. Reprint of 1919 edition published by Little, Brown, and Company.

Eberlein, Harold Donaldson, and Hubbard, Cortlandt Van Dyke. *Colonial Interiors, Federal and Greek Revival, Third Series,* Bonanza Books, NY, 1923.

French, Leigh, Jr. *Colonial Interiors, Colonial and Early Federal, First Series,* Bonanza Books, NY, 1923.

Garrett, Wendell. *Classic America, The Federal Style and Beyond,* Universe Publishing, NY, 1995.

Howells, John Mead. *Lost Examples of Colonial Architecture, Buildings that have disappeared or been so altered as to be denatured,* Dover Publications, NY, 1963.

Kelly, J. Frederick. *Early Domestic Architecture of Connecticut,* Dover Publications, NY, 1963. Reprint of the first edition, 1924.

Kimbal, S. Fiske. *Domestic Architecture of the American Colonies and of the Early Republic,* C. Scribner's Sons, NY, 1922.

Lane, Mills. *Architecture of the Old South,* Abbeville Press Publishers, NY, 1993.

Moore, Barbara W., and Weesner, Gail. *Beacon Hill, A Living Portrait,* Century Hill Press, Boston, MA, 1992.

Morrison, Hugh. *Early American Architecture, From the First Colonial Settlements to the National Period,* Dover Publications, NY, 1987.

Pierson, William H., Jr. *American Buildings and their Architects, The Colonial and NeoClassical Styles,* Oxford University Press, NY, 1986.

Sale, Edith Tunis. *Colonial Interiors, Southern Colonial and Early Federal, Second Series,* Bonanza Books, NY, 1923.

BIBLIOGRAPHIES

Hitchcock, Henry-Russell. *American Architectural Books: a list of books, portfolios, and pamphlets on architecture and related subjects published in America before 1895,* University of Minnesota Press, MN, 1962.

Montgomery, Charles F. *A List of Books and Articles for the Study of The Arts in Early America,* The Henry Francis du Pont Winterthur Museum, Winterthur, DE, 1970.

Montgomery, Charles F., and Kane, Patricia E. *American Art: 1750-1800 Towards Independence,* New York Graphic Society, Boston, MA, 1975. Section titled, "Suggestions for further reading."

CHARLES BULFINCH

Kirker, Harold. *The Architecture of Charles Bulfinch,* Harvard University Press, Cambridge, MA, 1969.

Kirker, Harold, and Kirker, James. *Bulfinch's Boston 1787-1817,* Oxford University Press, NY, 1964.

Place, Charles. *Charles Bulfinch, Architect and Citizen,* Da Capo Press, NY, 1968. Reprint of the 1925 edition published by Houghton Mifflin Co., NY.

FURNITURE

Barquist, David L. *American Tables and Looking Glasses in the Mabel Brady Garavan and other collections at Yale University*, Yale University Art Gallery, CT, 1992.

Dunbar, Michael. *Federal Furniture*, Taunton Press, Newtown, CT, 1986.

Fairbanks, Jonathan L., and Bates, Elizabeth Bidwell. *American Furniture 1620 to the Present*, Richard Marek Publishers, NY, 1981.

Kane, Patricia E. *300 Years of American Seating Furniture, Chairs and Beds from the Mabel Brady Garavan and other collections at Yale University*, Little, Brown, and Co., NY, 1976.

Ketchum, William C., Jr. *American Cabinetmakers Marked American Furniture, 1670-1940*, Crown Publishers, NY, 1995.

Montgomery, Charles E. *American Furniture, The Federal Period*, Viking Press, NY, 1966.

Nutting, Wallace. *Furniture Treasury*, volumes I and II in one. Macmillan Publishing Co., Inc., NY, 1974. Reprint of 1928 edition.

Sack, Albert. *The New Fine Points of Furniture, Early American, good, better, best, superior, masterpiece*, Crown Publishers, NY, 1993.

Stoneman, Vernon C. *John and Thomas Seymour Cabinetmakers in Boston, 1794-1816*, Special Publications, Boston, MA, 1959.

Ward, Gerald W. R. *American Case Furniture in the Mabel Brady Garavan and other collections at Yale University*, Yale University Art Gallery, CT, 1988.

MEASURED DRAWINGS AND PHOTOGRAPHS

Historic American Buildings Survey/Historic American Engineering Record (HABS) *American Memory,"* Library of Congress Website, http://memory.loc.gov/ammem/hhhtml/hhhome.html.

Howe, Lois L., and Fuller, Constance. *Details from Old New England Houses*, The Architectural Book Publishing Company, NY, 1913.

Kettell, Russel Hawes. *Early American Rooms 1650-1858*, Dover Publications, NY, 1967. Reprint of the 1936 edition.

Miner, Robert G. *Architectural Treasures of Early America Series*, 8 volumes consisting of material originally published as *The White Pine Series of Architectural Monographs*. Prepared by the staff of The Early American Society. Arno Press Inc., NY, 1977.

-Volume 1, *Early Homes of Massachusetts*
-Volume 2, *Colonial Architecture in Massachusetts*
-Volume 3, *Colonial Architecture in New England*
-Volume 4, *Early Homes of Rhode Island*
-Volume 5, *Early Homes of New England*

-Volume 6, *Early Homes of New York and the Mid-Atlantic States*
-Volume 7, *Colonial Homes in the Southern States*
-Volume 8, *Survey of Early American Design*

Mullins, Lisa C. *Architectural Treasures of Early America*, 16 volumes. From material originally published as *The White Pine Series of Architectural Monographs*. National Historical Society, Harrisburg, PA, 1987.

* most helpful volumes
-Volume 1, *Survey of Early American Design**
-Volume 2, *Early Architecture of the South*
-Volume 3, *New England by the Sea*
-Volume 4, *Colonial Architecture of the Mid-Atlantic*
-Volume 5, *The Homes of New York and Connecticut*
-Volume 6, *Early Architecture of Rhode Island*
-Volume 7, *Village Architecture of Early New England*
-Volume 8, *Early American Southern Homes*
-Volume 9, *The Evolution of Colonial Architecture*
-Volume 10, *Early American Community Structures*
-Volume 11, *Blueprints for America's Past*
-Volume 12, *The Southern Tradition*
-Volume 13, *Styles of the Emerging Nation**
-Volume 14, *The Grandeur of the South*
-Volume 15, *The Georgian Heritage*
-Volume 16, *Spirit of New England**

Wallis, Frank E. *American Architecture, Decoration, and Furniture of the 18ᵗʰ Century*, Paul Wenzel, NY, 1896.

Wallis, Frank E. *Old Colonial Architecture and Furniture*, George H. Polley and Co. Publishers, Boston, MA, 1887.

Ware, William Rotch. *The Georgian Period, a collection of papers dealing with Colonial or 18ᵗʰ Century architecture in the United States, together with references to earlier provincial and true colonial work*, Boston, MA, American Architecture and Building News Co., 1899-1902. 3 volumes in 12 parts. Reprinted in 1922 and 1923.

Whitehead, Russel F. *The White Pine Series of Architectural Monographs, 17 volumes of 6 issues each*. White Pine Bureau, St. Paul, MN, Published from 1915.

-Volume III, number 1, Brown, Frank C. *Three-Story Colonial Houses of New England*, 1917.
-Volume III, number 2, LeBoutillier, Addison B. *The Early Wooden Architecture of Andover, Massachusetts*, 1917.
-Volume III, number 3, Fisher, Richard Arnold. *Old Houses in and Around Newburyport, Massachusetts*, 1917.
-Volume III, number 5, Dow, Joy Wheeler. *The Bristol Renaissance*, 1917.
-Volume IV, number 2, Walker, C. Howard. *Some Old Houses on the Southern Coast of Maine*, 1918.
-Volume IV, number 6, Chappell, George S. *Colonial Architecture in Vermont*, 1918.

-Volume VIII, number 6, Hopkins, Alfred. *Fences and Fence Posts*, 1922.

-Volume IX, number 1, Fowler, Lemuel Hoadley. *Some Forgotten Farmhouses on Manhattan Island*, 1923.

-Volume X, number 2, Embury, Aymar II. *A Comparative Study of a Group of Early American Ornamental Cornices, Part One*, 1924.

-Volume X, number 3, Embury, Aymar II. *A Comparative Study of a Group of Early American Ornamental Cornices, Part Two*, 1924.

-Volume XII, number 5, Ferguson, A. E. *Early Dwellings in New Hampshire*, 1926.

-Volume XII, number 6, Patterson, William D. *Wiscasset, Maine*, 1926.

-Volume XIV, number 4, Chandler, Joseph Everett, *Some Charleston Mansions*, 1928.

-Volume XIV, number 6, Simons, Albert. *Edward-Smyth House*, 1928.

-Volume XVIII, number 2, Brown, Frank Chouteau. *Old Concord, Massachusetts*, 1932.

-Volume XVIII, number 3, Franklin, M. S. *Colonial Public Buildings in Salem, Massachusetts*, 1932.

-Volume XVIII, number 5, Brown, Frank Chouteau. *Interior Treatment of Period Windows*, 1932.

-Volume XX, number 2, Brown, Frank Chouteau. *Early Brickwork in New England*, 1934.

-Volume XX, number 6, Dean, Eldon L. *College and Educational Buildings in New England*, 1934.

-Volume XXII, number 2, Brown, Frank Chouteau. *Salem, Massachusetts*, 1937.

-Volume XXII, number 5, Parker, Roderick H. *Tiverton, Rhode Island*, 1936.

-Volume XXIII, number 3, Brown, Frank Chouteau. *Watertown, Massachusetts*, 1937.

-Volume XXIII, number 4, Cogswell, Charles. *Cambridge, Massachusetts Part One*, 1937.

-Volume XXIII, number 5, Cogswell, Charles. *Cambridge, Massachusetts*, 1937.

-Volume XXIII, number 6, Brown, Frank Chouteau. *Early Boston Churches*, 1937.

-Volume XXV, number 2, Brown, Frank Chouteau. *Entrance Halls and Stairways*, 1939.

-Volume XXV, number 5, Brown, Frank Chouteau. *Low Mantels and Fireplace Enframements from the 19th Century*, 1939.

-Volume XXVI, number 2, Brown, Frank Chouteau. *Door and Doorways from the 18th Century*, 1940.

-Volume XXVI, number 4, Brown, Frank Chouteau. *Gardner-White-Pingree House*, 1940.

-Volume XXVI, number 5, Brown, Frank Chouteau. *Interior Arched Openings found in NorthEastern Colonial Work*, 1940.

MUSEUMS

Hipkiss, Edwin. *Three McIntire Rooms from Peabody, Massachusetts*, Museum of Fine Arts, Boston, MA, 1931.

Metropolitan Museum of Art. *Measured drawings of Woodwork displayed in the American Wing*, NY, 1925.

Metropolitan Museum of Art. *Period Rooms in the Metropolitan Museum of Art*, Harry Abrams, Inc., NY, 1996.

Sweeney, John A. H. *The Treasure House of Early American Rooms*, A Winterthur Book. Viking Press, NY, 1963.

ORNAMENT SOURCES

The Decorators Supply Corporation. *Illustrated Catalogue of Period Ornaments*, 3610-12 South Morgan Street, Chicago, IL, 60609-1586, 312-847-6300. An excellent source for carved wood fiber, composition material, and plaster ornaments.

CustomMade.com. A Website listing woodworkers by specialty and location. <www. custommade.com>

PAINTING

Flexner, Ernst Richard. *America's Old Masters: Benjamin West, John Singleton Copley, Charles Wilson Peale, and Gilbert Stuart,* Dover Publication, NY, 1995.

PATTERN BOOKS

Benjamin, Asher. *The American Builder's Companion,* Dover Publications, NY, 1969. Reprint of the 6th edition of 1827.

Benjamin, Asher, and Raynerd, Daniel. *The American Builder's Companion*, Da Capo Press, NY, 1972. Reprint of 1st edition, 1806, published in Boston, MA.

Benjamin, Asher. *The Country Builder's Assistant,* Da Capo Press, NY, 1972. Reprint of 1st edition, 1797, printed in Greenfield, MA, by Adolf K. Placzek.

PRESERVATION

Maycock, Susan E., and Zimmerman, Sarah J. *Painting Historic Exteriors: Colors, Application, and Regulation. A Resource Guide for Historical Commissions, Historical Societies, Historic House Museums, Historic District Commissions, and Preservation Planning Staff,* Cambridge Historical Commission in cooperation with the Bay State Historical League, Cambridge, MA, 1998.

Moss, Roger W., editor. *Paint in America: the colors of historic buildings,* The Preservation Press, The National Trust for Historic Preservation, Lexington, MA, 1989.

SAMUEL MCINTIRE

Kimbal, Fiske. *Mr. Samuel McIntire, Carver, The Architect of Salem,* Peter Smith, Gloucester, MA, 1966. Reprint of 1940 edition published by The Southworth-Anthoensen Press, Salem, MA.

SILVER

Falino, Jeannine, and Ward, Gerald W. R. *New England Silver and Silversmithing, 1620-1815,* The Colonial Society of Massachusetts. University Press of Virginia, Charlotteville, VA, 2001.

Phillips, John Marshall. *American Silver,* Dover Publications, NY, 2001.

Rhode Island School of Design Museum. *The New England Silversmith, An Exhibition of New England Silver from the Mid-17th Century to the Present. Selected from New England Collections,* Providence, RI, 1965.

TEXTILES AND FLOORCOVERINGS

Fleming, Ernst Richard. *An Encyclopedia of Textiles from the Earliest times to the beginning of the 19th Century,* E. Weyhe, NY, 1927.

Nylander, Jane C. *Fabrics for Historic Buildings: A Guide to Selecting Reproduction Fabrics,* Preservation Press, John Wiley & Sons, Inc., NY, 1990.

Von Rosenstiel, Helene, and Winkler, Gail Caskey. *Floor Coverings for Historic Buildings: A Guide to Selecting Reproductions,* The Preservation Press. National Trust for Historic Preservation, Washington, DC, 1988.

WALLPAPER

Lynn, Catherine. *Wallpaper in America from the 17th Century to WWI,* W. W. Norton, NY, 1980.

Nylander, Richard C. *Wallpapers for Historic Buildings, A Guide to Selecting Reproduction Wallpapers,* Preservation Press, Washington, DC, 1992.

WEBSITES

The Federal Style Orders. <www.federalstyle.com>

Historic American Buildings Survey/Historic American Engineering Record (HABS). *American Memory,* Library of Congress Website, http://memory.loc.gov/ammem/hhhtml/hhhome.html.

Huculak and Associates. <www.caddpower.com>

Society for the Preservation of New England Antiquities. <www.SPNEA.org>

Zubi Graphics. <www.zubi.com>

II. GENERAL BACKGROUND ARCHITECTURE BOOKS

ROBERT ADAM

Adam, Robert, and Adam, James. *Ruins of the Palace of the Emperor Diocletian,* Royal Institute of British Architecture; Rare Book Collection; Microfilm, 1976.

Adam, Robert, and Adam, James. *The Works in Architecture of Robert and James Adam,* edited by Robert Ovresko, St. Martin's Press, NY, 1975.

Adam, Robert, and Adam, James. *The Works in Architecture of Robert and James Adam,* Alec Tiranti Ltd., London, 1959.

Beard, Geoffrey. *The Work of Robert Adam,* Bloomsbury Books, London, 1978.

Harris, Eileen. *The Furniture of Robert Adam*, Academy Editions, London and St. Martin's Press Inc., NY, 1973.

Harris, Eileen. *The Genius of Robert Adam: His Interiors,* Yale University Press, New Haven and London, 2001.

Parissien, Steve. *Adam Style*, The Preservation Press, Washington, DC, 1992.

Stillman, Damie. *Decorative Work of Robert Adam*, Academy Editions, London, 1973.

FURNITURE

Athineos, Doris. "Mr. Hepplewhite and Mr. Sheraton Rule," *Traditional Home* magazine, July 1998, pages 44-50.

Hepplewhite, George. *The Cabinet-Maker and Upholsterer's Guide*, Dover Publications, NY, 1969. Reprint of the 3rd edition, 1794, published in London by I. and J. Taylor.

Sheraton, Thomas. *The Cabinetmakers and Upholsterer's Drawing Book,* Dover Publications, NY, 1972. Reprint reproducing material from various editions between 1793 and 1802.

PATTERN BOOKS

Langley, Batty, and Langley, Thomas. *The Builder's Jewel or the Youth's Instuctor and Workman's Remembrancer,* Benjamin Bloom, Inc., NY, 1970. Reprint of 1746 edition.

Pain, William. *The Builder's Companion and Workman's General Assistant*, found in volume IV of Lisa C. Mullin's "*The Architectural Treasures of Early America*". Originally published by Pain, 1762.

Pain, William. *The Builder's Pocket-Treasure*, Gregg International Publishers, Ltd., England, 1972. Printed in London, reprinted in Boston by William Norman, 1794.

Pain, William, and Pain, James. *Decorative Details of the 18th Century*, A. Tiranti, London, 1948.

PERSPECTIVE AND PORPORTION

D'Espouy, Hector. *Greek and Roman Architecture in Classic Drawings*, Dover Publications, NY, 1999.

Hale, Jonathan. *The Old Way of Seeing*, Houghton Mifflin Co., Boston and NY, 1994.

Pozzo, Andrea. *Perspective in Architecture and Painting: An unabridged reprint of the English and Latin edition of the 1693 "Perspectiva Pictorum et Architectorum,"* Dover Publications, NY, 1989.

ORDERS OF ARCHITECTURE

Adam, Robert. *Classical Architecture*, Harry N. Abrams, Inc., NY, 1991.

Chambers, Sir William. *A Treatise on the Decorative Part of Civil Architecture*, Benjamin Bloom, NY and London, 1968. Reprint of the 3rd edition published in 1791 by Joseph Smeeton, London.

Chitham, Robert. *The Classical Orders of Architecture,* Rizzoli, NY, 1985.

Palladio, Andrea. *The Four Books of Architecture*, Dover Publications, NY, 1965. Reprint of 1738 edition published by Issac Ware.

Rattner, Donald M. *Parallel of the Classical Orders of Architecture*, Acanthus Press, NY, 1998.

Tzonis, Alexander, and Lefavre, Liane. *Classical Architecture, The Poetics of Order,* MIT Press, MA, 1986.

Vignola, Giacomo Barozzi da. *Canon of the Orders of Architecture,* Acanthus Press, NY, 1999. Reprint of 1572 edition.

Ware, William Robert. *The American Vignola, A guide to the Making of Classical Architecture*, Dover Publications, NY, 1994. Originally published by International Textbook Co., Scranton, PA, 1904-1913.

WEDGEWOOD

Kelly, Alison. *Decorative Wedgewood in Architecture and Furniture*, Country Life Limited, London, 1965.

Kelly, Alison. *The Story of Wedgewood*, Viking Press, NY, 1975.

About the CD-ROM

Introduction

This appendix provides you with information on the contents of the CD that accompanies this book. For the latest and most detailed information, please refer to the ReadMe file located at the root of the CD.

System Requirements

- A computer with a processor running at 120 Mhz or faster
- At least 32 MB of total RAM installed on your computer; for best performance, we recommend at least 64 MB
- A CD-ROM drive

Using the CD with Windows

To install the items from the CD to your hard drive, follow these steps:

1. Insert the CD into your computer's CD-ROM drive.
2. The CD-ROM interface will appear. The interface provides a simple point-and-click way to explore the contents of the CD.

If the opening screen of the CD-ROM does not appear automatically, follow these steps to access the CD:

1. Click the Start button on the left end of the taskbar and then choose Run from the menu that pops up.
2. In the dialog box that appears, type *d*:\setup.exe. (If your CD-ROM drive is not drive *d*, fill in the appropriate letter in place of *d*.) This brings up the CD Interface described in the preceding set of steps.

How to Use the CD Using the Mac OS

To install the items from the CD to your hard drive, follow these steps.

1. Insert the CD into your computer's CD-ROM drive. In a moment, an icon representing the CD you just inserted appears on your Mac desktop. Chances are, the icon looks like a CD-ROM.
2. Double click the CD icon to show the CD's contents.
3. Double click the file called License.txt. This file contains the end-user license that you agree to by using the CD. When you have finished reading the license, you can close the window that displayed the file.
4. Double click the Read Me First icon. This text file contains information about the CD's programs and any last-minute instructions you need to know about installing the programs on the CD that we don't cover in this appendix.
5. Most of the files included on the CD can be opened directly from the CD-ROM. If you would like to copy them from the CD onto your Mac's hard drive, simply drag them from their folder on the CD-ROM into an appropriate folder on your hard drive.

What's on the CD

Federal Style Patterns 1780-1820 is a comprehensive collection of pattern drawings of the Federal Style from 1780 to 1820, which is useful to architects, interior designers and preservationists. It's organized with patterns for cornices, door and window casings, chair rails, baseboards, mantels, and fences. The CD contains the drawings in the following formats: vector PDF, Postscript, DXF for PC, and PowerCadd for Mac.

Customer Care

If you have trouble with the CD-ROM, please call the Wiley Product Technical Support phone number at (800) 762-2974. Outside the United States, call 1(317) 572-3994. You can also contact Wiley Product Technical Support at **http://www.wiley.com/techsupport**. John Wiley & Sons will provide technical support only for installation and other general quality control items. For technical support on the applications themselves, consult the program's vendor or author.

To place additional orders or to request information about other Wiley products, please call (877) 762-2974.